How to Pass the
Professional Skills Tests for Initial Teacher Training (ITT)

PERFECT REVISION FOR THE NEW SKILLS TEST

How to Pass the
Professional Skills Tests for Initial Teacher Training (ITT)

1000+ practice questions

Chris Tyreman

KoganPage

LONDON   PHILADELPHIA   NEW DELHI

Publisher's note
Every possible effort has been made to ensure that the information contained in this book is accurate at the time of going to press, and the publishers and author cannot accept re-sponsibility for any errors or omissions, however caused. No responsibility for loss or damage occasioned to any person acting, or refraining from action, as a result of the material in this publication can be accepted by the editor, the publisher or the author.

First published in Great Britain and the United States in 2013 by Kogan Page Limited

120 Pentonville Road	1518 Walnut Street, Suite 1100	4737/23 Ansari Road
London N1 9JN	Philadelphia PA 19102	Daryaganj
United Kingdom	USA	New Delhi 110002
www.koganpage.com		India

© Chris Tyreman, 2013

ISBN   978 0 7494 7021 0
ESBN   978 0 7494 7022 7

British Library Cataloguing-in-Publication Data

A CIP record for this book is available from the British Library.

Typeset by Graphicraft Limited, Hong Kong
Print production managed by Jellyfish
Printed and bound in Great Britain by CPI Group (UK) Ltd, Croydon, CR0 4YY

Contents

Introduction

All candidates wishing to enter Initial Teacher Training (ITT) must pass the Professional Skills Tests in numeracy, literacy and reasoning. These tests are normally taken before the interview to identify the strongest candidates. Teacher training providers will be able to review your marks as part of the selection process, so a weak performance could find you screened out at an early stage.

This book will enable you to pass the tests at the first attempt. Of course it cannot, without some effort, miraculously pass the tests for you, but if you work steadily through each chapter you can succeed. To be successful you will need to demonstrate competency in a range of skills and knowledge that teachers are expected to have, regardless of the subject specialism. The new tests are more of a challenge than before and require greater cognitive ability.

Numeracy section

Candidates with a *recent* grade B or above in GCSE mathematics (higher tier) will be familiar with the topics and are best placed to pass first time with the least preparation. If you managed only a grade C or lower then you must prepare carefully. This book will help you to succeed whatever your level because it assumes that you have forgotten much of what you learnt at school or college, or that you never understood it in the first place. It builds on your existing knowledge using annotated examples and 'Warm-up exercises'. These are followed by 'Easy questions' with expanded answers, then more demanding examples are included together with 'More difficult questions' to prepare you fully for the most challenging test questions. You can dip into the book at any point to revise weak areas. However, each chapter assumes the knowledge of all the previous chapters, so there is value in starting at the beginning.

A calculator is not to be used for any section of the test, so we have included a separate chapter entitled 'Quicker mental calculations' to complement the basic arithmetic chapter. Some mathematical knowledge is presumed. To interpret numeracy questions you need to convert the language of the questions into mathematical operations. You should be familiar with the different ways that these operations can be denoted in question form, for example:

(×) multiply by, times, lots of, product of, twice, double, half, multiple, fraction
(÷) divide by, proportion, ratio, per/per cent, out of, each, factor
(+) add, total, plus, sum, tally, more than
(−) subtract, difference, take, less than

Use the pen and paper provided to jot down these key steps in a calculation. You are far more likely to make numerical errors if you rely too heavily on your memory. For the purposes of the numeracy test, mental arithmetic is not about working everything out in your head; it is arithmetic without the help of a calculator.

To interpret the graphs you must be able to work out the distance from one tick mark to the next along the axis, by dividing the scale by the number of tick mark intervals, as shown below:

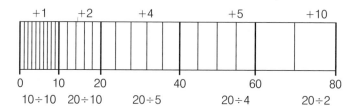

Reading from the above scale you should be able to identify the following numbers without too much difficulty: 7, 14, 28, 55 and 70. If you are unable to locate these numbers on the scale you may have a numeracy problem that requires remedial help.

Literacy section

Teacher training applicants are assumed to have a basic degree of literacy, so this book sets out to encourage candidates to develop skills that they already have. In the spelling section, for example, the 'rules of spelling' are reviewed and 'Warm-up exercises' and 'Easy questions' boost confidence in those words that candidates find difficult to spell. All the important punctuation marks are reviewed along with their correct and incorrect application. The grammar chapter of the book checks your ability to write grammatically correct sentences as well as to identify grammatical errors. A range of exercises and questions is used to identify weak areas in word selection and sentence construction.

The new tests check your ability to write continuous prose. Your essay will be human-marked, so in addition to spelling, punctuation and grammar, your work will be assessed for its overall composition and effect. The book explains how to plan and craft your essay to achieve the highest mark and includes exemplar essays.

Reasoning section

This new element of the selection tests is intended for pre-entry candidates and not for trainees who were expecting the QTS numeracy and literacy tests when they started their course. However, both the verbal and numerical reasoning components of this section are recommended for all applicants whatever their training status. The numerical reasoning questions provide excellent practice in the mental arithmetic skills needed for performing calculations quickly without using a calculator. The verbal reasoning tests take the form of comprehension exercises that require you to analyse and interpret, and these skills are valuable for the tests as a whole. A range of non-verbal reasoning tests (diagram tests) are included in this book. A strong performance in these tests is an indicator of intelligence (IQ) and problem-solving ability when faced with new concepts.

Download your FREE online resources for selected maths topics from: www.koganpage.com/ittresources

Part one

Numeracy

Chapter 1

Review of arithmetic

Feedback from trainee teachers suggests that some candidates need fuller explanations of the basic arithmetic processes that underpin the test questions. This book caters for those who find mathematics a difficult subject. It starts at a very low level and recognizes that if you get stuck you cannot just put up your hand to ask a question.

Some students may be tempted to skip the first few pages, indeed the entire first chapter. However, confidence with numbers is built on a sound knowledge of traditional numerical processes. Confident candidates can draw upon a wide range of mental strategies to solve numerical problems. A useful starting point is 'place value' as applied to whole numbers, written in both figures and words.

Place value

Large numbers (greater than nine) are built up with separate columns for hundreds, tens and units. Each column can have numbers ranging from nought to nine (0 to 9), but the value of each number in the column has a different meaning. The table below lists some numbers in words with their corresponding figures and place values:

Number in words	Number in figures*			
	TH	H	T	U
two hundred and six		2	0	6
five hundred and sixty-four		5	6	4
six hundred and thirty-two		6	3	2
six thousand two hundred	6	2	0	0

* TH = thousands; H = hundreds; T = tens; U = units

The figure 6 (underlined) has a different place value depending on which column it appears in. It can mean 6, 60, 600 or 6000:

In 206 the six means six UNITS (6 × 1 = 6).

In 564 the six means six TENS (6 × 10 = 60).

In 632 the six means six HUNDREDS (6 × 100 = 600).

In 6200 the six means six THOUSANDS (6 × 1000 = 6000).

Very large numbers are built up in the same way as for smaller numbers with columns for tens of thousands, hundreds of thousands and millions. For example:

200128 is two hundred thousand one hundred and twenty-eight.

2150235 is one million one hundred and fifty thousand two hundred and thirty-five.

Place values can be used to make simple mental arithmetic calculations without a pen and paper and to solve more complex calculations without the need for a calculator. The following questions are based on the simple concept of place value but in some instances they do require a little thought!

1 Warm-up exercise

1   Write 2540 in words.   Answer ....

2   In words, what is the place value of the underlined number in 25<u>4</u>0?
                                            Answer ....

3   In words, what is the place value of 0 in 2540?   Answer ....

4   In words, what is the place value of 0 in 2045?   Answer ....

5   In numbers, what is the place value of 1 in 515400?   Answer ....

6   In numbers, what is the place value of 5 in 512400?   Answer ....

7   Rearrange the figures in 34529 to give the largest possible number.
                                            Answer ....

8   Rearrange the figures in 34529 to give the smallest possible number.
                                            Answer ....

9   Write 51240000 in words.   Answer ....

10   In numbers and words, what is the place value of 5 in 51240000?
                                            Answer ....

The four processes of arithmetic

Addition

Traditionally numbers have been arranged underneath each other so that the units, tens and hundreds columns etc are kept in vertical alignment.

Example: 139 + 226

We align the numbers in columns and then add the units column (right-hand column) giving 6 + 9 = 15.

The number five is placed in the units column and the number ten is carried over as one 'ten' into the tens column.

```
H  T  U
1  3  9
2  2  6  +
_____
      5
_____
   1
```

Now we add the tens column (middle column, remembering to include the 'one' that has been carried: 1 + 2 + 3 = 6 (middle column):

```
1  3  9
2  2  6  +
_____
   6  5
_____
   1
```

Now we add the hundreds column: 2 + 1 = 3 (left-hand column):

```
1  3  9
2  2  6  +
_____
3  6  5
_____
   1
```

For the addition of three or more numbers, the method is the same. For example, 200 + 86 + 44 becomes

```
2  0  0
   8  6
   4  4  +
_____
3  3  0
_____
1  1
```

Subtraction

Subtraction is concerned with taking things away. Subtraction is the reverse of addition. The most important thing about subtraction is that the larger number is on top (above the smaller), so when subtracting you subtract the smaller number from the larger number.

As with addition, the numbers must be arranged underneath each other, so that the units, tens and hundreds columns are in line. After aligning the numbers, we subtract (take away) the columns vertically, starting at the right-hand end (units column). For example:

$$374 - 126$$

The first step is to align the numbers in columns with the larger number above the smaller number:

```
H  T  U
3  7  4
1  2  6  –
_____
```

The next step is to subtract the units (right-hand column), $4 - 6$, which we cannot do since six is larger than four.

To overcome this problem we borrow one from the tens column (this is the same as ten units) and add it to the four in the units column. So our sum now becomes:

$$14 - 6 \text{ (we can do)} = 8$$

So far we can write:

```
3  7  ¹4
1  2  6  –
_____
         8
_____
```

The next step is to pay back the 'one' we have just borrowed from the tens column. There are two methods for doing this and both are now explained.

Method 1 (traditional method)

In this method the ten is paid back to the bottom. For example:

```
3  7   ¹4
1  2¹  6  –
_____
          8
_____
```

Now we add the 1 and the 2 to make 3. The 3 is subtracted from the 7 to give to the 4. So the sum becomes:

```
3   7   ¹4
1   2¹  6   –
─────────────
    4   8
─────────────
```

Finally we subtract the 1 from 3 (in the hundreds column) to give 2:

```
3   7   ¹4
1   2¹  6   –
─────────────
2   4   8
─────────────
```

Method 2 (modern method)

In this method the ten borrowed is subtracted as a one at the top of the tens column $(7 - 1 = 6)$:

```
3   7⁶₁  4̶
1   2    6   –
─────────────
2   4    8
─────────────
```

Now try the following questions. *You must not use a calculator* for any questions in this book, except for the purposes of checking answers.

2 Warm-up exercise

Work out the following additions and subtractions:

1 $472 + 24 =$ *Answer* ....

2 $178 + 35 =$ *Answer* ....

3 $2830 + 250 + 67 =$ *Answer* ....

4 $957 - 340 =$ *Answer* ....

5 $1327 - 898 =$ *Answer* ....

6 $375 - 123 =$ *Answer* ....

7 $375 - 123 - 38 =$ *Answer* ....

8 $375 - 123 + 59 =$ *Answer* ....

Multiplication

Multiplication (or 'times') means 'lots of' and is a quick way of adding up numbers that have the same value. For example:

3

3

3

3

3+   5 lots of 3

15   5 × 3 = 15 (5 times 3 equals 15)

Note that 5 × 3 = 15 and also 3 × 5 equals 15:

3   5

3   5

3   5+

3   15

3+

15

This applies to all numbers that are multiplied together; it does not matter which way around you put them, the answer is the same. The answer 15 is known as the 'product' of 5 and 3 (or 3 and 5). To multiply two numbers you need to be familiar with your 'Times Tables' up to 10 by 10 (up to 12 by 12 is better). It is essential that you memorize these tables because calculators are not allowed in the examination room.

Multiplication table (try to memorize to at least 10 × 10)

	1	2	3	4	5	6	7	8	9	10	11	12
1	1	2	3	4	5	6	7	8	9	10	11	12
2	2	4	6	8	10	12	14	16	18	21	22	24
3	3	6	9	12	15	18	21	24	27	30	33	36
4	4	8	12	16	20	24	28	32	36	40	44	48
5	5	10	15	20	25	30	35	40	45	50	55	60
6	6	12	18	24	30	36	42	48	54	60	66	72
7	7	14	21	28	35	42	49	56	63	70	77	84

	1	2	3	4	5	6	7	8	9	10	11	12
8	8	16	24	32	40	48	56	64	72	80	88	96
9	9	18	27	36	45	54	63	72	81	90	99	108
10	10	20	30	40	50	60	70	80	90	100	110	120
11	11	22	33	44	55	66	77	88	99	110	121	132
12	12	24	36	48	60	72	84	96	108	120	132	144

The common times tables

2 times	3 times	4 times	5 times	6 times	7 times
$1 \times 2 = 2$	$1 \times 3 = 3$	$1 \times 4 = 4$	$1 \times 5 = 5$	$1 \times 6 = 6$	$1 \times 7 = 7$
$2 \times 2 = 4$	$2 \times 3 = 6$	$2 \times 4 = 8$	$2 \times 5 = 10$	$2 \times 6 = 12$	$2 \times 7 = 14$
$3 \times 2 = 6$	$3 \times 3 = 9$	$3 \times 4 = 12$	$3 \times 5 = 15$	$3 \times 6 = 18$	$3 \times 7 = 21$
$4 \times 2 = 8$	$4 \times 3 = 12$	$4 \times 4 = 16$	$4 \times 5 = 20$	$4 \times 6 = 24$	$4 \times 7 = 28$
$5 \times 2 = 10$	$5 \times 3 = 15$	$5 \times 4 = 20$	$5 \times 5 = 25$	$5 \times 6 = 30$	$5 \times 7 = 35$
$6 \times 2 = 12$	$6 \times 3 = 18$	$6 \times 4 = 24$	$6 \times 5 = 30$	$6 \times 6 = 36$	$6 \times 7 = 42$
$7 \times 2 = 14$	$7 \times 3 = 21$	$7 \times 4 = 28$	$7 \times 5 = 35$	$7 \times 6 = 42$	$7 \times 7 = 49$
$8 \times 2 = 16$	$8 \times 3 = 24$	$8 \times 4 = 32$	$8 \times 5 = 40$	$8 \times 6 = 48$	$8 \times 7 = 56$
$9 \times 2 = 18$	$9 \times 3 = 27$	$9 \times 4 = 36$	$9 \times 5 = 45$	$9 \times 6 = 54$	$9 \times 7 = 63$
$0 \times 2 = 20$	$10 \times 3 = 30$	$10 \times 4 = 40$	$10 \times 5 = 50$	$10 \times 6 = 60$	$10 \times 7 = 70$
$11 \times 2 = 22$	$11 \times 3 = 33$	$11 \times 4 = 44$	$11 \times 5 = 55$	$11 \times 6 = 66$	$11 \times 7 = 77$
$12 \times 2 = 24$	$12 \times 3 = 36$	$12 \times 4 = 48$	$12 \times 5 = 60$	$12 \times 6 = 72$	$12 \times 7 = 84$

8 times	9 times	10 times	11 times	12 times
$1 \times 8 = 8$	$1 \times 9 = 9$	$1 \times 10 = 10$	$1 \times 11 = 11$	$1 \times 12 = 12$
$2 \times 8 = 16$	$2 \times 9 = 18$	$2 \times 10 = 20$	$2 \times 11 = 22$	$2 \times 12 = 24$
$3 \times 8 = 24$	$3 \times 9 = 27$	$3 \times 10 = 30$	$3 \times 11 = 33$	$3 \times 12 = 36$
$4 \times 8 = 32$	$4 \times 9 = 36$	$4 \times 10 = 40$	$4 \times 11 = 44$	$4 \times 12 = 48$
$5 \times 8 = 40$	$5 \times 9 = 45$	$5 \times 10 = 50$	$5 \times 11 = 55$	$5 \times 12 = 60$
$6 \times 8 = 48$	$6 \times 9 = 54$	$6 \times 10 = 60$	$6 \times 11 = 66$	$6 \times 12 = 72$
$7 \times 8 = 56$	$7 \times 9 = 63$	$7 \times 10 = 70$	$7 \times 11 = 77$	$7 \times 12 = 84$
$8 \times 8 = 64$	$8 \times 9 = 72$	$8 \times 10 = 80$	$8 \times 11 = 88$	$8 \times 12 = 96$
$9 \times 8 = 72$	$9 \times 9 = 81$	$9 \times 10 = 90$	$9 \times 11 = 99$	$9 \times 12 = 108$
$10 \times 8 = 80$	$10 \times 9 = 90$	$10 \times 10 = 100$	$10 \times 11 = 110$	$10 \times 12 = 120$
$11 \times 8 = 88$	$11 \times 9 = 99$	$11 \times 10 = 110$	$11 \times 11 = 121$	$11 \times 12 = 132$
$12 \times 8 = 96$	$12 \times 9 = 108$	$12 \times 10 = 120$	$12 \times 11 = 132$	$12 \times 12 = 144$

Short multiplication

Multiplication of any number by a unit (1 to 9), for example: 6×5; 68×9; 390×7; 5240×3.

Example: what is 68×9? We rewrite this as:

```
6  8
9  ×
```

Multiplying the units gives $8 \times 9 = 72$ (see nine times table), so we have:

```
   6  8
      9  ×
   ─────
      2
      7
```

We multiply the 6 in the tens column by the 9 to give $6 \times 9 = 54$.

The 54 is added to the 7 previously carried, to give $54 + 7 = 61$. The 1 of the 61 is placed in the tens column and the 6 of the 61 is carried into the hundreds column:

```
   6  8
      9  ×
   ─────
   1  2
 6    7
```

Since there are no hundreds to multiply in the hundreds column, the figure 6 can be carried directly into this column, giving:

```
      6  8
         9  ×
   ────────
   6  1  2
 6       7
```

3 Warm-up exercise

1   $7 \times 9 =$ *Answer* ....

2   $12 \times 8 =$ *Answer* ....

3   $11 \times 12 =$ *Answer* ....

4   Multiply 20 by $6 =$ *Answer* ....

5   Multiply 23 by $4 =$ *Answer* ....

6   90 times 5 is   *Answer* ....

7 The product of 19 and 5 is   *Answer* ....

8 33 × 3 =   *Answer* ....

9 75 × 4 =   *Answer* ....

10 125 × 8 =   *Answer* ....

Long multiplication

Multiplying any number by a number greater than 9, eg 52 × 18; 120 × 50 etc. To multiply 52 × 18 we rewrite this as:

```
  5  2
  1  8  ×
 ─────

 ─────
```

We proceed in two steps as follows: first by multiplying the 52 by the 8 in the units column and second by multiplying the 52 by the 1 in the tens column.

First step: (multiply 52 by the 8) so we have:

```
    5  2
    1  8  ×
 ────────
  4  1  6
 ────────
     1
```

Second step: (multiply the 52 by the 1 in the tens column). Since we are now multiplying from the tens column we leave the units column blank which is the same as filling it with a 0. The sum is written on the line below 416.

```
       5  2
       1  8  ×
    ────────
  4  1  6
  5  2  0
```

We now add the two steps together, ie add 416 and 520 to give the final sum which is shown below:

```
       5  2
       1  8  ×
    ────────
  4  1  6
  5  2  0  +
 ─────────
  9  3  6
 ─────────
```

4 Warm-up exercise

Work out the following multiplication sums:

1   62 × 13   *Answer* ....

2   79 × 32   *Answer* ....

3   80 × 15   *Answer* ....

4   254 × 20   *Answer* ....

5   17 × 25   *Answer* ....

6   125 × 80   *Answer* ....

7   167 × 33   *Answer* ....

8   42 × 121   *Answer* ....

Multiplication by 10, 100 and 1000

To multiply a number by ten we add a nought to the number, for example: 5 × 10 = 50. This has the effect of moving the number one along to the left in the hundreds, tens and units columns (increasing its value ten times).

H	T	U			H	T	U
		5	× 10	=		5	0

Multiplication by 100 is the same except that you add two zeros. This moves the number two places to the left.

Example: 3 × 100 = 300:

H	T	U			H	T	U
		3	× 100	=	3	0	0

and 12 × 100 = 1200:

TH	H	T	U			TH	H	T	U
		1	2	× 100	=	1	2	0	0

(ie twelve hundred is one thousand two hundred)

To multiply by 1000 we add three zeros, so 8 × 1000 = 8000

TH	H	T	U			TH	H	T	U
			8	× 1000	=	8	0	0	0

18 × 1000 = 18000 (eighteen thousand):

TTH	TH	H	T	U			TTH	TH	H	T	U
			1	8	× 1000	=	1	8	0	0	0

In this case we have to go to the next column along – the tens of thousands column (TTH) – to give one ten thousand. Together with the eight thousands it gives us eighteen thousand.

5 Warm-up exercise

Work out the following multiplication by adding noughts (zeros):

1   28 × 10 =   *Answer* ....

2   6 × 1000 =   *Answer* ....

3   49 × 10 =   *Answer* ....

4   49 × 100 =   *Answer* ....

5   49 × 1000 =   *Answer* ....

Division

Division is the reverse of multiplication and is concerned with sharing (or dividing numbers into equal parts). For example, divide 195 by 3, ie 195 ÷ 3. We rewrite as follows:

$$3\overline{)195}$$

The first step is to divide the 1 by the 3. However, since 3 into 1 won't go, we have to carry the 1 into the next column:

$$3\overline{)1^195}$$ giving us 3 into 19

We now use the multiplication table in reverse to find how many 3s are in 19. To do this, start in the 3s column on the left-hand side and move along the horizontal row until you get to the number which is closest to but smaller than 19. The number is 18. Following the vertical row upwards gives us 6. So 3 goes into 19 six times with 1 left over (19 − 18 = 1[left over]). The 6 is placed at the top; the 1 is carried to the next column to make 15:

$$\frac{6}{3\overline{)1^19^15}}$$

Finally the 3 is divided into 15. The three times table shows us that 3 goes into 15 times exactly five times, so the finished sum is:

$$\begin{array}{r} 6\ 5 \\ \hline 3\overline{)1^19^15} \end{array}$$

So $195 \div 3 = 65$. The answer can be checked by multiplying it by the number that we have divided by ($65 \times 3 = 195$ – correct). The answer (65) is known as the *quotient*. The number we are dividing by (3) is the *divisor*, and the number we are dividing into (195) is the *dividend*. Note that if the dividend had been 196 instead of 195 then the answer would have been 65 *remainder* 1 (65 with 1 left over).

6 Warm-up exercise

Work out the following divisions:

1 $36 \div 9$ *Answer* ....

2 $248 \div 4$ *Answer* ....

3 $3\overline{)339}$ *Answer* ....

4 $5\overline{)265}$ *Answer* ....

5 $1230 \div 3$ *Answer* ....

6 $295 \div 5$ *Answer* ....

7 $1464 \div 6$ *Answer* ....

8 $1000 \div 8$ *Answer* ....

Long division (division by large numbers)

For example, 2064 divided by 48.

We write: $48\overline{)2064}$

First step: divide 2 by 48 – won't go

Second step: divide 20 by 48 – won't go

Third step: divide 206 by 48 – will go

48 into 206 will go, but we don't have a times table for 48 so we have to *build up a table ourselves*. This is done as follows:

$1 \times 48 = 48$
$2 \times 48 = 96$ $4 \times 48 = 192$ (the nearest to 206)
$3 \times 48 = 144$ $5 \times 48 = 240$ (too big)

Fourth step: work out the remainder. We know that 48 goes into 206 four times to leave a remainder of 14 (206 − 192).

```
        4
48)2064
   192−
    14
```

Fifth step: we now bring the 4 down to give 144:

```
        4
48)2064
   192−
   144
```

Sixth step: the 48 is divided into 144 to give 3 with no remainder (see 48 times table on the previous page)

```
       43
48)2064
   192 −
   144
   144 −
```

So 2064 ÷ 48 = 43.

7 Warm-up exercise

Work out the following long divisions:

1 360 ÷ 12   *Answer* ....

2 372 ÷ 12   *Answer* ....

3 18)792   *Answer* ....

4 20)900   *Answer* ....

5 72)1440   *Answer* ....

6 216 ÷ 36   *Answer* ....

7 950 ÷ 25   *Answer* ....

8 2680 ÷ 40   *Answer* ....

9 976 ÷ 16   *Answer* ....

10 4944 ÷ 24   *Answer* ....

Law of operations ('BIDMAS')

A calculation with two or more different arithmetic signs (operations) must be worked out in the correct sequence. Multiplication and division are always carried out before addition and subtraction. For example:

$$4 \times 3 + 6$$

Multiplication first: $4 \times 3 = 12$ followed by addition: $12 + 6 = 18$.

So $4 \times 3 + 6 = 18$.

If we carried out the addition part first $(3 + 6 = 9)$ and then multiplied by the 4, this would have given 36 $(4 \times 9 = 36)$ which is the wrong answer. For example:

$$25 - 12 \div 3$$

Division first: $12 \div 3 = 4$ followed by subtraction $25 - 4 = 21$.

So $25 - 12 \div 3 = 21$.

Where a calculation contains *only* addition and subtraction then each part is worked out in a sequence from left to right. For example:

$11 - 3 + 9 - 2$ becomes $11 - 3 = 8$ then $8 + 9 = 17$ then finally $17 - 2 = 15$.

Where a calculation contains only multiplication and division then each part is worked out *in sequence* from left to right. For example:

$10 \div 2 \times 6$ becomes $10 \div 2 = 5$ followed by $5 \times 6 = 30$.

8 Warm-up exercise

Work out the following (without using a calculator):

1   $12 \div 6 + 12$ *Answer* ....

2   $10 + 15 \div 5$ *Answer* ....

3   $3 \times 4 - 2$ *Answer* ....

4   $8 - 3 \times 2$ *Answer* ....

5   $10 + 20 \div 5$ *Answer* ....

6   $15 - 9 + 3$ *Answer* ....

7   $14 + 11 - 10 - 6 =$ *Answer* ....

8   $22 \times 4 \div 2 + 12 =$ *Answer* ....

9   $30 \div 6 \times 5 - 15 =$ *Answer* ....

10 $2 \times 3 \times 4 \times 5 \div 20 =$ *Answer* ....

11 $10 - 1 \times 3 - 1 =$ *Answer* ....

12 $9 + 3 \times 4 \div 2 - 1 =$ *Answer* ....

Some calculations include brackets to help to make sure that the arithmetic is carried out in the correct sequence. Where a calculation contains *brackets* then the sum inside the brackets must be worked out before anything else. For example:

$$12 \div (6 - 2)$$

First step: $(6 - 2) = 4$ Second step: $12 \div 4 = 3$

So $12 \div (6 - 2) = 3$

Without the brackets, $12 \div 6 - 2$ is $12 \div 6 = 2$, then $2 - 2 = 0$

When no arithmetic sign is placed outside the brackets then the calculation is *automatically taken as being times* ('$\times$').

So $9(6 + 5)$ means $9 \times (6 + 5)$ giving $9 \times 11 = 99$

The sequence of operations is **BIDMAS: B**rackets first, then ***I**ndices, **D**ivision or **M**ultiplication, and finally **A**ddition or **S**ubtraction (* eg squares and cubes, covered later).

9 Warm-up exercise

Calculate the following by working out the brackets first:

1 $9 + (5 \times 3)$ *Answer* ....

2 $14 - (10 + 2)$ *Answer* ....

3 $30 \div (3 \times 2)$ *Answer* ....

4 $4 \times (20 - 9)$ *Answer* ....

5 $10(10 - 9)$ *Answer* ....

6 $7 (15 \div 5)$ *Answer* ....

7 $3(10 + 6 \div 2)$ *Answer* ....

8 $3 + 6(4 \times 2 + 1)$ *Answer* ....

9 $2(23 - 17) \div 4$ *Answer* ....

10 $4 + 4(4 + 4)$ *Answer* ....

11 $90 \div 9(8 - 3 \times 2)$ *Answer* ....

12 $10 \times 2(60 \div 2 \times 15)$ *Answer* ....

Factors and multiples

The ability to break down (factorize) large numbers into smaller more manageable numbers, or factors, is an essential part of cancelling fractions. Factors and multiples are also useful for mental arithmetic calculations as discussed in a later chapter.

Factors are numbers that will divide into another number exactly, without leaving a remainder. A *divisor* is any number that you are dividing by; a divisor is a factor when it leaves no remainder. For example:

15 is a factor of 60 (60 divided by 15 = 4)

50 is a factor of 250 (250 divided by 50 = 5)

100 is a factor of 1000 (1000 divided by 100 = 10)

All the factors of a number are all of the whole numbers that will divide into it exactly. Take the number 36, for example. The factors of 36 are:

1 and 36;

2 and 18;

3 and 12;

4 and 9;

6 and 6.

Notice how the factors are found in pairs; pairing off in this way will help you to find the factors of large numbers, without missing any out. The factors of 36 can be listed as:

1 2 3 4 6 9 12, 18 and 36

The highest common factor (HCF) of two numbers is the highest of their common factors. For example: what is the highest common factor of 60 and 15?

15: factors = 1 3 5 15 (by pairing off)

60: factors = 1 2 3 4 5 6 10 12 15 20 30 60

The factors that are common to both 15 and 60 are:

1 3 5 15 and of these 15 is the highest, so 15 is the HCF of 60 and 15.

Example: what is the HCF of 16 and 20?

16: 1 2 4 8 16

20: 1 2 4 5 10 20

1, 2 and 4 are the common factors so 4 is the HCF of 16 and 20.

Finding factors

When looking for factors, the following tests can be applied to whole numbers (integers):

i) If the *last* digit is 0, 2, 4, 6, or 8 (ie it is an even number) then the number will divide by 2. For example, 576 will divide by 2 because 6 will divide by 2.

ii) If the *last* digit is 1, 3, 5, 7, or 9 (ie it is an odd number) then the number will not divide by 2 without leaving a remainder. For example, 575 will not divide by 2 without leaving a remainder (so 2 is not a factor of 575).

iii) If the *sum* of the digits is 3 the number will divide by 3. For example, 576 will divide by 3 because $5 + 7 + 6 = 18$ and 18 is divisible by 3.

iv) If the *last two* digits are divisible by 4 the number is divisible by 4.
For example, 128, 132, 136, 240, 244, 348, 552, 760, 964, 1012 etc.

v) If the *last* digit ends in 0 or 5 the number will divide by 5. For example, 1365 will divide by 5 because 65 will divide by 5; if you double a number ending in 5 it will divide by 10 (see vii).

vi) If the *sum* of the digits divides by 9 the number will divide by 9 (and also by 3 because 9 divides by 3). For example, 3474 will divide by 9 because $3 + 4 + 7 + 4 = 18$ and 18 is divisible by 9.

vii) If the last digit ends in 0 the number will divide by 10; if the last two digits are 00 the number will divide by 100 (and by 10), etc.

10 Warm-up exercise

Find the factors of the following numbers. Use the pairing-off method (1 and; 2 and; 3 and; 4 and; 5 and; 6 and; etc).

1 6 (four factors)   *Answer* ....

2 10 (four factors)   *Answer* ....

3 32 (six factors)   *Answer* ....

4 90 (twelve factors)   *Answer* ....

5 500 (twelve factors)   *Answer* ....

Find the highest common factor (HCF) of:

6 24 and 32   *Answer* ....

7 75 and 120   *Answer* ....

8 12 and 500   *Answer* ....

A *prime number* is a number that is *only* divisible by itself and one; a prime number has only two factors – the number itself and one. The lowest prime number is 2 (1 is not a prime number because it has only one factor – itself).

All the prime numbers below 50 are listed below:

2   3   5   7   11   13   17   19   23   29   31   37   41   43   47

Note: with the exception of 2, all the prime numbers are odd numbers (but not all odd numbers are prime numbers).

A factor that is a prime number is called a *prime factor*. To find the prime factors of any number we keep dividing by prime numbers – starting with the lowest prime number that will divide into it, and then progressing through until it will not divide by any prime number any further.

Example: what are the prime factors of 210?

$$210 \div 2 = 105$$
$$105 \div 3 = 35$$
$$35 \div 5 = 7$$
$$7 \div 7 = 1$$

So: 210 has the prime factors 2, 3, 5 and 7

$$210 = 2 \times 3 \times 5 \times 7$$

Example: express 2520 as a product of its prime factors.

As in the previous example we start dividing by the lowest prime number which is 2:

$$2520 \div 2 = 1260$$

1260 is an even number so it will divide by 2 again:

$$1260 \div 2 = 630$$

630 is an even number so it will divide by 2 again:

$$630 \div 2 = 315$$

315 is an odd number so it will not divide by 2 but it will divide by the next prime number which is 3:

$$315 \div 3 = 105$$

105 will divide by 3 again:

$$105 \div 3 = 35$$

35 will not divide by 3, but it will divide by the next prime number which is 5.

$$35 \div 5 = 7$$

7 is a prime number so it will not divide any further.

$$7 \div 7 = 1$$

So: $2520 = 2 \times 2 \times 2 \times 3 \times 3 \times 5 \times 7$

Note: finding the correct prime factors may involve 'trial and error' if the number is not divisible by the first prime factor you try.

$209 \div 2 = 104$ remainder 1, so 2 *is not* a prime factor of 209

$209 \div 3 = 69$ remainder 2, so 3 *is not* a prime factor of 209

$209 \div 5 = 41$ remainder 4, so 5 *is not* a prime factor of 209

$209 \div 7 = 29$ remainder 6, so 7 *is not* a prime factor of 209

$209 \div 11 = 19$ exactly so 11 is a prime factor of 209

From this we can see that 209 has the prime factors 11 and 19.

11 Warm-up exercise

Express the following numbers as a product of their prime factors (2, 3, 5, 7 etc):

1	6	*Answer*	**5**	81	*Answer* ....
2	30	*Answer*	**6**	216	*Answer* ....
3	63	*Answer*	**7**	125	*Answer* ....
4	420	*Answer*	**8**	343	*Answer* ....

A *multiple* of a number is the number multiplied by:

1 2 3 4 5 6 7 8 9 10 11 12 13 14 etc.

So a multiple is the 'times table' of a number. For example:

the multiples of 5 are:	5	10	15	20	25	30 etc.
the multiples of 6 are:	6	12	18	24	30 etc.	
the multiples of 10 are:	10	20	30	40	50 etc.	

Common multiples are those numbers which are common to a pair of numbers. For example: what are the first three common multiples of 5 and 10?

multiples of 5:	5	<u>10</u>	15	<u>20</u>	25	<u>30</u>
multiples of 10:	<u>10</u>	<u>20</u>	<u>30</u>	40	50

The common numbers are underlined; so the first three common multiples of 5 and 10 are: 10, 20 and 30. The lowest of these is 10, making it the lowest common multiple (LCM); it is the lowest number that both 5 and 10 will divide into exactly.

Example: find the lowest common multiple (LCM) of 3 and 9:

multiples of 3:	3	6	9	12	18
multiples of 9:	9	18	27	36	45

so the LCM of 3 and 9 is 9

Example: find the lowest common multiple (LCM) of 4 and 5:

4:	4	8	12	16	20	24
5:	5	10	15	20	25	

so LCM is 20

12 Warm-up exercise

Find the first four multiples of:

1 2   *Answer* ....

2 12   *Answer* ....

3 20   *Answer* ....

4 25   *Answer* ....

5 100   *Answer* ....

Find the lowest common multiple (LCM) of:

6 2 and 3   *Answer* ....

7 12 and 20   *Answer* ....

8 24 and 36   *Answer* ....

9 30 and 75   *Answer* ....

10 25 and 40   *Answer* ....

Rounding numbers

When rounding numbers we increase or decrease the answer to a sum to give the level of *accuracy* we want. For example, we can round answers to the nearest whole number, the nearest ten, the nearest hundred, the nearest thousand etc with any smaller numbers discarded (replaced with zeros).

To do this, you look at the column to the right of the column you are rounding to. If the number in that column is '5 or more' you round up and if it is less than 5 you round down. So 1, 2, 3, and 4 all round down, whereas 5, 6, 7, 8 and 9 all round up.

Example: work out 49 × 21 and round your answer to i) the nearest 10; ii) the nearest 100.

i)   49 × 21 = 1029 To round 1029 to the nearest ten you look at the column to the right of the tens column (ie the 9 units). This number is '5 or more' so you increase the number in the *tens column* by one to 3 (three tens is the nearest ten). So 1029 to the nearest ten is 1030.

ii) 49 × 21 = 1029. To round 1029 to the nearest hundred you look at the column to the right of the hundreds column (ie the two tens). This number is less than 5 so the number in the *hundreds column* remains the same ie 0 (no hundreds is the nearest hundred). So 1029 to the nearest hundred is 1000. The up/down split occurs at 1049. Numbers above 1049 round up to 1100, whereas numbers of 1049 and below round to 1000.

Example: round 82743 to i) the nearest ten, ii) nearest hundred, iii) nearest thousand.

i)   82743 – the 3 is less than 5 so the 4 remains the same (four tens) ie 82740 (the 43 becomes 40).

ii) 82743 – the 4 is less than 5 so the 7 remains the same (seven hundreds) ie 82700 (the 743 becomes 700).

iii) 82743 – the 7 is '5 or more' so the 2 is increased to 3 (three thousands) ie 83000 (the 2743 becomes 3000).

13 Warm-up exercise

Round the numbers to the level of accuracy given:

1	74 to the nearest ten	*Answer* ....
2	125 to the nearest ten	*Answer* ....
3	125 to the nearest hundred	*Answer* ....
4	140086 to the nearest hundred	*Answer* ....
5	140086 to the nearest thousand	*Answer* ....

To what level of accuracy have the numbers been rounded to?

6   7472 is 7500 to the nearest?   *Answer* ....

7   7476 is 7480 to the nearest?   *Answer* ....

8   22084 is 22100 to the nearest?   *Answer* ....

9   22084 is 22000 to the nearest?   *Answer* ....

10   220847 is 220000 to the nearest?   *Answer* ....

14 Warm-up exercise

1   Write out two thousand and twenty-two in figures.   *Answer* ....

2   Add 434 and 176.   *Answer* ....

3   Subtract 51 from 246.   *Answer* ....

4   Subtract 2750 from 5342.   *Answer* ....

5   Multiply 9 by 12.   *Answer* ....

6   Multiply 8 $\times$ 8.   *Answer* ....

7   Multiply 125 $\times$ 45.   *Answer* ....

8   Multiply 1053 $\times$ 141.   *Answer* ....

9   Multiply 105 by 100.   *Answer* ....

10   Multiply 25 by 10000.   *Answer* ....

11   Divide 121 by 11.   *Answer* ....

12   Divide 195 by 5.   *Answer* ....

13   Divide 3136 by 14.   *Answer* ....

14   Divide 1728 by 24.   *Answer* ....

15   Divide 1040 by 8.   *Answer* ....

16 $10 + 20 \div 2 =$ *Answer* ....

17 $20 \div 2 \times 10 =$ *Answer* ....

18 $10 + 4 - 5 + 7 =$ *Answer* ....

19 $8 \times 3 \div 4 \times 9 =$ *Answer* ....

20	$10(5 + 3) =$	*Answer* ....
21	$2(8 + 10 \div 2) =$	*Answer* ....
22	$3 \times 5(12 \div 3 + 6) =$	*Answer* ....
23	Find the factors of 20.	*Answer* ....
24	What are the prime factors of 20?	*Answer* ....
25	Find the factors of 42.	*Answer* ....
26	What are the prime factors of 42?	*Answer* ....
27	Write down the first 6 multiples of 6.	*Answer* ....
28	Write down the first 6 multiples of 9.	*Answer* ....
29	What is the lowest common multiple of 6 and 9?	*Answer* ....
30	What is the lowest common multiple of 20 and 25?	*Answer* ....
31	What is the lowest common multiple of 50 and 250?	*Answer* ....
32	What is the lowest common multiple of 10 and 12?	*Answer* ....
33	540 is 542 rounded to the nearest…	*Answer* ....
34	400 is 435 rounded to the nearest…	*Answer* ....
35	1000 is rounding 1450 to the nearest…	*Answer* ....

Tips for multiplication and division without a calculator

Multiplication

1   To multiply by 4, double the number twice.

2   To multiply by 5, multiply the number by 10 and halve the result.

3   To multiply by 6, multiply the number by 3 and double the result.

4   To multiply by 7 there is no easy method; however, you can multiply the number by 10 then subtract three times the original number.

5   To multiply by 8, double the number three times.

6   To multiply by 9, multiply the number by 10 and then subtract the original number.

7   To multiply by 20, multiply by 10 and then double the result.

8   To multiply by 25, multiply by 100 and divide by 4.

9   To multiply by 50, multiply by 100 and then halve the result.

Division

1   To divide by 4, halve the number and then halve the result.

2   To divide by 5, double the number then divide by 10.

3   To divide by 6, half the number and divide the result by 3.

4   To divide by 7, there is no easy method.

5   To divide by 8, halve the number, and then halve it twice more.

6   To divide by 9, divide the number by 3 and then by 3 again.

7   To divide by 20, divide by 10 and then halve the result.

8   To divide by 25, divide by 100 and then multiply by 4.

9   To divide by 50, divide by 100 and then halve the result.

More help with mental arithmetic can be found in Chapter 7, 'Quicker mental calculations'.

Chapter 2

Understanding fractions

We use fractions in everyday situations; for example, we talk about *half* an hour, *three-quarters* of a mile and *one-third* off the price. Despite these everyday uses, some people have difficulty with the concept of fractions and find problems involving fractions extremely difficult. One way to explain fractions is to say that the whole is divided into a number of *equal parts*, where we have one or more parts.

All fractions have a top and a bottom number. The bottom number, or *denominator*, tells us how many equal parts the whole is divided into. The top number, or *numerator*, tells us how many parts we have. So half an hour means that we *divide* the hour into two equal parts and we have one part.

Another way to understand fractions is to draw the whole, divide it up into equal parts and shade in the fraction. One-quarter is:

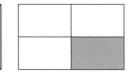

Similarly, the fraction three-quarters can be shown as:

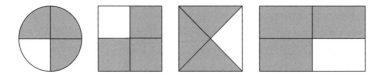

The above diagrams show how one-quarter added to three-quarters completes the whole.

An alternative way of looking at a fraction is to consider it as a division, where the horizontal bar separating the top and bottom numbers means divided by, for example:

$$\frac{1}{2} = 1 \div 2; \text{ (half = one whole divided by two)}$$

$$\frac{3}{4} = 3 \div 4; \text{ (three quarters = three wholes divided by four)}$$

$$\frac{1}{3} = 1 \div 3 \text{ (one third = one whole divided by three)}$$

Diagrams can be used to explain the division process. If four people *share equally* three pizzas they will receive three-quarters of a pizza each, which can be shown as follows:

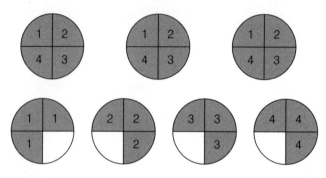

So three pizzas divided equally between four people is 3 ÷ 4 each, or three-quarters per person. Looking at the individual quarters we can see that there are twelve quarters in total and twelve quarters divided amongst four people is three quarters each.

When comparing the sizes of fractions with the *same denominator*, the largest fraction has the largest numerator so

$$\frac{3}{4} \text{ is greater than } \frac{2}{4} \text{ which is greater than } \frac{1}{4}$$

Cancelling (equivalent fractions)

Some fractions can be cancelled so as to express them in smaller numbers. The value of the fraction is *not altered by cancelling* and so is an 'equivalent fraction'.

For example, *four-sixths* can be expressed as a fraction having smaller numbers, by dividing *both* the top and bottom numbers by 2. This is known as *cancelling*.

$$\frac{4^{\div 2}}{6^{\div 2}} = \frac{2}{3}$$

Remember, the value of the fraction has not become smaller, only the numbers involved – this means that *four-sixths* and *two-thirds* are equivalent fractions:

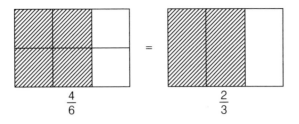

$$\frac{4}{6} \qquad \frac{2}{3}$$

Another example of cancelling is $\frac{8}{16}$. This fraction can be cancelled three times as follows:

$\frac{8}{16}$ can be cancelled to $\frac{4}{8}$ by dividing the 8 and the 16 by 2

$\frac{8}{16}$ can be cancelled to $\frac{2}{4}$ by dividing the 8 and the 16 by 4

$\frac{8}{16}$ can be cancelled to $\frac{1}{2}$ by dividing the 8 and the 16 by 8

So the equivalent fractions are $\frac{8}{16} = \frac{4}{8} = \frac{2}{4} = \frac{1}{2}$

If we cancel $\frac{8}{16}$ to $\frac{1}{2}$, this is known as cancelling a fraction to its lowest terms (it cannot be reduced any further):

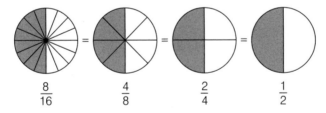

$$\frac{8}{16} \qquad \frac{4}{8} \qquad \frac{2}{4} \qquad \frac{1}{2}$$

When comparing the sizes of fractions with the *same numerator* we can see that the largest fraction has the smallest denominator:

$\frac{1}{2}$ is greater than $\frac{1}{4}$ which is greater than $\frac{1}{8}$ which is greater than $\frac{1}{16}$

1 Warm-up exercise

Cancel the following fractions to their lowest terms (use factors):

1 $\frac{3}{6}$ (divide the top and the bottom by 3) *Answer* ....

2 $\frac{15}{20}$ (divide the top and the bottom by 5) *Answer* ....

3 $\dfrac{12}{36}$ (divide top and bottom by 12, or by 3 and then by 4)   *Answer* ....

4 $\dfrac{40}{72}$ (divide top and bottom by 2, three times over)   *Answer* ....

5 $\dfrac{16}{24}$ (try dividing by small numbers like 2, 3 or 4)   *Answer* ....

6 $\dfrac{18}{30}$ (try dividing by 2 and then 3)   *Answer* ....

7 $\dfrac{10}{100}$ (numbers ending in zero always divide by 10)   *Answer* ....

8 $\dfrac{95}{100}$ (numbers ending in 5 always divide by 5)   *Answer* ....

9 $\dfrac{8}{12}$ (use the methods outlined earlier for factors and primes)   *Answer* ....

10 $\dfrac{40}{100}$ (use the methods outlined for factors and primes)   *Answer* ....

Addition and subtraction of fractions

Addition and subtraction of fractions can be dealt with together as the same 'rules' apply to both. Multiplication and division of fractions have different rules and will be explained separately. To be able to add or subtract fractions they must have the same denominators. Take the following example:

$$\frac{1}{8} + \frac{3}{8}$$

Both fractions have a denominator of 8. We write the denominator *once*, and then add the two top numbers:

$$\text{so } \frac{1}{8} + \frac{3}{8} = \frac{1+3}{8} = \frac{4}{8}$$

An example of subtraction is:

$$\frac{13}{16} - \frac{5}{16} = \frac{13-5}{16} = \frac{8}{16}$$

2 Warm-up exercise

Add/subtract the following fractions then cancel where possible:

1 $\dfrac{6}{8} + \dfrac{1}{8}$ *Answer* ....

5 $\dfrac{7}{9} - \dfrac{2}{9} + \dfrac{4}{9}$ *Answer* ....

2 $\dfrac{2}{6} + \dfrac{3}{6}$ *Answer* ....

6 $\dfrac{11}{12} - \dfrac{5}{12}$ *Answer* ....

3 $\dfrac{7}{10} + \dfrac{4}{10}$ *Answer* ....

7 $\dfrac{9}{15} + \dfrac{1}{15}$ *Answer* ....

4 $\dfrac{11}{12} + \dfrac{4}{12}$ *Answer* ....

8 $\dfrac{12}{40} - \dfrac{4}{40}$ *Answer* ....

When the fractions have different denominators we can still add or subtract them, but in order to do so we first of all have to find a *common denominator*, ie a number which both denominators will divide into. Take the following example:

$$\frac{1}{4} + \frac{3}{6}$$

The first fraction has a denominator of 4 and the second fraction has a denominator of 6. The *common denominator* is a number which both 4 and 6 will divide into. There are many numbers which both 4 and 6 will divide into. To find them we compare the four times table with six times table and see where they give us the same answer). From these tables, we can see that 4 and 6 have common denominators at 12, 24, 36 and 48. To make the working easier we choose the *lowest* of these – 12.

Four times table	Six times table
1 × 4 = 4	1 × 6 = 6
2 × 4 = 8	2 × 6 = **12**
3 × 4 = **12**	3 × 6 = 18
4 × 4 = 16	4 × 6 = **24**
5 × 4 = 20	5 × 6 = 30
6 × 4 = **24**	6 × 6 = **36**
7 × 4 = 28	7 × 6 = 42
8 × 4 = 32	8 × 6 = **48**
9 × 4 = **36**	9 × 6 = 54
10 × 4 = 40	10 × 6 = 60
11 × 4 = 44	11 × 6 = 66
12 × 4 = **48**	12 × 6 = 72

The tables show us that 12 is the lowest common denominator (LCD). To proceed with the sum, the next stage is to rewrite each fraction in terms of the common denominator, ie twelfths. So we re-write $\frac{1}{4}$ in twelfths and $\frac{3}{6}$ in twelfths.

To do this we divide the common denominator 12 by the denominators of the two fractions (4 and 6 in the above example) and then multiply the numerator of each fraction by the respective answer.

We rewrite $\frac{1}{4}$ in twelfths as follows:

$12 \div 4 = 3$ (common denominator 12 ÷ denominator of 4 = **3**)

$\mathbf{3} \times 1 = 3$ (answer 3 × numerator of 1 = 3)

So we have: $\frac{1}{4} = \frac{3}{12}$

Similarly $\frac{3}{6}$ in twelfths is rewritten:

$12 \div 6 = 2$ (common denominator 12 ÷ denominator of 6 = **2**)

$\mathbf{2} \times 3 = 6$ (answer 2 × numerator of 3 = 6)

So we have: $\frac{3}{6} = \frac{6}{12}$

The sum of $\frac{1}{4} + \frac{3}{6}$ now becomes: $\frac{3}{12} + \frac{6}{12} = \frac{9}{12}$

Subtraction of fractions with different denominators is carried out in exactly the same way.

Note that two (or more) numbers, even prime numbers, *always* have a common denominator. If we take any two numbers, for example 3 and 13, we can multiply them to find a common denominator: $3 \times 13 = 39$. The 3 goes into 39 thirteen times and the 13 goes into 39 three times, so 3 and 13 have 39 as a common denominator. When adding one-quarter and three-sixths in an earlier example we could have multiplied the denominators of 4 and 6 to give 24 and then worked in 24ths rather than in 12ths (the LCD). You can work with any common denominator but the LCD makes the numerators smaller and easier to work with, and the answer requires less cancelling. For example, 20ths and 25ths have a denominator of $20 \times 25 = 500$, but the LCD is only 100.

$$\frac{1}{20} + \frac{1}{25} = \frac{25}{500} + \frac{20}{500} = \frac{45}{500} = \frac{9}{100} \text{ (using the LCD of 500)}$$

$$\frac{1}{20} + \frac{1}{25} = \frac{5}{100} + \frac{4}{100} = \frac{9}{100} \text{ (using the LCD of 100)}$$

Note that if one denominator divides into the other denominator exactly then the larger denominator is the LCD of both denominators. For example, the denominators 2 and 12 have an LCD of 12 (because 2 divides into 12 six times and

12 divides into 12 once; 12 is the lowest number that 12 divides into exactly). So always check to see if the lowest denominator divides into the highest denominator when adding or subtracting fractions; if it does then you have the LCD straight away.

3 Warm-up exercise

Work out the *lowest common denominator* (LCD) only:

1 $\frac{1}{5}$ and $\frac{4}{15}$
Answer ....

2 $\frac{1}{4}$ and $\frac{2}{3}$
Answer ....

3 $\frac{13}{16}$ and $\frac{1}{8}$ and $\frac{3}{4}$
Answer ....

Calculate the following using the LCDs above:

4 $\frac{1}{5} + \frac{4}{15}$
Answer ....

5 $\frac{1}{4} + \frac{2}{3}$
Answer ....

6 $\frac{13}{16} + \frac{1}{8} - \frac{3}{4}$
Answer ....

4 Warm-up exercise

Work out the LCD and then *choose the largest fraction*. Try to work out the answers 'in your head' as far as possible:

1 $\frac{2}{3}$ and $\frac{3}{4}$
Answer ....

2 $\frac{2}{3}$ and $\frac{5}{9}$ and $\frac{11}{18}$
Answer ....

3 $\frac{1}{3}$ and $\frac{2}{5}$ and $\frac{11}{30}$
Answer ....

4 $\frac{5}{6}$ and $\frac{3}{4}$ and $\frac{7}{8}$
Answer ....

5 $\dfrac{30}{100}$ and $\dfrac{7}{25}$ and $\dfrac{16}{50}$ *Answer* ....

6 $\dfrac{75}{1000}$ and $\dfrac{7}{100}$ and $\dfrac{3}{50}$ *Answer* ....

Multiplication and division of fractions

Multiplication is straightforward. All you have to do is multiply the two numerators (top numbers) together and multiply the two denominators (bottom numbers) together. For example:

$$eg \; \frac{1}{5} \times \frac{2}{3} = \frac{1 \times 2}{5 \times 3} = \frac{2}{15}$$

So when multiplying fractions together the rule is:

$$\frac{\textit{Multiply the two top numbers}}{\textit{Multiply the two bottom numbers}}$$

The answer is always smaller than either of the original fractions and always between 0 and 1.

5 Warm-up exercise

Calculate the following and cancel the answer where possible:

1 $\dfrac{2}{3} \times \dfrac{1}{9}$ *Answer* ....   **6** $\dfrac{2}{3} \times \dfrac{3}{4}$ *Answer* ....

2 $\dfrac{4}{15} \times \dfrac{2}{3}$ *Answer* ....   **7** $\dfrac{3}{5} \times \dfrac{5}{9}$ *Answer* ....

3 $\dfrac{4}{7} \times \dfrac{4}{9}$ *Answer* ....   **8** $\dfrac{7}{20} \times \dfrac{5}{7}$ *Answer* ....

4 $\dfrac{2}{3} \times \dfrac{1}{9}$ *Answer* ....   **9** $\dfrac{2}{9} \times \dfrac{3}{9}$ *Answer* ....

5 $\dfrac{3}{5} \times \dfrac{1}{100}$ *Answer* ....   **10** $\dfrac{9}{10} \times \dfrac{1}{3}$ *Answer* ....

Division of fractions is similar except the fraction on the right-hand side must be:

(i) turned upside down (eg $\dfrac{3}{5}$ becomes $\dfrac{5}{3}$)

(ii) then multiplied with the fraction on the left-hand side eg $\dfrac{1}{5} \div \dfrac{3}{10} = ?$

Stage (i) $\dfrac{3}{10}$ becomes $\dfrac{10}{3}$

Stage (ii) $\dfrac{1}{5} \times \dfrac{10}{3} = \dfrac{10}{15}$

So when dividing fractions the rule is:

Turn the right-hand fraction upside down and then multiply the two fractions together.
This can be explained as follows: if we take 6 and multiply it by one-twelfth we have six twelfths, but if we take 6 wholes and divide them into twelfths we have 6 × 12 = 72:

$$\text{So } 6 \times \frac{1}{12} = \frac{6}{12} \text{ but } 6 \div \frac{1}{12} = 72 \left(6 \times \frac{12}{1} = 72\right)$$

We can see that any number divided by a fraction gives a larger number.

6 Warm-up exercise

Calculate the following divisions by turning the right-hand-side fraction upside down and *multiplying by it*:

1 $\dfrac{1}{6} \div \dfrac{1}{4}$ *Answer* ....

2 $\dfrac{1}{3} \div \dfrac{5}{9}$ *Answer* ....

3 $\dfrac{3}{16} \div \dfrac{1}{4}$ *Answer* ....

4 $\dfrac{3}{10} \div \dfrac{3}{5}$ *Answer* ....

5 $\dfrac{5}{12} \div \dfrac{1}{2}$ *Answer* ....

6 $\dfrac{12}{100} \div \dfrac{3}{10}$ *Answer* ....

7 $\dfrac{8}{1000} \div \dfrac{1}{5}$ *Answer* ....

8 $\dfrac{1}{250} \div \dfrac{4}{5}$ *Answer* ....

9 $\dfrac{2}{125} \div \dfrac{8}{75}$ *Answer* ....

10 $\dfrac{3}{7} \div \dfrac{9}{14}$ *Answer* ....

Improper fractions

Until now, we have worked with fractions that have denominators greater than the numerator (bottom greater than top). For example:

$$\frac{1}{4}, \frac{5}{6}, \frac{9}{10}, \frac{13}{16} - \text{these are known as 'vulgar fractions'.}$$

However, some fractions are *top heavy*, eg $\frac{17}{6}, \frac{9}{4}, \frac{65}{25}$ – the numerator is greater than the denominator. These fractions are known as 'improper fractions', and are added, subtracted, multiplied and divided in the same way as for vulgar fractions. For example:

$$\frac{5}{2} + \frac{7}{3} = \frac{15 + 14}{6} = \frac{29}{6}$$

$$\frac{9}{5} - \frac{10}{7} = \frac{63 - 50}{35} = \frac{13}{35}$$

$$\frac{9}{4} \times \frac{8}{5} = \frac{72}{20} = \frac{18}{5}$$

$$\frac{11}{4} \div \frac{9}{7} = \frac{11}{4} \times \frac{7}{9} = \frac{77}{36}$$

7 Warm-up exercise

Work out the following sums containing improper fractions, and cancel your answers where possible:

1 $\frac{7}{6} + \frac{11}{12}$ Answer ....

2 $\frac{14}{3} - \frac{9}{2}$ Answer ....

3 $\frac{5}{4} \times \frac{3}{2}$ Answer ....

4 $\frac{6}{5} \div \frac{12}{5}$ Answer ....

5 $\frac{12}{5} + \frac{5}{2}$ Answer ....

6 $\frac{5}{3} \times \frac{8}{5}$ Answer ....

7 $\frac{25}{6} \div \frac{15}{8}$ Answer ....

8 $\frac{75}{20} \times \frac{40}{3}$ Answer ....

Mixed fractions (or mixed numbers)

A mixed fraction consists of a whole number with a vulgar fraction. Examples of mixed fractions are:

$$1\frac{1}{2}, 2\frac{5}{6}, 5\frac{1}{3}, 3\frac{3}{4}$$

To be able to work out the problems containing mixed fractions we have to turn the mixed fraction into an improper fraction. To do this, we first separate the whole number from the *vulgar* fraction; for example:

$$1\frac{1}{2} \text{ is 1 whole and 1 half: } 1 + \frac{1}{2}$$

The next step is to write the whole number in terms of the fraction. In the above example, 1 is 2 halves, so

$$1 = \frac{2}{2}$$

We can now add the whole, expressed as a fraction, to the vulgar fraction:

$$1\frac{1}{2} = \frac{2}{2} + \frac{1}{2} = \frac{3}{2}$$

so $1\frac{1}{2}$ as an improper fraction is $\frac{3}{2}$.

Similarly, $2\frac{3}{4} = \frac{8}{4} + \frac{3}{4} = \frac{11}{4}$

This example can also be shown in diagram form:

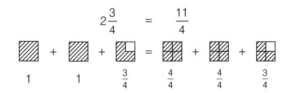

A more mathematical way of converting a mixed fraction to an improper fraction is as follows:

Step (i)   Multiply the whole number by the denominator of the vulgar fraction.

Step (ii)   Put the answer in step (i) over the denominator of the vulgar fraction.

Step (iii)   Combine the vulgar fraction with the answer in step (ii).

For example, express the mixed fraction $2\frac{1}{4}$ as an improper fraction:

Step (i) $2 \times 4 = 8$

Step (ii) $\frac{8}{4}$ (2 wholes = 8 quarters)

Step (iii) $\frac{8}{4} + \frac{1}{4} = \frac{9}{4}$

So $2\frac{1}{4}$ as an improper fraction is $\frac{9}{4}$.

8 Warm-up exercise

Convert the following mixed fractions to improper fractions and cancel where possible:

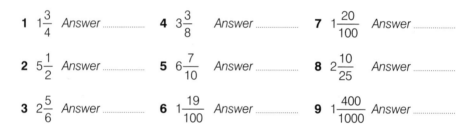

1 $1\frac{3}{4}$ *Answer* ....   **4** $3\frac{3}{8}$ *Answer* ....   **7** $1\frac{20}{100}$ *Answer* ....

2 $5\frac{1}{2}$ *Answer* ....   **5** $6\frac{7}{10}$ *Answer* ....   **8** $2\frac{10}{25}$ *Answer* ....

3 $2\frac{5}{6}$ *Answer* ....   **6** $1\frac{19}{100}$ *Answer* ....   **9** $1\frac{400}{1000}$ *Answer* ....

It is also possible to convert an improper fraction into a mixed fraction – the reverse of above. For example:

$$\frac{27}{8}, \frac{9}{2}, \frac{7}{3}, \frac{11}{10}, \text{ can be converted to mixed fractions.}$$

This is done as follows:

Step (i)   Divide the numerator by the denominator.

Step (ii)   Put the remainder (from the answer in step (i)) over the denominator of the improper fraction.

Step (iii)   Combine the whole number (from the answer in step (i)) with the answer in step (ii).

For example, express the improper fraction $\dfrac{21}{3}$ as a mixed fraction.

Step (i)
$$\overset{\text{5 remainder } \textbf{1}}{4\overline{)21}}$$

Step (ii) $\dfrac{1}{4}$

Step (iii)   combine 5 with $\dfrac{1}{4}$ to give $5\dfrac{1}{4}$

so $\dfrac{21}{4} = 5\dfrac{1}{4}$

9 Warm-up exercise

Convert the following improper fractions to mixed fractions:

1 $\dfrac{9}{2}$ *Answer* ....   **3** $\dfrac{16}{3}$ *Answer* ....   **5** $\dfrac{42}{8}$ *Answer* ....

2 $\dfrac{23}{4}$ *Answer* ....   **4** $\dfrac{50}{3}$ *Answer* ....   **6** $\dfrac{125}{10}$ *Answer* ....

Multiplication and division of fractions by whole numbers

Here it is helpful to rewrite the whole number as an *improper fraction with a denominator of 1*, before carrying out the calculation.

For example, 2, 3, 4, 5 etc can be rewritten as $\dfrac{2}{1}, \dfrac{3}{1}, \dfrac{4}{1}, \dfrac{5}{1}$:

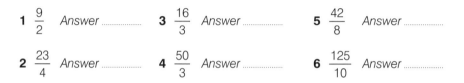

$$\frac{5}{6} \times \textbf{2} = \frac{5}{6} \times \frac{2}{1} = \frac{10}{6} = 1\frac{4}{6} = 1\frac{2}{3}$$

$$\frac{5}{6} \times \textbf{3} = \frac{5}{6} \times \frac{3}{1} = \frac{15}{6} = 2\frac{3}{6} = 2\frac{1}{2}$$

$$\frac{5}{6} \times \textbf{4} = \frac{5}{6} \times \frac{4}{1} = \frac{20}{6} = 3\frac{2}{6} = 3\frac{1}{3}$$

$$\frac{5}{6} \times \textbf{5} = \frac{5}{6} \times \frac{5}{1} = \frac{25}{6} = 4\frac{1}{6}$$

10 Warm-up exercise 10

Multiply or divide the following fractions by the whole numbers shown and express your answers as mixed fractions:

1   $\dfrac{1}{2} \times 5$ *Answer* ....

5   $\dfrac{50}{80} \times 12$ *Answer* ....

2   $\dfrac{3}{4} \times 6$ *Answer* ....

6   $\dfrac{3}{4} \div 5$ *Answer* ....

3   $\dfrac{7}{8} \times 4$ *Answer* ....

7   $\dfrac{4}{9} \div 16$ *Answer* ....

4   $\dfrac{9}{5} \times 6$ *Answer* ....

8   $\dfrac{5}{6} \div 20$ *Answer* ....

How to cross-cancel fractions

Often you can avoid large numbers in calculations by cancelling fractions *diagonally* rather than just top and bottom. Cross-cancelling helps to *simplify* the arithmetic. For example:

$\dfrac{7}{8} \times \dfrac{9}{14}$ Without cross-cancelling this becomes $\dfrac{63}{112}$

In cross-cancelling, the 7 can be cancelled diagonally with the 14 ('7 goes into 7 once and 7 goes into 14 twice'). The calculation then becomes $\dfrac{1}{8} \times \dfrac{9}{2}$ giving $\dfrac{9}{16}$ as the answer. For example:

$\dfrac{8}{15} \times \dfrac{5}{16}$ Without cross-cancelling this becomes $\dfrac{40}{240}$

In cross-cancelling, the 8 can be cancelled diagonally with the 16, and the 5 can be cancelled diagonally with the 15. The calculation becomes $\dfrac{1}{3} \times \dfrac{1}{2}$ giving $\dfrac{1}{6}$ as the answer.

It is difficult to cross-cancel 'in your head' so you would normally write the calculation as follows:

$$\dfrac{\overset{1}{\cancel{8}}}{\underset{3}{\cancel{15}}} \times \dfrac{\overset{1}{\cancel{5}}}{\underset{2}{\cancel{16}}} = \dfrac{1}{3} \times \dfrac{1}{2} = \dfrac{1}{6}$$

11 Warm-up exercise

Work out the following by cross-cancelling as a first step. Express your answers as mixed fractions or whole numbers:

1 $\dfrac{7}{3} \times \dfrac{3}{5}$ *Answer* ....

4 $\dfrac{3}{10} \times 100$ *Answer* ....

2 $\dfrac{51}{16} \times \dfrac{4}{3}$ *Answer* ....

5 $\dfrac{32}{40} \times 80$ *Answer* ....

3 $\dfrac{240}{50} \times \dfrac{5}{3}$ *Answer* ....

6 $\dfrac{36}{500} \times 1000$ *Answer* ....

(In the following divisions, cross-cancel *after* turning the right-hand-side number upside down.)

7 $\dfrac{5}{12} \div \dfrac{16}{24}$ *Answer* ....

12 $\dfrac{14}{216} \div \dfrac{28}{36}$ *Answer* ....

8 $\dfrac{17}{100} \div \dfrac{34}{50}$ *Answer* ....

13 $\dfrac{3}{4} \div \dfrac{375}{1000}$ *Answer* ....

9 $\dfrac{27}{100} \div \dfrac{3}{5}$ *Answer* ....

14 $\dfrac{48}{60} \div \dfrac{80}{360}$ *Answer* ....

10 $\dfrac{40}{150} \div \dfrac{64}{120}$ *Answer* ....

15 $\dfrac{15}{100} \div 60$ *Answer* ....

11 $\dfrac{30}{144} \div \dfrac{110}{132}$ *Answer* ....

12 Warm-up exercise

Work out the following by first converting the mixed fractions to improper fractions. The answers are all whole numbers:

1 $4\dfrac{1}{2} \times \dfrac{2}{3}$ *Answer* ....

4 $20 \div 2\dfrac{1}{2}$ *Answer* ....

2 $2\dfrac{4}{5} \times 5$ *Answer* ....

5 $1\dfrac{1}{3} \div \dfrac{1}{6}$ *Answer* ....

3 $4\dfrac{4}{9} \times 1\dfrac{4}{5}$ *Answer* ....

6 $2\dfrac{2}{3} \div \dfrac{8}{15}$ *Answer* ....

7 $5\frac{1}{4} \div 1\frac{3}{4}$ *Answer* ....   **9** $1\frac{200}{1000} \times 4\frac{1}{6}$ *Answer* ....

8 $\frac{45}{100} \times 2\frac{2}{9}$ *Answer* ....

Ratios and proportional parts

Ratios are similar to fractions and they show you how a whole is divided into parts. Examples of ratios are 5:2 (five parts to two parts), 3:1 (three parts to one part), 1:4 (one part to four parts), 3:2:6 (three parts to two parts to six parts). The ratio tells you how many parts in total are present in the whole.

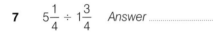 Example: a ratio of 5:2 means there are 7 parts in the whole (5+2). A ratio of 3:2:6 means there are 11 parts in the whole (3+2+6).

So for a ratio of 5:2 the whole is split into sevenths, and for a ratio of 3:2:6 the whole is split into elevenths. To find out how much each part of the ratio is of the whole we divide each part by the total number of parts.

So, 5:2 means that the whole is divided into $\frac{5}{7}$ and $\frac{2}{7}$

A ratio of 3:2:6 means that the whole is divided into $\frac{3}{11}$, $\frac{2}{11}$ and $\frac{6}{11}$

This is known as dividing a quantity into proportional parts.

For example: divide 60 in the ratio 3:1.

First step: Work out the number of parts in the whole, in this case: 3 + 1 = 4 (four quarters).

Second step: Work out the proportional parts (the fractions), these are $\frac{3}{4}$ and $\frac{1}{4}$.

Third step: Multiply the whole by the proportional parts: $\frac{3}{4} \times 60 = 45$; and $\frac{1}{4} \times 60 = 15$

So 60 in the ratio 3:1 is 45:15.

The proportional parts when added together give the whole:

45 + 15 = 60

Ratios can be simplified in a similar way to fractions by cancelling *both sides* by a common factor (eg by 2, by 3 etc).

Example: The ratio of boys to girls in a science class of 28 is 16:12. Express this ratio in its simplest terms.

16:12 = 8:6 = 4:3 ie there are 4 boys for every 3 girls

Example: the ratio of boys to girls in a class of 25 is 40:60. How many boys are there and how many girls are there? We can simplify this ratio by looking for common factors (numbers to divide by), in this example 10 and 2:

$40 \div 10 = 4; 60 \div 10 = 6;$

so 40 : 60 = 4:6, which reduces to 2:3 if we divide both sides by 2.

A ratio of 2:3 means that there are 5 parts in the whole (2 + 3) and the whole is split into two-fifths boys (2 parts) and three-fifths girls (3 parts).

$$\text{boys} = \frac{2}{5} \times 25 = 2 \times 5 = 10 \text{ boys}$$

girls = total – boys = 25 – 10 = 15 girls; (subtracting boys from the total is quicker than multiplying 25 by the fraction of girls)

Note that ratio of 40:60 does not mean that there are 100 pupils. There can be any number of pupils, fewer or more than 100. The lowest possible number of pupils is 5 (2 boys and 3 girls). Like a percentage, a ratio is just another way of expressing a fraction.

The method is the same when there are three terms. For example:

The ratio of girls to boys to teachers on a school trip is 5:4:1. Determine the number of girls, boys and teachers if 40 people went on the trip.

Method:

i)   Work out the total number of parts.

ii) Work out the proportional parts (fractions).

iii) Multiply the proportional parts by the whole.

First step: Number of parts = 5 + 4 + 1 = 10

Second step: Work out the proportional parts:

$$\frac{5}{10} ; \frac{4}{10} ; \frac{1}{10}$$

Third step: Multiply the whole by the proportional parts:

$$\frac{5}{10} \times 40 = 20 \text{ girls}; \frac{4}{10} \times 40 = 16 \text{ boys}; \frac{1}{10} \times 40 = 4 \text{ teachers}$$

In all three answers you are multiplying by 40 and dividing by 10, which is the same as multiplying by 4. In other words, there are 4 'people per part'. So instead of using fractions you can multiply the ratio 5:4:1 by 4 to give 20:16:4, which are the respective numbers of girls, boys and teachers.

In another type of ratio question, the total number in one of the proportions is given rather than the total number in the whole.

Example: if the ratio of boys to girl in a class is 5:4 and there are 20 boys, how many girls are in the class?

Here, we are not given the total number of pupils in the class, only the *number of boys*.

We have 5 parts equal to 18 boys, or $\dfrac{5}{9}$ class = 20

There are a few ways to tackle this problem; two non-algebra methods are explained.

i) Intuitive fractions method

We are asked to find the number of girls. We can see that the answer will be less than 20 because the number of girls equals 4 parts (boys are 5 parts). For every 5 boys there are 4 girls, so for every 1 boy there must be 4 ÷ 5, or 4/5 girl.

We have 20 boys so we must have $20 \times \dfrac{4}{5} = 4 \times 4 = 16$ girls.

ii) One-part first method

We have 5 parts equal to 20 boys. We can work out one-part by dividing five-parts by 5. Then we multiply one-part by 4 to give the number of girls (4 parts).

5 parts class = 20, so 1 part class = 20 ÷ 5 = 4 (one-ninth of the class = 4);

Girls = 4 parts = 4 × 4 = 16.

13 Warm-up exercise

1 Divide 60p in the ratio of 5:1   *Answer* ....

2 Divide £30 in the ratio of 2:3   *Answer* ....

3 Divide 125 in the ratio of 19:6   *Answer* ....

4 Divide 600 in the ratio of 3:2:1   *Answer* ....

5 Divide 250 in the ratio of 5:4:1   *Answer* ....

14 Warm-up exercise

1 Place the following fractions in order of size starting with the smallest fraction:

$$\frac{5}{20} \quad \frac{2}{20} \quad \frac{19}{20} \quad \frac{11}{20}$$

Answer ....

2 Place the following fractions in order of size starting with the smallest fraction:

$$\frac{5}{20} \quad \frac{5}{10} \quad \frac{5}{25} \quad \frac{5}{125}$$

Answer ....

3 Tick the two equivalent fractions $\frac{2}{3}, \frac{3}{5}, \frac{6}{9}, \frac{8}{10}$

Answer ....

4 Place the following fractions in order of size starting with the smallest fraction:

$$\frac{5}{10} \quad \frac{11}{20} \quad \frac{1}{5} \quad \frac{12}{40}$$

Answer ....

5 What is the missing numerator? $\frac{6}{10} = \frac{?}{5}$

Answer ....

6 What is the missing denominator? $\frac{2}{3} = \frac{8}{?}$

Answer ....

7 Reduce the fraction $\frac{5}{25}$ to its lowest terms.

Answer ....

8 Cancel the fraction $\frac{36}{60}$ to its lowest terms.

Answer ....

9 Reduce $\frac{15}{90}$ to its lowest terms.

Answer ....

10 Cancel $\frac{35}{100}$

Answer ....

11 Add $\frac{3}{6}$ and $\frac{2}{6}$

Answer ....

12 $\frac{1}{5} + \frac{2}{5} =$

Answer ....

13 Subtract $\frac{5}{8}$ from $\frac{7}{8}$ and simplify your answer.   *Answer* ....

14 $\frac{5}{9} - \frac{3}{9} =$ *Answer* ....

15 $\frac{5}{32} - \frac{1}{8} =$ *Answer* ....

16 Simplify $\frac{3}{4} - \frac{2}{3}$ *Answer* ....

17 $\frac{3}{4} \times \frac{1}{2} =$ *Answer* ....

18 What is $\frac{2}{3} \times \frac{1}{4}$ in its lowest terms?   *Answer* ....

19 $\frac{3}{10} \div 6 =$ *Answer* ....

20 What is $\frac{1}{4}$ of 24?   *Answer* ....

21 20 seconds are what fraction of 1 minute?   *Answer* ....

22 Convert $\frac{27}{7}$ to a mixed fraction.   *Answer* ....

23 Convert $4\frac{1}{2}$ to an improper fraction.   *Answer* ....

24 Write $\frac{18}{6}$ in its lowest terms.   *Answer* ....

25 Write $\frac{10}{4}$ in its lowest terms.   *Answer* ....

26 Multiply $\frac{1}{3}$ by 120   *Answer* ....

27 What is $\frac{2}{3}$ of 75?   *Answer* ....

28 $\dfrac{7}{8} \times 7 =$

Answer ....

29 Solve $\dfrac{33}{7} - 4$

Answer ....

30 $\dfrac{2}{7} \div \dfrac{2}{5} =$

Answer ....

31 Divide 36 in the ratio 5:7

Answer ....

32 In a maths class of 24 pupils the ratio of pupils at Key Stage 5 to Key Stage 6 in maths is 7:5. How many pupils are at Key Stage 5?

Answer ....

33 If the ratio of boys to girls in a class is 7:9 and there are 32 pupils, find:

i) the number of boys;

Answer ....

ii) the number of girls.

Answer ....

15 Easy questions

1 In a school of 185 pupils, one-fifth take free school meals. How many take free school meals?

Answer ....

2 In a secondary school with 900 pupils, four out of every five pupils own a mobile phone. How many pupils do not own a mobile phone?

Answer ....

3 A school has 290 boys and 310 girls. How many girls would you expect there to be in a representative sample of 120 pupils?

Answer ....

4 GCSE pupils take a double science or single science award. If double science is seven times more popular than single science, what fraction of the pupils takes single science?

Answer ....

5 Find the value of $6 \div 1\dfrac{1}{6}$

Answer ....

6   Find the value of $2\frac{1}{3} \div 4\frac{1}{5}$

Answer ....

7   The teacher to pupil ratio on a school trip is not to be less than one to fifteen. How many teachers are needed with 172 pupils?

Answer ....

8   Out of 144 who sat GCSE English, 90 achieved grades A to C. What fraction achieved grades A to C?

Answer ....

9   A school trip requires three 40-seater coaches to hold the pupils and teachers. Two of the coaches are full and the third coach is three-quarters full. How many teachers went on the trip if there was one teacher for every nine pupils?

Answer ....

10   The following table compares a school's A-level entries in chemistry, physics and biology according to sex:

	Chemistry	Physics	Biology
Boys	36	45	30
Girls	32	10	50

Indicate whether the statements are true or false:

i)   The ratio of boys to girls in chemistry was 8:9.

Answer ....

ii)   The ratio of girls to boys in physics was 2:9.

Answer ....

iii) The ratio of boys to girls in biology was 5:3.

Answer ....

11   On a food technology course:

i)   To make jam, the ratio of fruit (in kilograms) to water (in litres) to sugar (in kilograms) is 2:1:3. How much fruit is required to make 12 kilograms of jam?

Answer ....

ii)   To make bread, the ratio of flour to salt to yeast is 75:3:2 (by weight). How much yeast is required to make a loaf weighing 400 grams?

Answer ....

12   The pupil–teacher ratio on a school trip is 9 to 1. If there are three teachers on the trip, how many people are there on the trip?

Answer ....

13   There are 40 people on a school trip, including 4 teachers,
16 girls, with the remainder all boys. Find:

i) the ratio of teachers to girls;   *Answer* ....

ii) the ratio of boys to girls.   *Answer* ....

14   The ratio of girls to boys in a group is 6:10.
If there are 39 girls, how many pupils are there
in the group?   *Answer* ....

16 **More difficult question**

1   John took three tests on the same day, one in maths, one in English and one
in science. His marks in the three tests were in the ratio 4:6:8. If his total mark
was 126, calculate:

a) i)   the fraction of his mark that came
from maths;   *Answer* ....

ii)   his mark in English;   *Answer* ....

b)   the ratio of his mark in science to his mark
in maths and English combined.   *Answer* ....

Chapter 3

Understanding decimals

Decimal numbers are numbers that contain a decimal point (d.p.). Decimal fractions are decimal numbers smaller than one (nought point something); they are fractions of a whole number. The decimal point (.) separates the whole number from the decimal fraction.

Decimal in words	Decimal in figures			
	Units	Tenths	Hun.ths	Thou.ths
three point five eight	3.	5	8	
one point two five six	1.	2	5	6
nought point seven three	0.	7	3	

In the last example (a decimal fraction) we say *nought point seven three* not nought point seventy-three.

Necessary and unnecessary zeros

It is important to understand which zeros are needed and which are not when writing both whole numbers and decimals. Whole numbers such as 2, 10 and 250 should not be written as 2.0, 10.0 and 250.0 – the decimal point and nought after it are unnecessary and could lead to errors if misread as 20, 100 and 250. For a similar reason, a zero should always be placed in front of the decimal point when there is no other number (eg write 0.73 not .73).

The following are examples of unnecessary zeros:

0.30   0.300   0.3000   which should all be written as 0.3
0.850   0.8500   0.85000   which should be written as 0.85

The following are examples of necessary zeros:

    0.3   0.03   0.003   which all have different values
    0.802 0.8002 0.80002 which all have different values

1 Warm-up exercise

Write out the following numbers in figures:

1	twenty two point five	Answer ....
2	nought point two seven five	Answer ....
3	nought point nought two	Answer ....
4	two hundred point zero seven five	Answer ....
5	one hundred and two point three seven five	Answer ....

2 Warm-up exercise

Place the numbers (in columns a, b, c and d) in order of size, starting with the *smallest first*. Write a, b, c, d.

	(a)	(b)	(c)	(d)
1	2.5	0.25	0.3	0.025
2	0.05	0.1	0.08	0.75
3	3.025	3.25	3.05	3.04
4	6.20	6.02	6.026	6.22
5	10.01	10.101	10.011	10.11

Multiplication by powers of ten (×10, ×100, ×1000)

To multiply a decimal number by 10, 100, 1000 etc, you just move the decimal point (d.p.) to the *right* by however many *powers of ten* you have – or put another way, by how many noughts you have (a calculator is not required). To multiply:

    × 10 you move the decimal point (d.p.) 1 place to the right

    × 100 you move the d.p. 2 places to the right

    × 1000 you move the d.p. 3 places to the right

For example, what is 5.178 × 100?

>answer: 5.178 × 100 = 517.8
>similarly: 0.0235 × 10 = 0.235

Division by powers of ten (÷10, ÷100, ÷1000)

Just as in the multiplication of decimals, you can divide decimals by powers of ten (10, 100, 1000, etc) by moving the decimal point. This is simply the reverse of the multiplication case so when dividing you move the decimal point to the *left*. For example:

>25.34 ÷ 10   = 2.534
>   ÷ 100   = 0.2534
>   ÷ 1000 = 0.02534

Other examples are:

>256.98 ÷ 100   = 2.5698
>   ÷ 1000 = 0.25698

Similarly: 0.0037 ÷ 100 = 0.000037

3 Warm-up exercise

Work out the following multiplications and divisions. Hint: the number of zeros following the 1 is the number of places to move the decimal point – either to the right (to multiply) or to the left (to divide):

1   1.589 7 × 1000 =   *Answer* ....

2   7692105 ÷ 10000 =   *Answer* ....

3   31.729 × 100 =   *Answer* ....

4   0.175 ÷ 10 =   *Answer* ....

5   17.1703 × 1000 =   *Answer* ....

6   0.025 × 1000 =   *Answer* ....

7   0.0058 × 1000 =   *Answer* ....

8   0.0001 × 1000000 =   *Answer* ....

Addition, subtraction, multiplication and division of decimals

The addition and subtraction of decimal numbers is the same as for ordinary numbers. The only thing to remember is to keep the decimal points aligned; adding unnecessary zeros can help.

Example: 0.36 + 0.28 + 0.052 + 0.1

```
 0.360
 0.280
 0.052
 0.100+
 ─────
 0.792
 ─────
   1
```

The multiplication of decimals is similar to the multiplication of whole numbers, with an extra step to work out the position of the decimal point (d.p.). The 'golden rule' to find the position is:

Number of d.p.'s in the question = Number of d.p.'s in answer

Example: 4.21 × 3

4.21	two decimal places
3 ×	no decimal places
12.63	two decimal places in the answer.

Example: 0.002 × 0.03

0.002	three decimal places
0.03 ×	two decimal places
0.00006	five decimal places in the answer.

Note that all unnecessary zeros should be removed before you multiply the numbers together.

4 Warm-up exercise

Multiply the following decimal numbers. Treat these as whole numbers first and then add the decimal point as a second step:

1	3.2 × 2.8	*Answer* ....
2	3.08 × 6.5	*Answer* ....
3	0.095 × 3.74	*Answer* ....
4	0.002 × 2.72 (handy hint: place the 0.002 *below* the 2.72)	*Answer* ....
5	10.01 × 0.15	*Answer* ....
6	500 × 0.32 (handy hint: multiply 0.32 by 100 and then by 5)	*Answer* ....
7	75 × 0.04	*Answer* ....
8	33.4 × 3	*Answer* ....
9	800 × 2.54 (handy hint: multiply 2.54 by 100 and then by 8)	*Answer* ....
10	4000 × 3.50	*Answer* ....

The division of decimal numbers is carried out as per whole numbers, while leaving the decimal point in the same position.

Example: 24.369 ÷ 3

$$\begin{array}{r} 8.123 \\ 3\overline{)24.369} \end{array}$$ keep the decimal point in the same position when dividing a decimal number

If the number that you are dividing by contains a decimal point, for example 0.35 or 3.5, then it must be *converted to a whole number* before the division can take place. To do this, you must multiply *both* numbers by a power of ten, ie by 10, 100 or 1000 etc, to remove the decimal point from the number that you are dividing by.

Example: 4.5 ÷ 0.3 becomes 45 ÷ 3 by multiplying *both* of numbers by 10 to remove the decimal point from the 0.3

Similarly 9.375 ÷ 0.02 becomes 937.5 ÷ 2 by multiplying *both* of the numbers by 100 to remove the decimal point from the 0.02

These divisions can now be carried out as per whole numbers.

5 Warm-up exercise

Work out the following division involving decimal numbers. If the number you are *dividing by* contains a decimal point, this must be removed first (questions 4–11):

1	6.8 ÷ 4	*Answer* ....
2	62.25 ÷ 5	*Answer* ....
3	64.25 ÷ 8	*Answer* ....
4	6.8 ÷ 0.04	*Answer* ....
5	9.99 ÷ 0.3	*Answer* ....
6	5.55 ÷ 0.50	*Answer* ....
7	3.6 ÷ 0.6	*Answer* ....
8	9 ÷ 0.15	*Answer* ....
9	1.44 ÷ 1.2	*Answer* ....
10	125 ÷ 0.002	*Answer* ....
11	1000 ÷ 0.05	*Answer* ....
12	0.08 ÷ 5	*Answer* ....

How to round decimal numbers – decimal place (d.p.)

Sometimes the numbers you obtain from a calculation are longer than is required for a sensible answer. For example:

$$3.75 \times 4.01 = 15.0375$$

If this level of *accuracy* is not required then you can shorten the number by *rounding it off*. To do this, you decrease the number of numbers to the right of the decimal point, ie you decrease the number of decimal places (d.p.)

For example, a number such as 15.0375 that has four decimal places (four numbers to the right of the decimal point) can be rounded off so that it has 3, 2 or 1 d.p.

Method:

If the *number to the right* of the decimal place you are shortening to is 5 *or more*, then you increase the number in the decimal place by 1; if is less than 5 it remains the same. For example:

> Round off 15.0375 to three decimal places – ie 3 numbers to the right of the decimal point.
>
> Answer: the number to the right of the third decimal place is 5 (15.037<u>5</u>) so we increase the number in the third decimal place by 1.

15.0375 becomes 15.038
15.0375 = 15.038 correct to 3 d.p.

Other examples are:

> Round off 15.0375 to 2 decimal places
> Answer: 15.0375 to 2 d.p. = 15.04
>
> Round off 15.0375 to 1 decimal places
> Answer: 15.0375 to 1 d.p. = 15.0
>
> Round off 1.973 to 1 d.p.

> more than 5 so the
> 9 becomes a 10 (making 1 unit)

Answer 1.976 to 1 d.p. = 2.0 (one decimal place showing)

> Round off 1.973 to 2 d.p.

> less than 5 so the
> 7 remains the same

Answer 1.973 to 2 d.p. = 1.97 (two decimal places showing)

6 Warm-up exercise

From the five alternatives (1, 2, 3, 4, or 5) choose *one* which completes the statement:

1   6.08323 to 2 d.p. is   6.083   6.08   6.0   6.0832   6.09
                                     1   2   3   4   5

Answer ....

2   0.385426 to 5 d.p. is   0.38543   0.39   0.3854   0.385   0.4
                               1   2   3   4   5

Answer ....

3   0.754 to 1 d.p. is   0.75   0.7   0.754   0.8   1.0
                             1   2   3   4   5

Answer ....

4   7.956 to 2 d.p. is   7.95   8.0   7.96   7.9   7.956
                             1   2   3   4   5

Answer ....

7 Warm-up exercise

Work out the following and then *give your answer* to the number of decimal places shown:

1   25 ÷ 6 =   (to 2 d.p.)   *Answer* ....

2   100 ÷ 7 =   (to 4 d.p.)   *Answer* ....

3   3.45 × 3 =   (to 1 d.p.)   *Answer* ....

4   14.5 × 3 =   (to the nearest whole number = to 0 d.p.)

Answer ....

Work out the following and then give your answer to the nearest whole number:

5   325 ÷ 4 =   *Answer* ....

6   1279 ÷ 8 =   *Answer* ....

7   655 ÷ 10 =   *Answer* ....

8   100 ÷ 6   *Answer* ....

9   73 ÷ 22   *Answer* ....

10 400 ÷ 3   *Answer* ....

Conversion of decimals to fractions

In order to convert a decimal to a fraction you divide the numbers to the right of the decimal point by:

10 if one number is present

100 if two numbers are present

1000 if three numbers are present etc

then cancel the fraction to its lowest terms. For example:

$$0.5 = \frac{5}{10} = \frac{1}{2}$$

$$0.25 = \frac{25}{100} = \frac{1}{4}$$

$$0.125 = \frac{125}{1000} = \frac{1}{8}$$

8 Warm-up exercise

Convert the following decimal numbers to fractions using the method outlined above.

1	0.6	*Answer*			
2	0.75	*Answer*	**6**	0.08	*Answer* ....
3	0.625	*Answer*	**7**	0.95	*Answer* ....
4	0.9	*Answer*	**8**	1.75	*Answer* ....
5	0.001	*Answer*	**9**	2.375	*Answer* ....

Decimal fractions worth remembering (in ascending size)

0.01 = nought point nought one = one-hundredth = 1/100

0.05 = nought point nought five = one-twentieth = 1/20

0.1 = nought point one = one-tenth =1/10

0.125 = nought point one two five = one-eighth = 1/8

0.2 = nought point two = one-fifth = 1/5

0.25 = nought point two five = one-quarter = 1/4

0.33 = nought point three three = one-third = 1/3

0.375 = nought point three seven five = three-eighths = 3/8

0.5 = nought point five = one-half = 1/2

0.625 = nought point six two five = five-eighths = 5/8

0.67 = nought point six seven = two-thirds = 2/3

0.75 = nought point seven five = three-quarters = 3/4

0.8 = nought point eight = four-fifths = 4/5

0.9 = nought point nine = nine-tenths = 9/10

Conversion of fractions to decimals

In scientific work it is usually more convenient to express a fraction as a decimal. The method is straightforward. All you have to do is divide the denominator (bottom number) into the numerator (top number).

Example: express $\frac{1}{2}$ as a decimal number

First step: rewrite $\frac{1}{2}$ as $2\overline{)1}$

Second step: rewrite the 1 as 1.0000 by adding a string of zeros

$$2\overline{)1.0000}$$

This division is carried out in the same way as with ordinary numbers, leaving the decimal point in the same position.

2 into 1 won't go so you put a nought down and carry the 1 into the next column to make 10; 2 into 10 goes 5 times.

$$\frac{0.\ 5}{2\overline{)1.^{1}0000}}$$

So $\frac{1}{2}$ expressed as a decimal number is 0.5

Example: $\dfrac{5}{8}$ as a decimal $= 8\overline{)5.0000}$

$$= 8\overline{)5.^50^20^400}$$
$$\qquad\quad 0.\ 6\ 2\ 5$$
$$= 0.625$$

Example: $\dfrac{7}{400}$ as a decimal $= 400\overline{)7.0000}$

$$= 400\overline{)7.^700^{300}0^{200}0}$$
$$\qquad\qquad 0.\ 01\ \ 7\ \ 5$$
$$= 0.175$$

9 Warm-up exercise

Express the following fractions as decimal numbers:

1 $\dfrac{3}{10}$ *Answer* ....

2 $\dfrac{1}{4}$ *Answer* ....   **6** $\dfrac{7}{8}$ *Answer* ....

3 $\dfrac{2}{5}$ *Answer* ....   **7** $\dfrac{17}{20}$ *Answer* ....

4 $\dfrac{5}{4}$ *Answer* ....   **8** $\dfrac{21}{200}$ *Answer* ....

5 $\dfrac{3}{25}$ *Answer* ....   **9** $\dfrac{27}{15}$ *Answer* ....

Estimation with decimal numbers

An estimate (or rough idea) of an answer is useful in spotting any wrong answers in multiple choice tests. Take, for example, 3.15×1.92. This can be estimated. To do this, we approximate each of the number involved, as follows: 3.15 is approximately 3; 1.92 is approximately 2; so the answer is approximately 6 (3×2). The accurate answer is 6.048. So, we estimate a sum by increasing or decreasing the value of the numbers to give simple numbers that can be worked out in your head.

Example: $87.1 \div 9.2$. Here, we can approximate the 87.1 to 90 and the 9.2 to 9, so $87.1 \div 9.2$ becomes $90 \div 9$ giving an approximate answer of 10.

You can approximate a number to any other number you wish. However, the closer the estimated values are to the actual numbers the more accurate your estimated answer will be. To learn more about approximating, see the earlier section on rounding numbers.

Example: find an estimated answer for the following multiplication: 89×12.2

A very rough estimate for the answer is $100 \times 10 = 1000$

A more accurate estimate for the answer is $90 \times 12 = 1080$

The accurate answer (the actual value) is $89 \times 12.2 = 1085.8$

Estimating an answer in the above way is useful in making sure that your accurate answer is sensible, and therefore, likely to be correct.

10 Warm-up exercise

Use approximations to find the correct answers:

1 12.1×4.85
   a) 58.69   b) 92.5   c) 70.21   d) 36   *Answer* ....

2 $24.1 \div 9.6$
   a) 4.4   b) 2.51   c) 1.91   d) 3.7   *Answer* ....

3 $\dfrac{94.6 \times 0.51}{24.8}$
   a) 12.7   b) 4   c) 8.64   d) 1.95   *Answer* ....

11 Warm-up exercise

Work out the following problems:

1 $1.5897 \times 1000 =$ *Answer* ....

2 $31.729 \times 100 =$ *Answer* ....

3 $17.1703 \times 1000 =$ *Answer* ....

4 $7692105 \div 10000 =$ *Answer* ....

5 $0.175 \div 1000 =$ *Answer* ....

6 $0.0058 \div 1000 =$ *Answer* ....

7   Multiply 5.5 by 6   *Answer* ....

8   Multiply 22.75 by 4   *Answer* ....

9   Divide 120 by 0.05   *Answer* ....

12 Easy questions

1   Find the decimal number exactly half-way
between 2.02 and 2.03.   *Answer* ....

2   Express 0.45 as a fraction.   *Answer* ....

3   Write 25 thousandths as a decimal fraction.   *Answer* ....

4   Calculate 0.7 + 0.2 × 7.   *Answer* ....

5   Convert $\dfrac{23}{25}$ to a decimal fraction. *Answer* ....

13 More difficult questions

1   Divide 45.5 by 6 and give your answer
to 2 decimal places.   *Answer* ....

2   Calculate 0.3 × 0.4 ÷ 0.15 giving
your answer as a fraction.   *Answer* ....

3   Convert 0.875 to a fraction in its lowest term. *Answer* ....

4   Evaluate $\dfrac{2.7}{0.45} \times \dfrac{1}{12}$ *Answer* ....

5   Evaluate $\dfrac{1}{0.625}$ as a decimal number.   *Answer* ....

Chapter 4

Calculating percentages

A percentage (percentage sign is %) means 'out of one hundred'; in other words, something is split into a hundred equal parts and each part is one per cent. A percentage is basically a special case of a fraction. *All* percentage fractions have the same denominator, which is 100. All that changes is the top number. For example:

$$3\% = \frac{3}{100} \ (3 \div 100) \qquad\qquad 99\% = \frac{99}{100} \ (99 \div 100)$$

A percentage fraction can be cancelled to its lowest terms:

$$40\% = \frac{40}{100} \ (40 \div 100) \text{ which cancels to } \frac{4}{10} \text{ and finally to } \frac{2}{5}$$

$$12\% = \frac{12}{100} \ (12 \div 100) \text{ which cancels to } \frac{6}{50} \text{ and finally to } \frac{3}{25}$$

Percentages can also be written in decimal form. To do this we divide the percentage by 100, expressing the answer as a decimal. The easiest way to divide by 100 is to move the decimal point two places to the left. For example:

40% as a decimal: $40.0 \div 100 = 0.4$

Similarly, 99% as a decimal: $99.0 \div 100 = 0.99$

Similarly, 3% as a decimal: $03.0 \div 100 = 0.03$

How do you work out the percentage of something? To do this you must multiply the 'something' by the percentage fraction. For example:

Find 25% of 60

First step: $25\% = \frac{25}{100} = \frac{1}{4}$ $\qquad\qquad$ Second step: $\frac{1}{4} \times 60 = \frac{60}{4} = 15$

Another method is to convert the percentage to a decimal fraction as a first step. For example:

Find 25% of 60

First step: 25% = 25 ÷ 100 = 0.25   Second step: 0.25 × 60 = 15

In the above example, the fraction method of working out the answer was easier than the decimal method but in some cases the reverse is true.

How to express numbers as percentages

We have seen that percentage means out of 100, so:

$$100\% = \frac{100}{100} = 1$$

This means that we can write any number as a percentage, without affecting its value, by multiplying it by 100%, ie by 1.
    Whole numbers can be converted to percentages as follows:

2 × 100% = 200% (ie 2 wholes is 200%)

Similarly 10 × 100% = 1000% (ie 10 wholes is 1000%)

Fractions can be converted to percentages in the same way. For example:

Example: $\frac{1}{4}$ × 100% = 25%   similarly $\frac{3}{10}$ × 100% = 30%

Decimal fractions can be converted to percentages in the same way, ie by multiplying by 100%, for example:

0.15 × 100% = 15%   0.01 × 100% = 1%

0.995 × 100% = 95.5%   1.1 × 100% = 110%

Working out percentage change from the original number

Sometimes you will have to compare old and new figures in terms of a percentage change. The change is always calculated as a percentage of the original number, not the final number. For example:

A new car is priced at £20,000. After one year the value has dropped to £14,000. Find the percentage depreciation in terms of the original cost.

After one year the car is worth £14,000.

So it depreciates by $20000 - 14000 = 6000$

$$\% \text{ depreciation} = \frac{\text{depreciation}}{\text{original cost}} \times 100\%$$

$$= \frac{6000}{20000} \times 100\%$$

$$= \frac{6}{20} \times 100\% = \frac{3}{10} \times 100\% = 30\%$$

Find the percentage increase in price if the price rises from £60 to £75.

Increase in price $= 75 - 60 = £15$

$$\% \text{ increase} = \frac{\text{increase in price}}{\text{original price}} \times 100\%$$

$$= \frac{15}{60} \times 100\% = 25\%$$

Find the percentage decrease in price when the price drops from £75 to £60.

$$\% \text{ decrease} = \frac{\text{decrease in price}}{\text{original price}} \times 100\%$$

$$= \frac{15}{75} \times 100\% = 20\%$$

Note how £60 to £75 is a 25% increase whereas £75 to £60 is a 20% decrease, even though the change is £15 in both instances; this is because of the different starting values (denominators).

Working out the original price from the percentage change

It is easy to work out the new price when you know the percentage change but working out the original price from the new price requires a little more thought.

In the first instance (working out the new price) you simply multiply the new price by the percentage discount subtracted from 100%. For example:

An e-book reader is priced at £169. The price is reduced by 20% in a sale. What is the sale price?

£169 $\times (100 - 20)\% = $ £169 $\times 80\% = $ £169 $\times 0.8 = $ £135.20

Alternatively, you can work out how much the 20% price reduction comes to before subtracting it from the full price: £169 $\times 20\% = $ £169 $\times 0.2 = $ £33.80 discount, then the sale price is given by £169 $-$ £33.80 $= $ £135.20 as before.

Working out the original price knowing the discounted price is more difficult. You are being asked to *find the* 100% price starting with the discounted price. For example:

An e-book reader is priced at £100 in a sale where the price has been dropped by 10%. What was the normal price before the sale?

Here, it is tempting to add 10% to the sale price of £100, ie £10 to get £110, but this is incorrect; if we had started at £110 and taken 10% off the price then the discount would have come out at £110 × 10% = £11 and the sale price would be £99 not £100. To find the correct starting price you need to *divide by the sale price percentage, expressed as a decimal*.

Sale price = £100. We are told that this is the normal full price less 10% so we can say that:

£100 = (100% – 10%) of the normal price;

so £100 = 90% of the normal price or 0.9 multiplied by the original price.

To get back to the original 100% price (original price × 1.0) we need to divide by 0.9 (dividing any given number by a number smaller than one increases the given number).

We need to *divide the discounted price by 0.9* (0.9 ÷ 0.9 gets us back to 1.0 or 100%); so original full price = £100 ÷ 0.9

To make the division easier we remove the decimal as follows:

£100 ÷ 0.9 = £1000 ÷ 9 = £111.11.

You can check this by multiplying the full price of £111.11 by 90% to get the discounted price of £100.

You also need to be careful when answering questions that ask for the *'percentage point increase'*, which is the difference between the percentages, not the percentage change. Consider the following example:

Comparing two year groups, 60% of pupils gained grades A–C in GCSE maths in 2011 and 80% gained grades A–C in 2012. Calculate:

i) the percentage point increase in GCSE maths grades A–C from 2011 to 2012.

ii) the percentage increase in GCSE maths grades A–C from 2011 to 2012.

i) 80% – 60% = 20% (a 20 percentage point increase)

ii) percentage increase = change in percentage ÷ by original percentage
= 20 ÷ 80 × 100% = 0.25 × 100% = 25% improvement

1 Warm-up exercise

Convert the following percentages to both fractions AND decimals:

1 20% *Answer* ....

2 25% *Answer* .... **6** 45% *Answer* ....

3 10% *Answer* .... **7** 35% *Answer* ....

4 75% *Answer* .... **8** 22% *Answer* ....

5 90% *Answer* .... **9** 2% *Answer* ....

Work out the following percentages using either the fractions method or the decimal method.

Use the fractions method:

10 50% of 180 *Answer* ....

11 30% of 200 *Answer* ....

12 10% of 250 *Answer* ....

13 5% of 250 *Answer* ....

Use the decimal method:

14 62.5% of 200 *Answer* ....

15 $2\frac{1}{2}$% of 1000 *Answer* ....

Convert each decimal or fraction to a percentage by multiplying it by 100%:

16 0.5 *Answer* .... **21** 0.005 *Answer* ....

17 0.015 *Answer* .... **22** $\frac{1}{5}$ *Answer* ....

18 0.75 *Answer* .... **23** $\frac{9}{25}$ *Answer* ....

19 1.05 *Answer* .... **24** $\frac{1}{8}$ *Answer* ....

20 1.0 *Answer* .... **25** $\frac{17}{20}$ *Answer* ....

Find the percentage change in going from:

26   £100 to £150   *Answer* ....

27   £50 to £30   *Answer* ....

28   £150 to £60   *Answer* ....

29   £75.00 to £56.25   *Answer* ....

30   If 20% of applicants fail a test, how many applicants
        pass the test if there are 32400 test takers?   *Answer* ....

2 Easy questions

1   In a school, 320 pupils sat GCSE English Language and 65% achieved
       grade C or below. How many achieved grade B or above?

                                                              Answer ....

2   What is 37.5% as a fraction?

                                                              Answer ....

3   An 11–18 comprehensive school has 1500 on roll, including 180 A-level
       students. What percentage of the pupils on roll are A-level students?

                                                              Answer ....

4   A total of 240 sat GCSE English. If 45% of the pupils achieved grade D or
       below, how many pupils achieved grade C or above?

                                                              Answer ....

5   An 11–18 comprehensive school has 1550 on roll, including 310 A-level
       students. What percentage of the pupils on roll are A-level students?

                                                              Answer ....

6   A school with 950 has an occupancy rate of 94%.
       How many more pupils could it take?

                                                              Answer ....

7   A pupil gained 30 marks out of 50 in one maths test and 16 marks out of 25
       in a second maths test. What was the average percentage for the two tests
       assuming they were weighted equally?

                                                              Answer ....

8   A geography school trip costs £70 and the deposit is £14. What percentage
       of the cost is the deposit?

                                                              Answer ....

9   In a primary school, 5% of half-day sessions were missed through absence. If there were 380 half-day sessions, how many were missed through absence?

Answer ....

10   The highest mark in a maths test was 46 correct answers out of 50 questions and the lowest mark was 25 correct answers out of 50. What is the difference between the highest and lowest marks in percentage points?

Answer ....

11   In a year group, 7 out of every 10 pupils achieved Key Stage 2. What percentage of the pupils failed to achieve Key Stage 2?

Answer ....

12   A test has a pass mark of 70%. If there are 35 questions, what is the minimum number of correct answers necessary to pass?

Answer ....

Chapter 5

Aspects of algebra

Algebra is the use of letters instead of numbers; often the letters describe the 'general case' of something as part of an *algebraic expression*. The letters *x* and *y* are the most common letters chosen. Letters are known as *variables* because their values can be varied; numbers have fixed values and are *constants*. When a constant is placed in front of a variable, as in the *term* 5*x*, the constant is called a *coefficient*. Many of the processes that apply to ordinary numbers (addition, subtraction etc) also apply in algebra. There are five aspects of either algebra or subjects directly related to algebra that you need to know: (i) directed numbers; (ii) substitution; (iii) removing brackets and simplifying; (iv) factorizing; (v) transposing equations; vi) solving linear equations.

Directed numbers

Directed numbers by themselves are not actually algebra; however, you need to be able to use them fully to solve many algebraic problems. Directed numbers are concerned with both positive and negative numbers. You will already be familiar with some negative numbers, for example temperature – when the temperature drops below freezing, the value becomes negative, eg minus five degrees Celsius ($-5\,°C$).

The four basic rules of ordinary numbers (addition, subtraction, multiplication and division) also apply to directed numbers. To understand the concept of directed numbers, it is often easier to refer to a number line that has positive numbers to the right and negative numbers to the left, with a zero placed in the middle. Number lines are used in the examples below.

Example: $3 + 2 = 5$ $(+3 + 2 = +5)$

$$\xrightarrow{+2}$$
$$-9\ -8\ -7\ -6\ -5\ -4\ -3\ -2\ -1\ 0\ +1\ +2\ +3\ +4\ +5\ +6\ +7\ +8\ +9$$

Example: $5 - 3 = 2 \; (+5 - 3 = +2)$

$$-3$$

$-9 \; -8 \; -7 \; -6 \; -5 \; -4 \; -3 \; -2 \; -1 \; 0 \; +1 \; +2 \; +3 \; +4 \; +5 \; +6 \; +7 \; +8 \; +9$

Example: $-7 + 3 = -4$

$$+3$$

$-9 \; -8 \; -7 \; -6 \; -5 \; -4 \; -3 \; -2 \; -1 \; 0 \; +1 \; +2 \; +3 \; +4 \; +5 \; +6 \; +7 \; +8 \; +9$

Example: $7 - 9 = -2$

$$-9$$

$-9 \; -8 \; -7 \; -6 \; -5 \; -4 \; -3 \; -2 \; -1 \; 0 \; +1 \; +2 \; +3 \; +4 \; +5 \; +6 \; +7 \; +8 \; +9$

Example: $-2 - 6 = -8$

$$-6$$

$-9 \; -8 \; -7 \; -6 \; -5 \; -4 \; -3 \; -2 \; -1 \; 0 \; +1 \; +2 \; +3 \; +4 \; +5 \; +6 \; +7 \; +8 \; +9$

Example: $-7 + 13 = 6$

$$+13$$

$-9 \; -8 \; -7 \; -6 \; -5 \; -4 \; -3 \; -2 \; -1 \; 0 \; +1 \; +2 \; +3 \; +4 \; +5 \; +6 \; +7 \; +8 \; +9$

Example: $-7 - (-9) = 2$ (seven subtract minus nine equals two)

$$- (-9)$$

$-9 \; -8 \; -7 \; -6 \; -5 \; -4 \; -3 \; -2 \; -1 \; 0 \; +1 \; +2 \; +3 \; +4 \; +5 \; +6 \; +7 \; +8 \; +9$

Two negatives make a positive (subtracting a negative is like adding a positive)

Example: $9 + (-5) = 4$ (nine add minus five equals four)

$$+ (-5)$$

$-9 \; -8 \; -7 \; -6 \; -5 \; -4 \; -3 \; -2 \; -1 \; 0 \; +1 \; +2 \; +3 \; +4 \; +5 \; +6 \; +7 \; +8 \; +9$

A positive and a negative make a negative (negative dominates; adding a negative is like subtracting a positive)

Example: $9 - (+5) = 4$ (this is the same as $9 - 5$)

$$- (+5)$$

$-9 \; -8 \; -7 \; -6 \; -5 \; -4 \; -3 \; -2 \; -1 \; 0 \; +1 \; +2 \; +3 \; +4 \; +5 \; +6 \; +7 \; +8 \; +9$

1 Warm-up exercise

Work out the following additions and subtractions and include the sign in your answer where necessary. Note: if no sign is placed in front of a number then it is assumed to be a positive number (5 means +5, 9 means + 9 etc):

$$-9\ -8\ -7\ -6\ -5\ -4\ -3\ -2\ -1\ 0\ +1\ +2\ +3\ +4\ +5\ +6\ +7\ +8\ +9$$

1 $6 + 2 =$ *Answer* ....

2 $6 - 2 =$ *Answer* ....

3 $-6 + 2 =$ *Answer* ....

4 $-6 - 2 =$ *Answer* ....

5 $-2 + 6 =$ *Answer* ....

6 $-16 + 2 =$ *Answer* ....

7 $-16 - 2 =$ *Answer* ....

8 $-5 + 8 =$ *Answer* ....

9 $-5 + 4 =$ *Answer* ....

10 $-5 - 4 =$ *Answer* ....

11 $-5 + (- 4) =$ *Answer* ....

12 $-5 - (-4) =$ *Answer* ....

13 $-7 + 3 =$ *Answer* ....

14 $-7 + (-3) =$ *Answer* ....

15 $-7 - (-3) =$ *Answer* ....

16 $72 + (+28) + (-23) =$ *Answer* ....

17 $-36 - 64 - (-90) =$ *Answer* ....

18 $-22 + 28 - 16 =$ *Answer* ....

19 $15 - 45 - 70 =$ *Answer* ....

20 $85 + (- 50) - 55 =$ *Answer* ....

The principle that two negatives combine to make a positive, and a negatively signed number dominates a positively signed number, also applies to the multiplication and division of numbers, as per the following examples:

$-12 \times 3 = -36$

$-12 \times -3 = 36$

$12 \div -3 = -4$

$-12 \div 3 = -4$

$-12 \div -3 = 4$

$-12 \times -3 \times -2 = -72 \ (-12 \times -3 = +36; 36 \times -2 = -72)$

$-12 \times -3 \times -2 \times -2 = 144 \ (-72 \text{ from the above}, \times -2 = +144)$

Multiplication signs are omitted if brackets are used:

$(-12)(-3)(-2)$ means $-12 \times -3 \times -2$

In an earlier example we showed that $-7 + 13 = 6$.

$$\xrightarrow{\hspace{3cm} +13 \hspace{3cm}}$$

$-9\ -8\ -7\ -6\ -5\ -4\ -3\ -2\ -1\ 0\ +1\ +2\ +3\ +4\ +5\ +6\ +7\ +8\ +9$

If the 13 is placed on the far left we can rewrite the equation as follows: $+\,13\,-7 = 6$, and then drop the unneeded positive sign with the 13 to give $13\,-7 = 6$.

$$\xleftarrow{\hspace{3cm} -7 \hspace{3cm}}$$

$-4\ -3\ -2\ -1\ 0\ +1\ +2\ +3\ +4\ +5\ +6\ +7\ +8\ +9\ +11\ +12\ +13\ +14\ +15$

If we move the minus seven to the other side of the equals sign it becomes plus seven because $13 = 6 + 7$, which shows that *a number (or letter) changes its sign when moving from one side of an equation to the other*, ie from -7 on the left-hand side to $+7$ on the right-hand side. Similarly, we can see that $13 - 6 = 7$, where the 6 on the right-hand side becomes -6 when move to the left-hand side. The simplest example following this rule is:

$1 = 1; 1 - 1 = 0; 0 = 1 - 1$; by moving the ones from one side to the other.

The ability to move numbers and letters from one side on an equation to the other is a very useful skill in algebra and in equations in general.

2 Warm-up exercise

Work out the following multiplications and divisions:

1 $6 \times 2 =$ *Answer* ....

2 $6 \times (-2) =$ *Answer* ....

3 $-6 \times (3) =$ *Answer* ....

4 $-6 \times (-3) =$ *Answer* ....

5 $-6 \times (-3) \times (-2) =$ *Answer* ....

6 $-2 \times (-4) \times 5 =$ *Answer* ....

7 $-15 \div 5 =$ *Answer* ....

8 $-15 \div (-5) =$ *Answer* ....

9 $20 \div (-5) =$ *Answer* ....

10 $20 \div (-5) \times (-1) =$ *Answer* ....

11 $-20 \div (-5) \times (-1) =$ *Answer* ....

12 $20 \div (-5) \div (-2) =$ *Answer* ....

Substitution

The first real skill of algebra involves substituting numbers for the letters. For example:

If $x = 5$ and $y = 7$ find:

a) $x + y$ $(5 + 7 = 12)$

b) $2x - y$ $(2 \times 5 - 7 = 3)$

c) $x^2 + 3y - 3$ $(5 \times 5 + 3 \times 7 - 3 = 25 + 21 - 3 = 43$; remembering to follow the BIDMAS rules)

If $x = 2$ and $y = -2$, find:

a) $x + y$ $(2 + -2 = 0$; for clarity this is best written as $2 + (-2) = 0)$

b) $x - y$ $(2 - -2 = 4$; for clarity this is best written as $2 - (-2) = 4)$

c) xy (x times y) $(2 \times (-2) = -4)$

Removing brackets and simplifying

Another skill is removing brackets and simplifying, also known as *expanding* an expression and *collecting like terms*. A term outside a bracket multiplies each of the terms inside the bracket, moving from left to right:

$3(y - 5z)$ = 3 times y plus 3 times $-5z$; = $3y - 15z$ (negative sign dominates)

Similarly: $-2y(6 - 3x + z) = -12y + 6xy - 2yz$ (negative times positive is negative and negative times negative is positive)

Simplifying is a process of collecting like terms together. So for example:

$2x + 3x + 4y + 5y + 6z + 7z = 5x + 9y + 13z$

Similarly: $5(x + 3y) - 3x + y$; expand the brackets first: $5x + 15y - 3x + y$, then collect like terms to give $2x + 16y$

Factorizing

This is the reverse of expanding an expression. By factorizing we can condense an algebraic expression by placing common factors outside a bracket; the factors multiply all the terms inside the bracket. For example, in $2x + 16y$ both terms have a factor of 2, so we can take this outside a bracket to give:

$2x + 16y = 2(x + 8y)$.

Similarly $-12y + 6xy - 2yz$ has 2 and y as common factors to all three terms so we can take these outside a bracket together as follows to give:

$-12y + 6xy - 2yz = 2y(-6 + 3x - z)$, which can be tidied up by placing the x term before the negative terms: $2y(3x - z - 6)$.

Transposing equations

A further skill is that of rearranging a formula (an equation with two or more variables). Take the following formula for example:

$x = y + y$

To make y the subject of the formula, subtract z from *both sides* of the equation to *leave y on its own*:

$x - z = y + z - z$

to give $x - z = y$ ie $y = x - z$

To make z the subject of the formula, subtract y from both sides of the equation to *leave z on its own*:

$$x - y = y + z - y$$

gives $x - y = z$ ie $z = x - y$

Example: Find x if $3x + y = z$ (x is the subject of the formula).

Step 1: subtract y from both sides:

$$3x + y - y = z - y$$
$$3x = z - y$$

Step 2: divide both sides of the equation by 3 to give x on its own:

$$\frac{3x}{3} = \frac{z - y}{3} \quad \text{so} \quad x = \frac{z - y}{3}$$

Solving linear equations

Linear equations have letters with a power of one – there are no squared terms. Examples of linear equations can be found in mathematics, science and everyday life. Typical examples are:

temperature conversion;

speed, distance and time;

ratio and proportion;

maps and scales;

VAT and income tax;

electrical power.

Examples of linear equations and algebraic manipulation are:

Calculate distance travelled (D) from speed (S) and time (T):

$D = ST$ (and $T = D \div S$; $S = D \div T$)

Calculate power in Watts (W) from volts (V) and amps (A):

$W = VA$ (and $V = W \div A$; $A = W \div V$)

The following formula is more difficult to rearrange because it requires more than one step. Your ability to find solutions to problems will increase if you can move letters and numbers around easily from one side of an equation to the other. The 'golden rule' is that whatever you do on one side of the equation you must do on the opposite side of the equation to maintain the balance.

To convert temperature from Celsius to Fahrenheit and vice versa:

$$F = \frac{5}{9}C + 32 \text{ and } C = \frac{5}{9}(F - 32)$$

eg Rearrange $F = \frac{5}{9}C + 32$ to leave C on its own.

i) Subtract 32 from *both sides* to give: $F - 32 = \frac{5}{9}C + 0$

ii) Now multiply *both sides* by $\frac{5}{9}$ to give $\frac{5}{9}(F - 32) = \frac{5}{9} \times \frac{9}{5}C$

Multiplying in this way gets rid of the fraction in front of the C because it is cancelled to leave 1, as follows:

$\frac{5}{9}(F - 32) = 1 \times C$ so we now have C on its own.

The final expression reads $\frac{5}{9}(F - 32) = C$, though we would normally write this

as $C = \frac{5}{9}(F - 32)$, by putting the variable we want on the left-hand side of the

equation. In words, to convert degrees Fahrenheit to degrees Celsius you subtract thirty-two from the temperature in Fahrenheit ('brackets first'), then multiply by five and divide by nine.

Key point: when solving linear equations put all the variables on the left of the equation and all the number terms on the right of the equation.

For example: Rearrange $C = \frac{5}{9}(F - 32)$ to leave F on its own.

i) Multiply both sides by $\frac{9}{5}$ to give $\frac{9}{5}C = F - 32$ in a single step.

ii) Add 32 to both sides to give $\frac{9}{5}C + 32 = F$ ie $F = \frac{9}{5}C + 32$

In words, to convert degrees Celsius to degrees Fahrenheit you multiply the temperature in Celsius by nine then divide by five (or vice-versa) and then add thirty-two.

Finally in this section we will look at how algebra can be used to solve simple maths problems. The method is always the same: i) let x be the unknown; create an equation for x; iii) solve the equation by getting x on its own.

Example: When 3 is added to a number and the total is multiplied by 2 the answer is 50. What is the number?

Let x be the number:

i) Add 3 to x: $x + 3$

ii) Multiply the total by 2: $2(x + 3)$; the answer is 50, so $2(x + 3) = 50$

iii) Expand the bracket and solve by getting x on its own:
we have $2(x + 3) = 50$; expanding the bracket gives $2x + 6 = 50$;
now subtract 6 from both sides to leave x on its own: $2x + 6 - 6 = 50 - 6$
ie $2x = 44$; finally divide both sides by 2 to get $x = 22$.

Check the answer by substituting x into the question.

When 3 is added to 22 and the total is multiplied by 2 the answer is 50.

Example: a school library contains 185 books. If the number of non-fiction books is four times the number of fiction books, how many non-fiction books are there?

We can solve this problem by formulating *two algebraic expressions* from the information provided. To do this we need to describe the number of books, both non-fiction and fiction, using letters. Rather than choosing x and y it makes sense to select letters that relate to the types of books so we will use N for non-fiction and F for fiction. Four different methods of solution are described below.

The number of non-fiction books is four times the number of fiction books. We can express this relationship algebraically as

i) $N = 4F$

ii) The library contains 185 books, comprising non-fiction and fiction books. We can express this relationship algebraically as $N + F = 185$

First method

We can solve an equation with one unknown but not with two unknowns. To solve $N + F = 185$ we need to *eliminate* one unknown (variable). We are asked for N so we need to eliminate F. We know that $N = 4F$ (given in i)), ie $4F = N$ and $F = N/4$ (dividing both sides of the equation by 4, to get F on its own).

$N + F = 185$ becomes $N + N/4 = 185$ (substituting N/4 for F leaves an equation with only one variable (N)). In words, we have N plus a quarter of N equals 185, meaning that one and a quarter N equals 185; you can also write N as four quarters ie 4N/4, then if you add in the single quarter (N/4) you get 5N/4:

$$N + \frac{N}{4} = 1\frac{1}{4}N \text{ ; or } N + \frac{N}{4} = \frac{4N}{4} + \frac{N}{4} = \frac{5N}{4}$$

The final expression is:

$\dfrac{5N}{4} = 185$; and if we multiply both sides by 4 we get $5N = 185 \times 4$; $5N = 740$

Dividing both sides of the equation by 5 gives $N = 740/5 = 148$, so the number of non-fiction books is 148.

Second method

We can solve an equation with one unknown but not with two unknowns. To solve $N + F = 185$ we need to *eliminate* one unknown (variable). We can eliminate either variable because it is easy to find the second variable by subtracting the first variable from 185. We need to compare the two expressions:

i) $N = 4F$

ii) $N + F = 185$

The goal is an equation with only one variable as in the first method. We can replace the N in ii) with the 4F in i) because we know that the N is given by $N = 4F$, so ii) becomes: $4F + F = 185$.

We now have $5F = 185$, giving $F = 185/5$ ie $F = 37$. Having found F it is easy to find N because we know that $N + F = 185$; we have $N + 37 = 185$, so subtracting 37 from both sides gives:

   $N + 37 - 37 = 185 - 37$; $N = 185 - 37$; $N = 148$ as in the first method.

Third method

Starting from the two expressions:

i) $N = 4F$

ii) $N + F = 185$

We can eliminate one variable, in this case N by *subtracting one equation from the other equation*. For example, we can subtract ii) from i). To do this we subtract everything on the left side of equation i) from the left side of equation ii); and subtract everything on the right side of equation i) from everything on the right side of equation ii), as follows:

   $N + F = 185$

   $N = 4F$

   $N + F - N = 185 - 4F$; so $F = 185 - 4F$; now if we add 4F to both sides
      (to leave 185 on its own) we get:

   $F + 4F = 185 - 4F + 4F$; so $5F = 185$ and $F = 37$; then $N = 148$ as before.

If the subtraction of one equation from another equation seems confusing, then consider the following simple example that uses numbers only:

i) $10 = 4 + 6$

ii) $25 = 20 + 5$

Subtracting i) from ii) gives $25 - 10 = 20 + 5 - (4 + 6)$; expanding the brackets gives $25 - 10 = 25 - 10$, which is correct. An equation is like a balance with the same amount on each side, so we can add and subtract two equations and the balance is maintained.

Fourth method

This method is a variation on the third method. Instead of subtracting the two equations we add them (which is easier than subtracting), but we need to multiply one equation by minus one first. Starting from the two expressions:

i) $N = 4F$

ii) $N + F = 185$

multiply every term in equation ii) by minus one (we could just as easily have chosen equation i) to give:

iii) $-N - F = -185$

Now *we can add* (instead of subtract) equations i) and iii) to eliminate N:

$$N = 4F$$
$$-N - F = -185$$
$$N - N - F = 4F - 185 \text{ to give:}$$

iv) $-F = 4F - 185$

There are two (or more) ways to solve iv). We can:

a)   add F to both sides to give $F - F = 4F + F - 185$, from which $0 = 5F - 185$, then add 185 to both sides to give $185 + 0 = 5F - 185 + 185$, so $185 = 5F$ and $5 = 37$ as before, etc.

b)   use the method outlined in directed numbers to move the letters and numbers to the opposite side of the equation, changing the negative signs into positive signs. We have $-F = 4F - 185$, so we can move the $-F$ to the right-hand side to get $+F$ and we can move the -185 to the left-hand side to get $+185$, which gives us $185 = 4F + F$, ie $185 = 5F$ etc as before.

In algebra you look for the easiest method, which in the above example is the second method.

In an intuitive method, without algebra, it is possible to see that the library is split into five equal parts, with four parts non-fiction and one part fiction. In other words, the library is four-fifths non-fiction books and one-fifth fiction books, so the number of non-fiction books is 4/5 × 185, which, dividing 185 by 5 first, becomes 37 × 4 or 148; noting that each one-part (each one-fifth) is 37 books.

Example: a rectangular playing field measures 1200 metres around the perimeter. If the playing field is twice as long as it is wide, how wide is it?

We can solve this problem by formulating two algebraic expressions from the information provided. Rather than use x for length and y for width, it makes sense to choose letters that relate to the measurements we want, so in this case we will choose L for length and W for width. The field is twice as long as it is wide. We can express this relationship algebraically as:

i) L = 2W

ii) The field is rectangular so the two long sides plus the two short sides must add up to 1200 metres: L + L + W + W = 1200; collecting like terms then factoring gives:

2L + 2W = 1200; factorizing this expression gives
2(L+W) = 1200; dividing both sides of the equation by 2 gives
L+W = 600

iii) We can solve an equation with one unknown but not with two unknowns. To solve L+W = 600 we need to *eliminate* one unknown (variable). We are asked for W so we need to eliminate L. We know that L = 2W (given in i)), so

L+W = 600 becomes
2W + W = 600 (substituting 2W for L leaves an equation with only one variable (W)); collecting like terms gives:
3W = 600; dividing both sides of the equation by 3 gives
W = 200.

The above example demonstrates the basic steps involved in solving a simple problem where there are two unknowns and one unknown can be expressed in terms of the other unknown. Problems like this one can sometimes be solved intuitively; the rectangle can be split into two L-shaped pieces, one length attached to width. We can see that these two sides must add up to 600 metres and that for the length to be twice the width the length must be 400 metres and the width 200 metres.

Finally, note that all the algebra techniques outlined in this chapter can be applied to any type of number, including fractions and decimals, and the methods by which letters are moved around an equation apply equally to numbers.

Example: The cost £C of advertising in a magazine is worked out using the formula: C = 0.25n + 1.25 where n is the number of words in the advertisement:

a) What is the cost of an advertisement that has 92 words?

b) If the cost of another advertisement is £54.50, how many words are in it?

a) Method to calculate C when n = 92:

> i) Simplify the equation to remove the decimal points by multiplying by 4 (or multiply by 100 and then divide by 25).
> ii) Insert the value of 92.
> iii) Calculate C using arithmetic shortcuts.

> i) $4C = n + 5$
> ii) $4C = 92 + 5 = 97$
> iii) $C = 97 \div 4 = (100 - 3) \div 4 = (100 \div 4) - (3 \div 4) = 25 - 3/4$
> $= £25 - £0.75 = £24.25$

b) Method to calculate n when C = £54.50:

> i) We have $4C = n + 5$ (from i) above) so rewrite this with n on the left of the equation (no algebra involved).
> ii) Get n on its own.
> iii) Substitute the known value of C.

> i) $n + 5 = 4C$
> ii) Subtract 5 from both sides of the equation (or move the 5 to the other side while changing the sign, whichever you prefer), to give $n = 4C - 5$.
> iii) Finally substitute the value of 54.50 given for C into the equation $n + 5 = 4C$ to get $n = 4 \times 54.50 - 5$

so $n = 4(50 + 4 + 0.5) - 5 = (200 + 16 + 2) - 5 = 213$ words (check: $C = 0.25n + 1.25$; $C = 213 \times 0.25 + 1.25 = 53.25 + 1.25 = 54.5$; checked with a calculator).

Example:

Find y given that $\dfrac{2}{7} = \dfrac{4}{9y}$

Method: 'cross-multiply' bottom and top diagonally, then solve: $2 \times 9y = 4 \times 7$

So $18y = 28$, then $9y = 14$, giving $y = 14/9$ or $1\dfrac{5}{9}$

Note: cross-multiplication is a quick way of multiplying both sides of the equation by the common denominator, which in this example is $63y$ ($7 \times 9y$). If you are still uncertain as to why this method works then consider the 7; we remove it from the bottom on the left (remove divide by 7 = increase left side by 7) and place it on the right = increase the right side by 7 (so both sides have been multiplied by 7). We have done the same for the 9y.

3 Warm-up exercise

Solve each equation for x:

1 $x + 2 = 5$ *Answer* ....

2 $x - 2 = 5$ *Answer* ....

3 $3x = 45$ *Answer* ....

4 $3x - 6 = 30$ *Answer* ....

5 $-x + 17 = 8$ *Answer* ....

6 $x - y = 5$ *Answer* ....

7 $2x + 3x = 15$ *Answer* ....

8 $9x + 7 = 4x + 67$ *Answer* ....

9 $0.5x = 11$ *Answer* ....

10 $2.5x = 10$ *Answer* ....

11 $32 = 14 - 2x$ *Answer* ....

12 $\frac{1}{2}x = 24$ *Answer* ....

13 $\frac{2}{3}x = 25 - y$ *Answer* ....

4 Warm-up exercise

Simplify the following expressions:

1 $3(x + 2) = 14$ *Answer* ....

2 $5(x - 1) = 10$ *Answer* ....

3 $3(x - 4) + 2(x + 3) = 4$ *Answer* ....

4 $2(x - y) + 3(x + 4y) - 5 = 0$ *Answer* ....

5 $7x(x + 2y) + 6y(x + y) = 0$ *Answer* ....

6 $\frac{4}{5}x(15x + 20) =$ *Answer* ....

5 Warm-up exercise

Factorize completely the following expression (employ brackets):

1	$2x + 2y =$	*Answer* ....
2	$10x - 15y =$	*Answer* ....
3	$2xy + 2y =$	*Answer* ....
4	$4x + 5y + 8x + 13y =$	*Answer* ....
5	$2x^2 + 4x =$	*Answer* ....
6	$10x^2 - 35 =$	*Answer* ....
7	$9x - 12x^2 =$	*Answer* ....
8	$42xy - 35y =$	*Answer* ....
9	$3(x + 9) + 5(x - 1) + 2 =$	*Answer* ....

6 Easy questions

1   Given that $x = 9$ and $y = -4$, find the value of:

    i) $3x - y$

    ii) $2(x + y)^2$

2   Use the formula $S = 0.5(u + v)t$ to find S when:

    i) $u = 5, v = 15$ and $t = 6$

    ii) $u = 0, v = 30$ and $t = 0.5$

3   If $3x + 2y = 44$, and $x = 12$, then $y =$

4   If $2x - 3y = 29$, and $x = 10$, then $y =$

5   If $5x(y + 1) = 200$, and $y = 19$, then $x =$

6   Solve the equation $11x - 6(x - 2) = 18$

7   Solve the equation $3x(2x - 5) - 5x(x - 3) = 16$

8   Solve the following pair of equations:

    a) $x = 2y$

    b) $3x + 2y = 20$

9   Solve the following pair of equations:

   a) $x + 2y = 10$;

   b) $4x + 2y = 19$

10 A number is multiplied by 20 and 45 added on. If the answer is 325, what is the number?

7 More difficult questions

1   Find x given that $\dfrac{4}{5x} = \dfrac{3}{10}$

2   A bus leaves college and stops three times to unload students. Half the students get off at the first stop, half the *remainder* get off at the second stop, and all the remaining students get off at the third and final stop. If 12 students get off at the final stop, and the number of students on the bus when it leaves college is given by S:

   a) Find, in terms of S, the number of students who get off the bus:

   i)   at the first stop;
   ii) at the second stop;
   iii) at the third stop.

   b) Hence find the total number of students on the bus when it leaves the college.

3   A taxi firm charges a fixed cost (FC) of £2.40 when a passenger enters the taxi and a variable cost (VC) of 20 pence per quarter-mile travelled.

   a) Write:

   i)   the variable cost in pounds for a journey of distance x, where x is measured in quarter-miles (VC =);
   ii) a formula for the cost C in pounds for travelling a distance x miles (ie C =).
   iii) Rearrange the formula to express the distance x in terms of C (ie x =).

   b) Hence calculate how far a passenger can travel in miles for a fare of £10.

Chapter 6

....

Money and exchange rates

Candidates should be familiar with the decimal system of money and the symbols used, for example 1 pound (£1) = 100 pence; five pounds = £5; and ten pence = 10p. Since £1 = 100p, all sums of money can be written as decimals, with a point separating the pounds from the pence columns. So, for example, five pounds can be written as £5.00; three pounds and twenty pence as £3.20; eighteen pounds and five pence as £18.05 (there are always two columns for the pence figures). A letter p is not used in amounts that contain pounds, so we write £10.50 not £10.50p.

To convert pounds to pence we multiply by 100 and to convert pence to pounds we divide by 100, so £2.50 = 250p (simply move the point 2 places to the right) and 135p = £1.35 (move the point 2 places to the left). Also note that:

$$£0.50 = 0.5 \times 100p = 50p; £0.05 = 0.05 \times 100p = 5p$$

We can add and subtract money by writing each amount in the same form, either as pence or pounds. The decimal point format is used with test questions that involve money; the pound sign is optional. For example:

$$£3.45 + 65 \text{ pence} = £3.45 + £0.65 = £4.10$$

$$\text{or } £3.45 + 65 \text{ pence} = 345p + 65p = 410p = £4.10$$

1 Warm-up exercise

Coinage analysis – make up the amounts given using the fewest number of coins (mental arithmetic). The first amount has been done.

£ amount \\ coin	£1	50p	20p	10p	5p	2p	1p
22p			1			1	
45p							
632p							
882p							
99p							
£1.74							
£2.65							
£3.79							
£4.50							
£5.96							

2 Easy questions

1   A school can buy 20 books at £7.50 pence each or borrow the books from a library service at a cost of £50. How much money will be saved by borrowing the books?   *Answer* ....

2   A school can buy 10 books at £9.95 each or borrow the books from a library service at a cost of £40. How much money will be saved by borrowing the books?

Answer ....

3   School dinners cost £1.85 each. A pupil pays in advance for a week's dinners. What is the correct change in pence out of a £10 note?

Answer ....

4   A sponsored walk by 500 pupils raised £6950 for charity. What was the average amount raised per pupil?   *Answer* ....

5   How many school books at £8.75 each can be bought on a budget of £100?

Answer ....

6   A school charges 6p per A4 page for photocopying, 30p for binding and 25p for a clear cover. What is the cost of two 100-page books bound with clear front and back covers?

Answer ....

7   A school teacher hires a minibus at £50 per day plus the cost of the petrol used. The minibus uses one litre of fuel for every 10 kilometres travelled. If fuel costs one £1.50 per litre, how much would it cost for a one-day round trip of 200 kilometres?   *Answer* ....

Foreign exchange rates

Many other countries use a decimal system of currency, similar to our own, most notably 1 US dollar = 100 cents. Pounds can be exchanged for the currency of another country by referring to the exchange rate. Up-to-date exchange rates are displayed in banks and in the financial pages of newspapers.

The exchange rate shows how many units of foreign currency can be exchanged (or bought) for one pound. Examples are given below (these rates vary from day to day):

euro: 1.16 euro (€) = £1; there are 0.86 pounds per euro

United States: 1.51 dollars ($) = £1; there are 0.66 pounds per dollar

Switzerland: 1.41 francs (SFr) = £1; there are 0.71 pounds per Swiss franc

To calculate the amounts of foreign currency, use the formula:

Foreign currency = British Currency (£) × Exchange rate

Example: if £200 is exchanged for US dollars and the exchange rate is £1 = $1.5, how many dollars will be received?

£1 = $1.5 so £200 = 200 × $1.5 = $300

Example: £1000 is changed for euros at a rate of £1 = €1.16

£1 = €1.16 so £1000 = 1000 × €1.16 = €1160

Foreign currency can be converted back to English money using the same exchange rates. For example:

2100 Swiss francs (SFr) are exchanged for pounds at a rate of £1 = SFr 1.4. How many pounds will be received?

£1 = SFr 1.4 so 1SFr = £1/1.4; then 2000 SFr = 1 × 2100/1.4 = 21000/14 (to remove the decimal point); cancel both sides by 7 to give 3000/2 = 1500 SFr

3 Easy questions

1   A ski trip to Austria costs £800 per pupil and requires a 25% deposit. What is the deposit in Austrian schillings (S) if £100 buys S1600?

Answer ....

2   A ski trip to Switzerland costs £600 and requires a 25% deposit. What is the deposit in Swiss francs (SFr) if £2 = 3SFr?

Answer ....

3   A school trip abroad costs £720 per pupil with a 15% deposit. How much is the deposit to the nearest euro if there are 1.16 euros to the pound?

Answer ....

4   A school trip to Poland costs £375 per person. The teacher converts pounds to zlotys at a rate of 0.2 Zl per pound. What is the cost of the trip in zlotys for 28 people?

Answer ....

5   A gap year student returns to the UK from South Africa and exchanges 1100 rand (R) to pounds (£) at an exchange rate of 1 rand = £0.07. How much does the student get back?

Answer ....

6   A teacher exchanged pounds (£) for euros (€) and received 2645 euros. How many pounds did the teacher have if the exchange rate is £1 = €1.15?

Answer ....

7   A tourist exchanges £150 for $250 Canadian dollars. What is the exchange rate for pounds to dollars?   Answer ....

8   A student orders £400 of US dollars online and is charged £5 for the transaction. How much will the student receive if the exchange rate is £1 = $1.50?   Answer ....

9   The rate of exchange between the Swedish krona (K) and British pound (£) is 9.75 K = £1. Calculate:

a) the number of krona received in exchange for £100;

b) the number of pounds exchanged for 97500 K.

Answer ....

10   On a school trip to Paris a teacher runs out of euros. She exchanges £250 for euros at an exchange rate of 8.8 euros for every £10. The teacher spends 176 euros and at the end of the trip exchanges the remaining euros back into pounds at the same exchange rate. Calculate how many pounds she has left over at the end of the trip.   Answer ....

4 More difficult questions

1   Before going on holiday to the United States, a teacher changed some pounds into dollars. The exchange rate between US dollars ($) and British pounds (£) was £1 = $1.5. The fee for the transaction was £3.50 plus 2% of the number of pounds exchanged. If the teacher was charged £10 for the transaction, how many pounds did she exchange?

Answer ....

2   On Saturday, Susan, Michael and Aziz exchange some foreign currency at the same bank. The rate of exchange from dollars ($) to pounds (£) is £1 = $1.5 and the rate of exchange from euros (€) to pounds (£) is £1 = €1.15.

a) Susan exchanged £300 into euros. Calculate how many euros she received.

Answer ....

b) Michael exchanged $750 into pounds. Calculate how many Pounds he received.

Answer ....

c) Aziz exchanged €230 into dollars. Calculate how many dollars he received.

Answer ....

d) What is the exchange rate for euros into dollars?

Answer ....

Chapter 7

Quicker mental calculations

This chapter does not teach specialist arithmetic shortcuts. All the techniques outlined below use the arithmetic explained earlier, so no new knowledge is required. You still need to be familiar with your 'times tables', so if memorizing these is a problem then you will have to find ways around this. For example: if you are unsure whether $7 \times 9 = 63$ then you can multiply 7 by 10 to give 70 and then subtract 7 times 1 to get $70 - 7 = 63$; we know this is correct because we have learnt $7 \times 9 = 7(10 - 1)$, from Chapter 5 on algebra. If you have memorized the times tables to 10×10 rather than 12×12 you will have to split number 12 into $10 + 2$ so that, for example, 12×11 becomes $(10 + 2) \times 11$, which is $110 + 22 = 132$. This chapter explains simple arithmetic techniques like those outlined above to provide candidates with a range of strategies to tackle arithmetic calculations without a calculator and with limited time.

Addition

When adding small numbers it is convenient to add to the nearest 10 first to avoid carrying anything over. So, for example, $64 + 28$ becomes $64 + 26 (+2) = 90 (+ 2)$; alternatively you can add the tens first: $6 + 2 = 8$ tens or 80, before adding the units, $4 + 8 = 12$, to give $80 + 12 = 92$. In a variation of this method you can move some units from one number to the other, so that one number ends in zero. In the above example we subtract 4 units from 64 to get 60, then add the 4 units to the other number (28) to give $64 + 28 = 60 + 32 = 92$.

To add larger numbers, the traditional method is to align the numbers in columns beneath each other, which takes time. In an alternative method, we can split numbers into convenient building blocks based on place value. Take for example 6142 added to 9531:

Slow method: 9531
                  6142 +
                  ─────
                  15673
                  ─────

In the slow method, each column has to be added in turn starting with the units.

Quicker method: 15000
                     600
                      70
                       3 +
                  ─────
                  15673
                  ─────

To add the numbers 6142 and 9532 using place values we start with the thousands column and work towards the units column: 15000 (9+6), six hundred (5+1) and seventy (3+4) three (1+2). In this way the calculation is carried out in your head without using pen and paper, or a calculator. The method is less useful if a digit needs to be carried over.

If a digit is to be carried over as in, for example, 75 + 46, we can break the addition into two smaller steps so that one number ends in a zero, as explained earlier. In this example we would write 75 + 46 = 80 + 41 = 121. The alternative method is to add to the next hundred, in which case we would borrow 25 from the 46 to get 75 + 46 = 75 + 25 + 21 = 100 + 21 = 121. Whichever method you choose, you need to find an easy first step. To add 1245 and 2900 an obvious solution is to borrow 100 from 1245 to add to 2900 to make 3000, so the addition becomes: 1245 + 2900 = 1145 + 3000 = 4145, which is much easier.

Subtraction

To subtract numbers more quickly we can adopt a similar approach to addition, by using the nearest ten, hundred or thousand. In this method you subtract a larger number than you need and then add back the difference to the number you are subtracting from, to 'balance the books'. Take for example 264 −38:

Slow method: 26^{1}4
                  3,8 −
                  ────
                  226
                  ────

In this slow method, we need to borrow one from the tens column (to make 14) then pay it back:

Quicker method: 266
                    40 −
                  ────
                  226
                  ────

Here we add 2 to 38 to make 40 as a first step, and to maintain the balance we add 2 to 264 to make 266. We can now carry out the subtraction mentally without difficulty because subtracting a number ending in zero is easy and there is nothing to borrow or pay back. This method needs to be modified slightly where borrowing is unavoidable, for example 266 − 78. Here it is better to subtract 100 and pay back the difference of 22:

$$266 - 78 = 266 - 100 + 22 = 166 + 22 = 188$$

Similarly: $2350 - 185 = 2350 - 200 + 15 = 2150 + 15 = 2165$

To check a subtraction you can use the method of *adding back*. Here you mentally add back to your answer the number that was subtracted. For example:

$266 - 78 = 188$; check this by adding back: $188 + 78 = 266$
(noting that this can written as $190 + 78 - 2 = 268 - 2 = 266$)

Similarly, $202 - 95 = 107$ $(107 + 95 = 102 + 100 = 202)$
$$720 - 130 = 590 \ (590 + 130 = 600 + 120 = 720)$$
$$27p - 19p = 8p \ (8p + 19p = 7p + 20p = 27p)$$

Multiplication

We can multiply numbers using the place value method described for addition.

To multiply 532 by 3 we can write:

$$(500 \times 3) + (30 \times 3) + (2 \times 3) = 1500 + 90 + 6 = 1596$$

Similarly, 9537 can be multiplied by 3 as follows:

$27000 + 1500 + 90 + 21 = 28000 + 590 + 21 = 28611$ (noting that we can add 21 to 590 by borrowing 10 from 21 to give $600 + 11 = 611$)

Multiplying by 10, 100 or 1000 is always easy, so try to break down numbers into factors of 10, or build up numbers so they end with a zero before proceeding with a multiplication. For example:

$26 \times 35 = 26 \times 10$ three times with half of 26×10 (because 5×26 is half of 10×260); expressed mathematically $26 \times 35 = 26(10 + 10 + 10 + 5)$ which is $260 \times 3 + 130 = 780 + 130 = 910$

$26 \times 49 = 26 \times 50$ less 26 times 1, and $26 \times 50 = 13 \times 100$; so we have $26 \times 49 = 1300 - 26 = 1300 - 100 + 74 = 1274$

An easier and quicker way of multiplying by decimals is to transfer the decimal point to the larger number. Take 0.036×2500, for example:

Slow method: 2500
    $0.036 \times$ 3 d.p. here
    ─────
    15000
    75000
    ─────
    90000 so 3 d.p. in the answer $= 90.000$ (ie 90)

Quicker method: when multiplying larger numbers by decimal numbers, shift the decimal point to the larger number by multiplying the decimal number by a power of ten and dividing the larger number by the same power of ten. For example:

   2500×0.036 is rewritten as 36×2.5

Here we have multiplied the 0.036 by 1000 and divided the 2500 by 1000.
    We now have 36×2.5 which can be rewritten as $36(2 + 0.5) = 72 + 18 = 90$. Shifting the decimal point in this way gives you a feel for the likely size of the answer and helps in avoiding mistakes. You can move the decimal point as many places as you like, and in any direction you like as long as you move it the same number of places in the opposite direction for the other number. In the above example we could have multiplied the 0.036 by 10000 (four decimal places to the right) to get 360 and divided the 2500 by 10000 (four decimal places to the left) to get 0.25, having spotted that one-quarter of 36 is 9.

Division

Place values can also be used to aid division. Take, for example, $864 \div 4$:

Slow method: 21 6
             ─────
             $4\overline{)86^24}$

Quicker method (brackets included for clarity):
   $864 \div 4 = (800 \div 4) + (60 \div 4) + (4 \div 4)$
         $= 200 + 15 + 1 = 216$

Instead of breaking down numbers according to place values, you split numbers into convenient chunks that are easier to divide. For example:

   $168 \div 12$

We do not know the answer to this straight off but we do know that 12×10 is 120 and that 48 added to 120 equals 168; we also know that $12 \times 4 = 48$.
   $168 \div 12 = (120 + 48) \div 12 = 10 + 4 = 14$

In an alternative approach, we could have also used factors to cancel the numbers to smaller values. For example:

$$168 \div 12 = 84 \div 6 \text{ (dividing both numbers by 2)}$$
$$= 42 \div 3 \text{ (dividing both numbers by 2 again)}$$
$$= 14$$

Percentages

With small percentages it can be convenient to move the denominator of 100 across to the number we are trying to calculate the percentage of. For example:

Slow method:

$$2.5\% \text{ of } 50 = \frac{2.5}{100} \times 50 = 0.025 \times 50 = 0.25 \times 5 = 1.25$$

Quicker method: the percentage denominator of 100 can be moved across to the number we want the percentage of (ie 50 in the above example) to give a recognizable fraction or multiplier (eg one-half). For example:

2.5% of 50 becomes 50% of 2.5 = a half of 2.5 = 1.25

6% of 25 becomes 25% of 6 = a quarter of 6 = 1.5

4% of 250 becomes 250% of 4 = 2.5 × 4 = 10

Mixed fractions

Calculations involving mixed fractions ('mixed number fractions') require the whole number to be converted into a top-heavy fraction that can be added to the proper fraction before any multiplication takes place. For example, calculate:

$$2\frac{3}{4} \times 2\frac{1}{2}$$

Slow method: first number: $2\frac{3}{4}$ = 2 wholes and 3 quarters; 1 whole is 4 quarters so 2 wholes = 8 quarters; add the 3 quarters to make 11 quarters: $\frac{11}{4}$;

second number: $2\frac{1}{2}$ = 2 wholes and 1 half; 1 whole is 2 halves so 2 wholes = 4 halves; add the single half to make 5 halves; $\frac{5}{2}$

now multiply $\frac{11}{4}$ and $\frac{5}{2}$: $\frac{11}{4} \times \frac{5}{2} = \frac{55}{8} = 6\frac{7}{8}$ (because 6 eights are 48 with 7 left over)

Quicker method: first number: $2\dfrac{3}{4}$: multiply the 2 wholes by the denominator of 4, to give 8, then add the 3; put the total over the denominator: $\dfrac{8+3}{4} = \dfrac{11}{4}$;

second number: $2\dfrac{1}{2}$: multiply the 2 wholes by the denominator of 2, to give 4, then add the 1; put the total over the denominator: $2\dfrac{1}{2} = \dfrac{4+1}{2} = \dfrac{5}{2}$;

finally $\dfrac{11}{4} \times \dfrac{5}{2} = \dfrac{55}{8} = 6\dfrac{7}{8}$ as before.

Chapter 8

Indices and roots

Squares of numbers

The square of a number is a number multiplied by itself, and is shown by a small 2 placed above the number. For example:

$$4^2 \text{ (four squared) means } 4 \times 4 \text{ so } 4^2 = 16$$

$$\text{Similarly, } 9^2 \text{ (four squared) means } 9 \times 9 \text{ so } 9^2 = 81$$

$$\text{A larger example is: } 500^2 = 500 \times 500 = 250000$$

An example of squaring a decimal fraction is:

$$0.06^2 = 0.06 \times 0.06 = 0.0036$$

An example of squaring a fraction is:

$$\left(\frac{3}{4}\right)^2 = \frac{3}{4} \times \frac{3}{4} = \frac{9}{16}$$

An example of squaring a mixed number is:

$$\left(2\frac{1}{4}\right)^2 = 2\frac{1}{4} \times 2\frac{1}{4} = \frac{9}{4} \times \frac{9}{4} = \frac{81}{16} = 5\frac{1}{16}$$

1 Warm-up exercise

Find the squares of the following numbers:

Example: $\dfrac{8}{3}$ $\left(\dfrac{8}{3}\right)^2 = \dfrac{8}{3} \times \dfrac{8}{3} = \dfrac{64}{9} = 7\dfrac{1}{9}$

1   7   *Answer* ....

2   120   *Answer* ....

3   0.4   *Answer* ....

4   2.5   *Answer* ....

5 $1\dfrac{3}{4}$ *Answer* ....

6 $2\dfrac{1}{3}$ *Answer* ....

Cubes of numbers

The cube of a number is a number multiplied by itself twice and is shown by a small 3 placed above the number. For example, 2^3 (two cubed) means $2 \times 2 \times 2$ so $2^3 = 8$.

Similarly $3^3 = 3 \times 3 \times 3 = 27$.

A larger example is:

$$40^3 = 40 \times 40 \times 40 = 64000$$

An example of cubing a decimal fraction is:

$$0.1^3 = 0.1 \times 0.1 \times 0.1 = 0.001$$

Another example is:

$$0.03^3 = 0.03 \times 0.03 \times 0.03 = 0.000027$$

An example of cubing a fraction is:

$$\left(\dfrac{3}{4}\right)^3 = \dfrac{3}{4} \times \dfrac{3}{4} \times \dfrac{3}{4} = \dfrac{27}{64}$$

Another example is:

$$\left(\dfrac{7}{10}\right)^3 = \dfrac{7}{10} \times \dfrac{7}{10} \times \dfrac{7}{10} = \dfrac{343}{1000}$$

2 Warm-up exercise

Find the cubes of the following numbers:

Example: $2\dfrac{1}{2}$ $\left(2\dfrac{1}{2}\right)^3 = 2\dfrac{1}{2} \times 2\dfrac{1}{2} \times 2\dfrac{1}{2} = \dfrac{5}{2} \times \dfrac{5}{2} \times \dfrac{5}{2} = \dfrac{125}{8} = 15\dfrac{5}{8}$

1   6   *Answer* ....

2   20   *Answer* ....

3   0.3   *Answer* ....

4   1.1   *Answer* ....

5 $1\dfrac{1}{2}$ *Answer* ....

Square roots and cube roots of numbers

Square roots of numbers

The square root of a number is a number that when squared gives the original number, and is shown by a square root sign ($\sqrt{}$) placed at the left of the number. For example, the square root of 9 equals 3, because $3^2 = 9$.

Example: find the square root of 25

$$\sqrt{25} = 5 \text{ because } 5 \times 5 = 25$$

Example: find the square root of $\dfrac{25}{16}$

$$\sqrt{\dfrac{25}{16}} = \dfrac{\sqrt{25}}{\sqrt{16}} = \dfrac{5}{4} \text{ because } \dfrac{5^2}{4^2} = \dfrac{25}{16}$$

To work out the square roots of numbers you need to know the squares of numbers and then work backwards. To work out the square root of a large number, for example 250000, it is necessary to split this (factorize it) into smaller numbers whose square roots we know.

So $250000 = 25 \times 100 \times 100$

Then $\sqrt{250000} = \sqrt{25 \times 100 \times 100}$
$= \sqrt{25} \times \sqrt{100} \times \sqrt{100}$
$= 5 \times 10 \times 10$
$= 500$

Example: find the square root of 490000

$$490000 = 49 \times 100 \times 100$$

Then $\sqrt{490000} = \sqrt{49 \times 100 \times 100}$

$$= \sqrt{49} \times \sqrt{100} \times \sqrt{100}$$
$$= 7 \times 10 \times 10$$
$$= 700$$

Example: find the square root of 900

$$900 = 9 \times 10 \times 10$$

Then $\sqrt{900} = \sqrt{9 \times 100}$

$$= \sqrt{9} \times \sqrt{100}$$
$$= 3 \times 10$$
$$= 30$$

3 Warm-up exercise

Find the square roots of the following numbers:

Example: 810000

$$\sqrt{810000} = \sqrt{81 \times 100 \times 100}$$
$$= \sqrt{81} \times \sqrt{100} \times \sqrt{100}$$
$$= 9 \times 10 \times 10$$
$$= 900$$

1   36   *Answer* ....

2 $\dfrac{9}{25}$ *Answer* ....

3 $\dfrac{49}{4}$ *Answer* ....

4   6400   *Answer* ....

5   144   *Answer* ....

6   14400   *Answer* ....

Cube roots of numbers

The cube root is a number that when cubed gives the original number, and is shown by a cube root sign, placed at the left of the number ($\sqrt[3]{\ }$).

Example: the cube root of 8 or $\sqrt[3]{8} = 2$, because $2^3 = 8$

Example: find the cube root of $\dfrac{64}{125}$

$$\sqrt[3]{\dfrac{64}{125}} = \dfrac{\sqrt[3]{64}}{\sqrt[3]{125}} = \dfrac{4}{5} \text{ because } \dfrac{4^3}{5^3} = \dfrac{64}{125}$$

To work out the cube roots of numbers you need to know the cubes of numbers and work backwards.

4 Warm-up exercise

Find the cube roots of the following numbers:

Example: find $\sqrt[3]{1000}$ Answer: 10 because $10^3 = 1000$

1 $\sqrt[3]{27}$ *Answer* ....

2 $\sqrt[3]{\dfrac{1}{27}}$ *Answer* ....

3 $\sqrt[3]{216}$ *Answer* ....

4 $\sqrt[3]{216000}$ *Answer* ....

Index laws (exponents)

We have looked at squares and cubes, which are the most well-known *indices*. However, it is possible to raise any number to any *index number* we want, for example we can have 6^5, 10^{12}, $16^{1/2}$ and 4^{-2}. Note that the terms 'indices', 'index number', 'exponent' and 'power' can be used interchangeably in the context of maths. There are a few rules that are worth remembering. These rules are explained using 'powers of 10', though they apply to all numbers (all base numbers).

$10^5 \times 10^2 = 10^{5+2} = 10^7$ (add the indices)

$10^5 \div 10^2 = 10^{5-2} = 10^3$ (subtract the indices)

$(10^3)^2 = 10^{3 \times 2} = 10^6$ (multiply the indices)

$10^{-6} = 1/10^6$ (invert and change the negative sign to a positive sign)

$10^{1/2} = \sqrt{10}$; $10^{1/3} = \sqrt[3]{10}$

$10^{1/2} + 10^{1/2} = 10^1 = 10$ (any number to the power of 1 is itself)

$10^0 = 0$ (and any number to the power of zero is zero)

$\sqrt{10} \div \sqrt{5} = \sqrt{(10 \div 5)} = \sqrt{2}$

$\sqrt{12} = \sqrt{(4 \times 3)} = \sqrt{4} \times \sqrt{3} = 2 \times \sqrt{3} = 2\sqrt{3}$

   (split the base number into numbers with known roots)

Example

Find the value of n in each of the following equations.

1 $2^n = 16$ $n = 4$ because n = $2^2 = 4$; $2^3 = 8$, $2^4 = 16$

2 $16^n = \dfrac{1}{4}$ $n = -2$ because $16^{-2} = 1/\sqrt{16} = 1/4$

3 $2^n = \dfrac{1}{16}$ $n = -4$ because $2^{-4} = 1/2^4 = 1/16$

4 $16^n = 2$ $n = 0.25$ or ¼ because $n^{1/4} = \sqrt[4]{16}$ = square root of
$\sqrt{16} = \sqrt{4} = 2$

5 Easy questions

Solve the following or find the value of *n*:

1 $6^3 =$ *Answer* ....

2 $6^3 - 6^2 =$ *Answer* ....

3 $6^2 \times 6^3 = 6^n$ *Answer* ....

4 $6^2 (6^3) = 6^n$ *Answer* ....

5 $10^3 - 6^2 =$ *Answer* ....

6 $3^n = 27$ *Answer* ....

7 $2^4 =$ *Answer* ....

8 $2^{-4} =$ *Answer* ....

9 $64 \times 2^{-5} =$ *Answer* ....

10 $3^7 \div 3^4 = 3^n$ *Answer* ....

6 More difficult questions

Solve the following or find the value of *n*:

1 $2^{40} \times 2^{-38} =$ *Answer* ....

2 $25^n = \dfrac{1}{5}$ *Answer* ....

3 $2^n = \dfrac{1}{32}$ *Answer* ....

4 $2^{-n} = \dfrac{1}{16}$ *Answer* ....

Chapter 9

Measurement

The most important metric measurements are weight, length and volume. SI units (international system) are in most cases the same as metric units, all being based on units of ten.

Weight

The basic unit of weight is the gram (g). All metric weights are based on this. There are four weights you are likely to encounter:

Name	Symbol
Kilogram	kg
Gram	g
Milligram	mg
Tonne	t

$1\,kg = 1000\,g$; $1\,g = 1000\,mg$; $1\,t = 1000\,kg$

Length

The basic unit of length is the metre (m). All metric lengths are based on this. There are four lengths you may encounter:

Name	Symbol
Kilometre	km
Metre	m
Centimetre	cm
Millimetre	mm

1 km = 1000 m; 1 m = 100 cm; 1 cm = 10 mm

Volume of liquids and gases (capacity)

Quantities of liquids and gases are measured in litres (l) and millilitres (ml) where 1 l = 1000 ml. You may also come across:

decilitre (dl) = one-tenth of a litre = 100 ml

centilitre (cl) = one-hundredth of a litre = 10 ml

cubic centimetre (cc or cm³) = one-thousandth of a litre = 1 ml

Adding and subtracting metric units

When working out sums with metric units it is important that all the numbers have the same units. For example, add 5 cm to 2 m:

2 m + 5 cm = 2 m + 0.05 m = 2.05 m

1 g + 25 mg = 1 g + 0.025 g = 1.025 g

0.6 g − 500 mg = 600 mg − 500 mg = 100 mg

Areas

The metric units of area are square metre (m²), square centimetre (cm²) and square millimetre (mm²).

Area of a square of side length a = a × a = a²

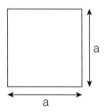

Area of a rectangle = length (l) × breadth (b) = l × b

The area of any triangle is found by multiplying half the base by the vertical height:
Area of a triangle = ½ base × vertical height = ½ bh

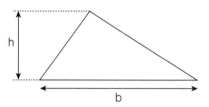

Area of a circle of radius r = πr^2 (pi r squared) where π = 3.142 (to 3 d.p.). Pi is sometimes expressed as a fraction because its value is very close to 22/7.

The area of a circle is sometimes given as $\pi D^2/4$ (pi D squared over 4) because

$$r^2 = r \times r = \frac{D}{2} \times \frac{D}{2} = \frac{D^2}{4}$$

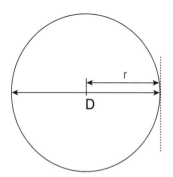

Borders

The area of any border is given by: area of the outside shape minus area of the inside shape. For example:

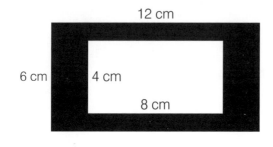

12 cm

6 cm

4 cm

8 cm

Area of border = area outer rectangle − area inner rectangle

$$= 12 \times 6 - 8 \times 4$$
$$= 72 - 32 = 40 \text{ cm}^2$$

Perimeters

The perimeter of any shape is the distance all the way around the outside of the shape. Examples are:

Perimeter of a square = 4 × length of side

Perimeter of a rectangle = 2 × length × breadth

Perimeter of a circle = circumference: $C = 2\pi r = \pi D$

Volumes of solids

Volume is a measure of the space taken up by a three-dimensional object. It is measured in units cubed (units^3) and the standard units of volume are the cubic metre (m^3), cubic centimetre (cm^3) and the cubic millimetre (mm^3).

The most common solids have a prism shape, which means they have the same cross-section throughout their length.

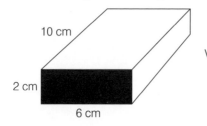

10 cm

2 cm

6 cm

Volume = area of front face × length
= 2 × 6 × 10 = 120 cm^3

Scales

These are used when something very large is drawn in reduced form. Typical examples are maps and scale drawings of houses (blueprints). Scales are usually given in the form of a ratio of length (or distance) on the scale drawing to a length (or distance) on the real thing. Scales can vary enormously, from, for example, one-quarter scale (eg house floor plans) to one fifty-thousandth scale (eg for maps).

Scales can be shown as either a fraction, eg 1⁄4, or as a proportion, ie 1:4 (one to four), meaning that one unit of length on the drawing represents four units of length on the real thing. A map scale given as 1⁄50000 or 1:50000 means that one unit of length on the map is equivalent to 50000 units on the ground, ie 1 cm on the map = 50000 cm on the ground = 500 m = 0.5 km. So 1 cm on the map equals 0.5 km on the ground (a '2 cm to 1 km' map). The most popular map scale is 1:25000 scale which is the same as 1 cm : 0.25 km or (a '4 cm to 1 km' map).

Another way to show a map scale is to use a graphic. Here the scale will remain true even if the size of the map is changed by photocopying.

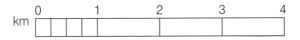

1 Easy questions

1 A school playground measures 16 m by 12.5 m.
What is its area in metres squared?   *Answer* ....

2 How many pieces of card measuring 30 cm by 20 cm can be cut from a
sheet measuring 1.5 m × 1.5 m?   *Answer* ....

3 A fence is to be erected around a school playing field. The field is
rectangular in shape and measures 120 m by 90 m. What length of fence will
be needed?   *Answer* ....

4 A pupil is 1.6 m tall. If there are 2.5 cm to the inch, how tall is the pupil in
inches?   *Answer* ....

5 A school wildlife pond is to be 4 m diameter. What is the diameter of the
pond on a 50:1 scale drawing?   *Answer* ....

6 In a school run, a pupil completed 3 miles around a 400 m track. How many
laps of the track were completed if one mile is equivalent to 1.6 km?
          Answer ....

7 If one gallon is equivalent to 4.5 litres, how many gallons are there in one
litre? Give your answer as a fraction.   *Answer* ....

8   The average weight of a class of 11-year-old pupils is 40 kg.
What is this in pounds if 1 kg = 2.2 lb?   *Answer* ....

2 More difficult question

1   a) A photocopier contains 5 reams of paper stacked on top of each other.
If each ream contains 500 sheets and the stack is 27.5 cm high, find the
thickness of 1 sheet in millimetres, giving your answer as a decimal.

Answer ....

b) Each sheet measures 300 mm by 200 mm.

i)   Find the surface area of one side of one sheet, giving your answer
in square metres.

Answer ....

ii) A football pitch measures 100 metres by 70 metres. Find the minimum
number of reams of paper needed to cover the entire surface of the
pitch with paper.

Answer ....

c) i)   Find the weight of a single sheet of paper in grams if each ream
weighs 2.4 kg.

Answer ....

ii) Hence find the weight of the paper expressed in terms of grams per
metre squared (g/m^2).

Answer ....

Chapter 10

···

Averages

You might have a group of numbers (data set) and wish to find a single number that best represents the group, ie a central value. The most common method is to calculate the arithmetic *mean*.

Mean

To find the mean (commonly known as 'the average'), you add all the numbers together then divide the total by the number of numbers. For example:

What is the mean height of the following group of pupils?

    1.55 m   1.62 m   1.57 m   1.65 m   1.51 m

The mean is the sum total of the heights divided by five:

$$\frac{1.55 + 1.62 + 1.57 + 1.65 + 1.51}{5} = 7.9\,m \div 5 = 1.58\,m$$

Alternatives to the mean are the median and mode. These two values are calculated as follows.

Median

The median is the middle number in a group of numbers that have been placed in ascending numerical order, from smallest (on the left) to largest (on the right). From the previous example:

1st	2nd	3rd	4th	5th
1.51	1.55	1.57	I.62	1.65

The median is given by the number positioned in the middle of the group, which in this case is the third number, ie 1.57 m. For example:

What is the median average of the following numbers?

4.3   10   3   7.5   5   9   6.7   5

First step: rearrange in ascending order, repeating any numbers where necessary:

3   4.3   5   5 ↑ 6.7   7.5   9   10

There is an even number of numbers in this group and, therefore, no 'middle value' as such.

Second step: To find the 'middle value' you work out the mean of the two middle numbers:

$$\frac{5 + 6.7}{2} = 11.7 \div 2 = 5.85 = \text{median of the group}$$

To locate the middle position of a large group of numbers (n), add 1 and divide by 2, ie (n + 1) ÷ 2.

Example: you have 51 numbers. The middle position (median) is found by adding 1 and dividing by 2: (51+1) ÷ 2 = 26th number.

Example: you have 50 numbers. The middle position is found by adding 1 and dividing by 2: (50+1) ÷ 2 = 25.5, so you have to average the 25th and 26th numbers to find the median.

Mode

The mode is the value that occurs most often (most frequently). For example:

What is the mode of the following group of numbers?

3   4   7   3   4   5   3   9   8   6   3

In the above example, the mode (modal value) is 3 because it occurs most frequently – four times. If two values are equally popular then the group is said to be 'bi-modal'. For example:

5   5   7   8   3   7   4   1   2 – the modal values are 5 and 7.

If more than two numbers occur equally most frequently in a group then the mode would not be used as a way of expressing the average value.

Range

The range measures the spread of the data ie the maximum value minus the minimum value. For example:

5   5   7   8   3   7   4   1   2   range = 8 − 1 = 7

Weighted average

In a weighted average some test scores count more than others towards the overall result. Weighted averages are used in coursework and in university degree classification. Examples of degree course weighting are:

1:3:5 first year = 1/9; second year = 3/9; final year = 5/9; of total marks

1:3 second year = 25%; final year = 75%; of total marks

1:2 second year = 0.33; final year = 0.67; of total marks

The weighted average is calculated as follows:

i)   Convert each mark or score to its percentage (eg 16 correct answers out of 20 marks = 80%).

ii)   Multiply each percentage mark by its weight (expressed as a fraction, percentage or decimal).

iii) Sum the results, giving your answer as a percentage.

The following equations show you how to work out the weighted average (overall mark) of the three examples given above.

1:3:5 Overall mark = (1/9 Yr1 % + 3/9 Yr2 % + 5/9 Yr3 %)
(uses fractions)

1:3 Overall mark = 25% Yr2 % + 75% Yr3 %
(uses percentages)

1:2 Overall mark = 0.33 Yr 1 + 0.67 Yr 2
(uses decimals)

If you are not given an equation then you need to:

i)   calculate each mark as a percentage (out of 100);

ii)   multiply the mark out of 100 by its percentage weight;

iii) add the results of the two (or more) together.

For example, a student scores 16 out of 20 in Test 1 and 32 out of 50 in Test 2. If the tests are weighted 25% for Test 1 and 75% for Test 2, what is the overall percentage?

Step i)   Test 1 = 16/20 = 80%; Test 2 = 32/50 = 64%

Step ii)   80 × 25% weighting = 20%; 64 × 75% weighting = 48%

Step iii) 20% + 48% = 68%

1 Warm-up exercises

Work out the average of the following group of numbers:

1   2, 3, 4   *Answer* ....

2   9, 7, 2, 6, 1   *Answer* ....

3   20, 30, 40   *Answer* ....

4   47, 3, 22, 8, 16, 6   *Answer* ....

5   100, 110, 120, 130   *Answer* ....

2 Warm-up exercises

Find the modal value:

1   12, 10, 14, 15, 11, 9, 7, 14, 13   *Answer* ....

2   1, 2, 1, 1, 4, 3, 2, 2, 3, 1, 3, 1, 3, 2   *Answer* ....

Find the median:

3   12, 10, 14, 15, 11, 9, 7, 14, 13   *Answer* ....

4   12, 10, 14, 15, 11, 9, 7, 14   *Answer* ....

Find the range:

5   12, 10, 14, 15, 11, 9, 7, 14, 13   *Answer* ....

3 Easy questions

1   If the average of the following set of numbers is 6, what is the value of x?

3, 10, x, 5, 8   *Answer* ....

2   If the average of the following set of numbers is 16, what is the value of y?

20, y, 13, 15, 9, 22, 17, 11   *Answer* ....

3   If the mean average of the following numbers is 8, what is the mode if x is a positive integer?

7, 10, 8, x, 9, 8, 6, 10, 7   *Answer* ....

4 In the following set of numbers the mean is 5. What is the median if x is a positive integer?

7, 3, 5, 8, 7, x, 4, 4, 6, 8, 2, 2, 8   *Answer* ....

5 In an evaluation test, scores ranged from 1 to 5 as shown in the table below. What is the mean score?

Score	Frequency
1	5
2	1
3	3
4	1
5	0

Answer ....

6 A class of 25 pupils were asked how many siblings they had. The results are shown in the table below.

Siblings	0	1	2	3	4
Number of pupils	7	8	6	3	1

Calculate:

a) the mean number of siblings;   *Answer* ....

b) the modal number of siblings;   *Answer* ....

c) the median number of siblings.   *Answer* ....

Example: The mean age of the 11 members of a female hockey team is 24 years:

a) When one member of the hockey team is sent to the 'sin bin' (penalty box), the mean average of the rest of the team is 23 years. How old is the player who was 'sin binned'?

b) The modal age of the 11 players is 21 and the median age of the 11 players is 22. The two youngest players are both aged 20. What is the maximum possible age of the oldest player?

a) Before 'sin bin': total of ages = 11 members × 24 years each = 264 years

After 'sin bin': total of ages = 10 members × 23 years each = 230 years

The 'sin binned' player reduces the age total from 264 to 230, so she is:

264 − 230 = 34 years old

b)   To find the oldest player (age x), place the players in ascending order with the youngest first and the oldest last. You can number them from 1 to 11 and then add in the known ages. The table shows the oldest and the two youngest.

1	2	3	4	5	6	7	8	9	10	11
20	20									X

The median age is 22, which is player 6, so we can enter this value.

1	2	3	4	5	6	7	8	9	10	11
20	20				22					X

The question asks for the maximum possible age of the oldest player; this means that *all the remaining values must be as low as possible*, so players 3, 4 and 5 are all aged 21, which is stated to be the modal value. Player 7 is 22 (lowest it can be), but not player 8 because three 22s would make the group bi-modal; so player 8 is 23, as is player 9 (lowest it can be). Player 10 is aged 30 ('sin binned').

1	2	3	4	5	6	7	8	9	10	11
20	20	21	21	21	22	22	23	23	30	x

We add all the ages and subtract the total from 264 to find x. Total of known ages $= 20 \times 2 + 21 \times 3 + 22 \times 2 + 23 \times 2 + 30 = 223$
    Finally, $x = 264 - 223 = 41$; the maximum possible age of the oldest player is 41.

4 More difficult questions

1   Ten numeracy test scores range from 1 to 10 inclusive. Given that the mean score is 5, the median is 5 and the mode is 6:

a)   Complete the following table of scores.

1					5				10

b)   If the lowest score was 3, calculate:

i)   the mean;   *Answer* ....

ii)   the median;   *Answer* ....

iii)   the mode.   *Answer* ....

2   The table shows the number of portions of fruit and vegetables eaten by some children at lunch time.

Number of portions	0	1	2	3	4
Number of children	x	16	8	2	1

a) If the modal number of portions is 1, what is the maximum value of x?

Answer ....

b) If the median value is 1 portion, what is the maximum value of x?

Answer ....

c) Calculate the value of x given that the mean average is 1.0 portions.

Answer ....

3   The table shows the number of pupils absent from school over a 31-day period in five class-intervals. For example, on 8 days there were 10, 11, 12, 13 or 14 pupils absent.

Number of pupils	0–4	5–9	10–14	15–19	20–25
Number of days	4	5	8	10	4

a) Which is the modal class interval?

Answer ....

b) In which class-interval does the median lie?

Answer ....

c) Calculate an estimate of the mean number of students absent from the school per day.

Answer ....

Chapter 11

··

Speed, distance and time

For the purposes of travel, speed is measured in miles per hour (mph) or kilometres per hour (km/h), distance is measured in miles or kilometres, and time is measured in hours, minutes and seconds, though you will also be familiar with days, weeks, months and years. At the start of this chapter, distance, speed and time calculations are considered without reference to any equations; non-formula methods are useful when calculators are not allowed. The latter part of the chapter looks at the distance–speed–time triangle as an aid to choosing the correct formula when working out more difficult problems.

Distance

Distance is speed times time. However, we can replace a difficult multiplication with simple arithmetic steps. We do this by considering what happens in *1 hour* (the unitary method) and then what happens for longer or shorter periods in relation to 1 hour.

Example: a coach travels a constant speed of 40 miles per hour for 2 hours and 45 minutes. What distance will it cover?

Consider 1 hour: *40 miles in 1 hour*

80 miles in 2 hours (40 × 2)

20 miles in 30 minutes (40 × ½)

<u>10</u> miles in 15 minutes (40 × ¼)

So total = <u>110</u> miles in 2 hours and 45 minutes

Example: a cyclist travels at a constant speed of 12 mph for 20 minutes. How far will the cyclist travel?

Consider 1 hour: 12 miles in 1 hour.

So 4 miles travelled in 20 minutes (12 ÷ 3)

The time period of 20 minutes is one-third of an hour so we multiply 12 miles by one-third; alternatively, we can see that there are three periods of 20 minutes in 1 hour, so we simply divide 12 miles by three to give 4 miles (which is the same as multiplying by one-third).

To make distance calculations quickly, it helps if you can convert times in minutes to fractions of one hour (60 minutes) easily. A list of common fractions is shown below. To calculate the distance travelled in a given time, you multiply the distance travelled in 1 hour by the appropriate fraction of 1 hour (or you divide by the number of time periods in 1 hour).

For 30 minutes (2 periods per hour):	multiply distance by $\frac{1}{2}$ (or divide by 2)
20 minutes (3 periods per hour):	multiply distance by $\frac{1}{3}$ (or divide by 3)
15 minutes (4 periods per hour):	multiply distance by $\frac{1}{4}$ (or divide by 4)
12 minutes (5 periods per hour):	multiply distance by $\frac{1}{5}$ (or divide by 5)
10 minutes (6 periods per hour):	multiply distance by $\frac{1}{6}$ (or divide by 6)
6 minutes (10 periods per hour):	multiply distance by $\frac{1}{10}$ (or divide by 10)
5 minutes (12 periods per hour):	multiply distance by $\frac{1}{12}$ (or divide by 12)
4 minutes (15 periods per hour):	multiply distance by $\frac{1}{15}$ (or divide by 15)
3 minutes (20 periods per hour):	multiply distance by $\frac{1}{20}$ (or divide by 20)
2 minutes (30 periods per hour):	multiply distance by $\frac{1}{30}$ (or divide by 30)
1 minute (60 periods per hour):	multiply distance by $\frac{1}{60}$ (or divide by 60)

For less obvious times we can use combinations of known times, for example: 26 minutes = 20 minutes (divide by 3) + 6 minutes (divide by 10).

Example: how far will you travel in 26 minutes at 45 mph?

Split 26 minutes into 20 minutes and 6 minutes, then we have:

45 miles in 1 hour
15 miles in 20 minutes
+ 3 miles in 6 minutes
= 18 miles in 26 minutes

Example: how far will a cyclist travel in 42 minutes if he cycles at a constant speed of 10 mph? Split 42 minutes into 30 minutes and 12 minutes, then we have:

10 miles in 1 hour
5 miles in 30 minutes
+ 2 miles in 12 minutes
= 7 miles in 42 minutes.

1 Warm-up exercise

1 How far will a car travel in 10 minutes at a constant speed of 66 mph?

Answer ....

2 How far will a cyclist travel in 5 minutes at a constant speed of 12 mph?

Answer ....

3 How far will a coach travel at 40 mph in 15 minutes?

Answer ....

4 How far will a pedestrian travel at 3 mph for 40 minutes?

Answer ....

5 How far will you travel at 10 mph for 2 hours and 15 minutes?

Answer ....

6 How far will you travel at 24 km per hour for 25 minutes?

Answer ....

7 How far does a plane travel in 1 minute at a speed of 780 mph?

Answer ....

8 How far does a ferry travel in 2.25 hours at 36 mph?

Answer ....

Converting between kilometres and miles

You will always be told how to convert from distances measured in metric units to distances measured in imperial units, and vice versa. However, the basics are worth remembering. A mile is approximately 1600 metres, and a kilometre is 1000 metres, so 1 mile = 1.6 kilometres; multiplying both sides of the equation by five gives 5 miles = 8 kilometres, so 1 kilometre = 5/8 mile (approximately 0.62 miles).

Many calculations that require a conversion will make use of the 5/8 ratio, as in:

5 miles = 8 km; 10 miles = 16 km; 20 miles = 32 km; 25 miles = 40 km;
50 miles = 80 km; 100 miles = 160 km etc

Example: a school bus makes a round trip of 32 km. How far is this in miles if one kilometre is equivalent to five-eighths of a mile?

$$1\,km = 5/8 \text{ mile}$$
$$8\,km = 5 \text{ miles}$$
$$16\,km = 10 \text{ miles}$$
$$32\,km = 20 \text{ miles}$$

Example: a student walks 2 miles to university. How far is this in kilometres if 5 miles are equivalent to 8 kilometres?

$$5 \text{ miles} = 8\,km$$
$$1 \text{ mile} = 8/5\,km = 1.6\,km$$
$$2 \text{ miles} = 3.2\,km$$

Example: a pupil travels 15.6 km to school. What is this distance in miles if 1 mile is equivalent to 1.6 km?

$$1 \text{ mile} = 1.6\,km$$
$$5 \text{ miles} = 8\,km$$
$$1\,km = 5/8 \text{ mile}$$
$$15.6\,km = 15.6 \times 5/8 = 78/8 = 9\frac{6}{8} = 9\frac{3}{4} \text{ miles}$$

2 Warm-up exercise

1   If 1 km is approximately 0.62 miles, how far is 30 kilometres?

Answer ....

2   A school coach makes a journey of 320 km.
How far is this in miles if one kilometre is five-eighths of a mile?

Answer ....

3   A school coach makes a journey of 360 km.
How far is this in miles if one kilometre is five-eighths of a mile?

Answer ....

4   A cyclist covers a distance of 1.5 miles.
How far this is in kilometres if 5 miles are equivalent to 8 km?

Answer ....

Speed

To calculate the speed you need to know the distance travelled and the time taken. Speeds use miles per hour or kilometres per hour, so if we find the distance travelled in 1 hour (the *unitary* method) then this is the speed.

Example: what is our speed if we cover 96 miles in 1 hour and 20 minutes?

We need to find the distance travelled in 1 hour.

We have:	96 miles in 1 hour 20 minutes
	96 miles in 80 minutes
	48 miles in 40 minutes
	24 miles in 20 minutes
Total:	72 miles in 60 minutes

Or 72 miles in 1 hour = *72 mph*

Example: a journey of 5 kilometres takes 24 minutes at a constant speed. Calculate the speed in kilometres per hour (km/h).

Again we need to find the distance travelled in 1 hour (60 minutes).

We have:	5 km in 24 minutes
	2.5 km in 12 minutes

Choosing the period of 12 minutes is helpful because there are five periods of 12 minutes in 1 hour (see earlier), so we can multiply 2.5 by 5 to find the *distance we would have covered had the journey lasted 1 hour.*

5 km in 12 min	$= 2.5 \times 5$ km in 1 hour
	$= (2 \times 5) + (0.5 \times 5)$
	$= 10 + 2.5$ km in 1 hour
	$= 12.5$ km in 1 hour = *12.5 kmh*

Example: what speed covers 250 km in 2 hours and 30 minutes?

We need to find the distance travelled in 1 hour (60 minutes).

We have:	250 km in 2 hours 30 minutes
	500 km in 5 hours
	100 km in 1 hour = *100 kmh*

Here we doubled the time to remove the half hour.

Example: what speed covers 240 km in 2 hours and 40 minutes?

We need to find the distance travelled in 1 hour (60 minutes).

We have:	240 km in 2 hours 40 minutes
	240 km in 160 minutes
	120 km in 80 minutes
	60 km in 40 minutes
	30 km in 20 minutes
Total:	*90 kmh*

Example: what speed covers 240 km in 2 hours and 40 minutes?

Alternative method:

We need to find the distance travelled in 1 hour (60 minutes).

We have: 240 km in 2 hours 40 minutes
Multiply by three: 720 km in 6 hours 120 minutes
                        720 km in 8 hours = *90 kmh*

Here we tripled the time so that the minutes would be divisible by 60, giving us a whole number of hours.

3 Warm-up exercise

1   What speed covers 84 miles in 3 hours?   *Answer* ....

2   What speed covers 25 miles in 30 minutes?   *Answer* ....

3   What speed covers 7 miles in 10 minutes?   *Answer* ....

4   What speed covers 21 km in 45 minutes?   *Answer* ....

5   What speed covers 140 km in 2 hours and 20 minutes?

                                                             Answer ....

6   What speed covers 12 miles in 40 minutes?   *Answer* ....

7   What speed covers 16 miles in 15 minutes?   *Answer* ....

8   What speed covers 25 km in 45 minutes?   *Answer* ....

9   What speed covers 132 km in 1 hour and 50 minutes?

                                                             Answer ....

Time

You should be able to express any period of time in a smaller or larger unit based on the conversions shown below:

60 seconds (s) = 1 minute (min); seconds to minutes = divide by 60

60 minutes (min) = 1 hour (h, hr); minutes to hours = divide by 60

24 hours = 1 day (d); hours to days = divide by 24; 28, 29, 30 or 31 days = 1 month; 365 days = 1 year; 366 days = 1 leap year

13 weeks = 1 quarter; 52 weeks = 1 year; 12 months = 1 year

p.a. = per annum = per year; a.m. = before noon; p.m. = afternoon

GMT = Greenwich Mean Time

Candidates should be familiar with both the 12-hour clock (which has two 12-hour periods – a.m. and p.m.) and the 24-hour clock, which finishes at midnight, ie midnight = 2400 hours (twenty-four hundred hours) and starts again at 0000 (zero hundred hours); noon (midday) = 1200 hrs (twelve hundred hours).

Times can be converted from the 12-hour clock to the 24-hour clock by rewriting the time as a four-digit number and adding 12 hours to all p.m. times. For example:

8.30 a.m. = 0830 hrs (O eight thirty hours)

1 p.m. = 1 + 12 hrs = 1300 hrs (thirteen hundred hours)

10.45 p.m. = 10.45 + 12 hrs = 2245 (twenty-two forty-five hours)

Likewise, times on the 24-hour clock can be converted to 12-hour clock times by subtracting 12 hours from all afternoon times (ie those greater than 1200 hrs); for example, 2050 hours = 2050 − 12 hrs = 8.50 pm.

Example: a school coach arrived at the Tate Gallery at 1300 hours. The journey took 1 hour and 55 minutes, excluding a 25-minute break. What time was it when the coach set out?

Total time taken = 1 hour 55 minutes + 25 minutes break = 2 hrs 20 min; (here you add 5 minutes to get to 2 hours and then add the remaining 20 minutes to get to 2 hours and 20 minutes). So we know that the coach must have set out 2 hours and 20 minutes before its arrival time of 1300 hrs. Subtracting hours and minutes in a single step is not easy, so *subtract more time than you need, in complete hours, and then add back the extra minutes* as follows: 1300 hrs − 2 hrs 20 min is 1300 hrs − 3 hrs + 40 min = 1000 hrs 40 min or 1040 hours.

4 Warm-up exercise

1   How many seconds are there in eight and three-quarter minutes?

Answer ....

2   How many minutes are there in three hours and twenty-five minutes?

Answer ....

3   How many days are there in 168 hours?   Answer ....

4   Convert 6.30 a.m. to a 24-hour clock time.   Answer ....

5   Convert 9.15 p.m. to a 24-hour clock time.   Answer ....

6   Convert 2245 hours to a 12-hour clock time.   Answer ....

7   Add 3 hours and 25 minutes to 1445 hours.   Answer ....

8   Subtract 1 hour and 42 minutes from 1410 hrs.   Answer ....

5 Easy questions

1   A school coach arrives at the Tate Gallery at twelve hundred hours.
The journey took two hours and twenty-five minutes excluding
a fifteen-minute break. At what time did the coach set out?

Answer ....

2   An exam finished at twelve twenty-five hours having lasted one
and three-quarter hours. At what time did the exam start?

Answer ....

3   Teachers at a school have four hours and twelve minutes of contact time
per day. What is the contact time per week?   *Answer* ....

4   A pupil aged eleven years and four months has a reading age eighteen
months below his actual age. What is his reading age?

Answer ....

5   A school day starts at eight-fifty a.m. and finishes at three-thirty p.m.
Breaks total one hour and fifteen minutes. What is the maximum number
of half-hour lessons possible per day?

Answer ....

6   School lessons start at a quarter past nine. There are ten lessons per day
lasting thirty minutes each and breaks that total ninety minutes.
What time does the school day finish?

Answer ....

7   A school day ends at five past three. There are two lessons in the afternoon
each lasting fifty minutes with a ten-minute break in between. At what time
does the first afternoon lesson begin?

Answer ....

To calculate the time for a journey you need to know the distance travelled and the
speed of travel. The methods employed to calculate time using 'a non-formula'
method are similar to those to calculate speed, in that we start with a time period of
1 hour (unitary method), but instead of calculating the distance travelled in 1 hour
(the speed) we calculate the time taken to cover the required distance.

Example: how long will it take to travel 144 miles at 36 mph?

We have   36 miles in 1 hour

72 miles in 2 hours

144 miles in 4 hours

Example: how long will it take to travel 14 km at 42 kmh?

We have   42 km in 1 hour

21 km 30 minutes

7 km in 10 minutes

= 14 km in 20 minutes

The alternative method of solving distance, speed and time calculations is to use the following three equations or formulae:

$$\text{Speed} = \frac{\text{Distance}}{\text{Time}} \qquad \text{Time} = \frac{\text{Distance}}{\text{Speed}} \qquad \text{Distance} = \text{Speed} \times \text{Time}$$

$$S = \frac{D}{T} \qquad\qquad T = \frac{D}{S} \qquad\qquad D = S \times T$$

If your algebra is up to scratch, you need only remember that 'distance is speed times time', because you can manipulate this equation to get either Time on its own (divide both sides by Speed) or Speed on its own (divide both sides by Time). However, many candidates will find it easier to refer to the distance–speed–time triangle.

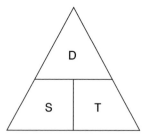

Example (used earlier): how long will it take to travel 14 km at 42 kmh?

To use the triangle, place the tip of your finger over the *variable* you need, in this case Time, to leave 'Distance over Speed', meaning Distance divided by Speed.

$$T = \frac{D}{S} = \frac{14}{42} = \frac{7}{21} = \frac{1}{3} \text{ hour} = 20 \text{ minutes}$$

6 Easy questions

Use the SDT triangle where necessary. Take 1 mile to be 1.6 km:

1   What distance is covered in 4 hours and 20 minutes at 60 mph?

Answer ....

2   What distance is covered in 4 hours and 20 minutes at 72 mph?

Answer ....

3   A school trip to the Tate Gallery took two hours and fifteen minutes by coach, travelling at an average speed of forty miles per hour. How far away was the Gallery?   *Answer* ....

4   What speed in miles per hour covers 44 kilometres in 30 minutes?

Answer ....

5   What speed in kilometres per hour covers 17.5 miles in 35 minutes?

Answer ....

6   What speed in miles per hour covers 66 kilometres in 45 minutes?

Answer ....

7   What time will it take to travel 6 miles at a speed of 6 kilometres per hour?

Answer ....

8   How long will it take to drive 140 km at 70 mph?   *Answer* ....

9   A coach leaves Birmingham at 1130 hrs. What time will it arrive at Manchester airport, 80 miles away, if it averages 60 mph?

Answer ....

Average speed for two journeys at different speeds

Care needs to be taken when calculating average speeds. If a car travels from A to B at 40 mph and then from B to A at 60 mph, the average speed might appear to be 50 mph; however, this is not the case. Average speed is calculated as follows:

$$\text{Average speed} = \frac{\text{Total distance travelled}}{\text{Total time taken}}$$

Example: a car travels from A to B, a distance of 80 miles, at a constant speed of 40 mph, and then returns from B to A at a constant speed of 60 mph. What was the average speed?

Method:

Divide total distance by total time:

i)   total distance = 80 + 80 = 160 miles

ii)   total time = time to travel from A to B and time to travel from B to A

For A to B: $T = \dfrac{D}{S} = \dfrac{80}{40} = 2$ hours

For B to A: $T = \dfrac{D}{S} = \dfrac{80}{60} = \dfrac{8}{6} = \dfrac{4}{3} = 1\dfrac{1}{3}$ hour

Total time = A to B added to B to A = $2 + 1\dfrac{1}{3} = 3\dfrac{1}{3}$ hrs

Total distance = 160 miles

Average speed = total distance ÷ total time

$$= 160 \div 3\dfrac{1}{3} = 160 \div \dfrac{10}{3} = 160 \times \dfrac{3}{10} = 16 \times 3 = 48 \text{ mph}$$

7 More difficult question

1   A coach travels from Chester to Liverpool at 36 mph before returning to Chester at 28 mph. If the distance between the two cities is 33.6 kilometres, calculate, by any method:

a)   the distance from Chester to Liverpool in miles, if 5 miles are equivalent to 8 kilometres;   *Answer* ....

b)   the average speed for the round trip.

Answer ....

Chapter 12

Charts, graphs and tables

These provide a simple and efficient way of displaying school data. In some questions the answer can be read directly from the diagram. However, the majority of questions need to be interpreted carefully to ensure that the correct data is located, before any mathematical operations are applied.

Pie charts

These charts are not the most accurate way of displaying data but they do show at a glance the relative sizes of component parts. A full circle (360°) represents 100 per cent of the data, so 180° = one-half (50%), 120° = one-third (33.3%) and 90° = one-quarter (25%) etc. Reading information from pie charts is easy but marks are lost when the candidate fails to look at the text in a key or sub-heading, for example the total number of pupils in the sample.

Now attempt the single-step warm-up questions associated with the pie charts on the next page.

1 Warm-up exercise

Figure 12.1 Distribution of children's expenditure aged 7 to 15

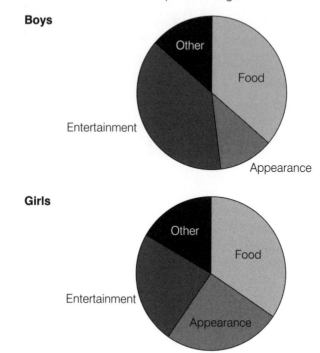

With reference to Figure 12.1:

1   What is the most popular area of girls' spending?   *Answer* ....

2   What is the least popular area of boys' spending?   *Answer* ....

3   In which area do boys and girls spend
    a similar proportion of their money?   *Answer* ....

4   What percentage of girls' spending is
    taken up by appearance?   *Answer* ....

5   Girls spend twice as much as boys on appearance.
    What fraction of boys' expenditure is taken up
    by appearance?   *Answer* ....

2 Warm-up exercise

Figure 12.2 Grade of staff in higher educational institutions

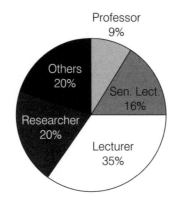

Total: 160,000

With reference to Figure 12.2:

1   What percentage of the staff are researchers?   *Answer* ....

2   What fraction of the staff are researchers?   *Answer* ....

3   What fraction of the staff are lecturer grade?   *Answer* ....

4   What fraction of the staff are senior lecturer grade?   *Answer* ....

5   What is the combined total of lecturers and
     senior lecturers as a decimal fraction of the whole?   *Answer* ....

6   How many staff are researchers?   *Answer* ....

7   How many more senior lecturers and researchers
     combined are there than lecturers?   *Answer* ....

8   How many staff are professors?   *Answer* ....

9   If there are five times as many male professors
     as female professors, how many female professors are there?
     Answer ....

3 Easy question

Figure 12.3 Pie charts showing the distribution of A-level grades in two different schools, A and B

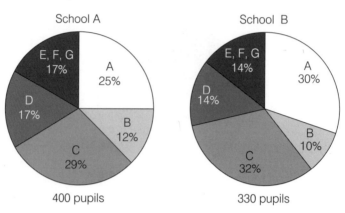

School A

E, F, G
17%
A
25%
D
17%
B
12%
C
29%

400 pupils

School B

E, F, G
14%
A
30%
D
14%
B
10%
C
32%

330 pupils

Say whether the statement is true or false:

1   School B achieved more A grades than School A.

Answer ....

2   The number of pupils achieving grade C
or above in School A was 264.   *Answer* ....

3   The A–C pass rate in School B was 6%
above that in School A.   *Answer* ....

Bar charts

Bar graphs (bar charts) are useful for comparing different categories of data, for example GCSE subjects, or school results in different years. The bars can be drawn vertically or horizontally. The height (or length) of each bar is read off the scale on the axis and corresponds to the size of the data.

4 Warm-up exercise

Figure 12.4 School subject by popularity

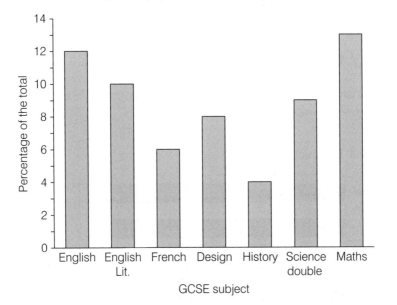

With reference to Figure 12.4:

1   Which subject is the most popular?   *Answer* ....

2   Which subject is the fifth most popular?   *Answer* ....

3   Which subject is three times more popular than history?
                                                                                               Answer ....

4   Which subject is two-thirds as popular as science double?
                                                                                               Answer ....

5   What proportion of the total shown is taken up by English literature?
        Give your answer as a fraction in its lowest terms and also as a decimal.
                                                                                               Answer ....

6   What proportion of the total shown is taken up by English and maths
        together? Give your answer as a fraction in its lowest terms.
                                                                                               Answer ....

7   What is the ratio of pupils taking English literature to pupils taking English?
        Give your answer in its lowest terms.   *Answer* ....

8   If 180 pupils take English, how many take English literature?
                                                                                               Answer ....

9   What percentage of the total shown is taken up by all seven subjects?

Answer ....

10   What decimal fraction of the total is taken up by subjects other than those shown in the chart?   *Answer* ....

5 Easy question

The bar chart in Figure 12.5 shows the percentage of pupils achieving grades A* to C in five popular subjects.

Figure 12.5 Bar chart of grades achieved in five subjects

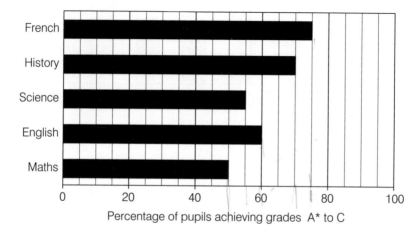

Percentage of pupils achieving grades A* to C

With reference to Figure 12.5:

1   If 180 pupils took GCSE maths, how many achieved grades A* to C?

Answer ....

2   One-third as many pupils took history as took maths. How many pupils achieved grades A* to C in history?   *Answer* ....

3   If English and maths were equally popular, how many more pupils gained grades A* to C in English than in maths?

Answer ....

4   If 54 pupils achieved grades A* to C in French, how many pupils took French?   *Answer* ....

6 Easy question

The bar chart shows Key Stage 2 Level 4 performance in English versus proportion of pupils eligible for free school meals in a local authority's schools for 2000 and 2004.

Figure 12.6 Key Stage 2 Level 4 performances versus free school meals

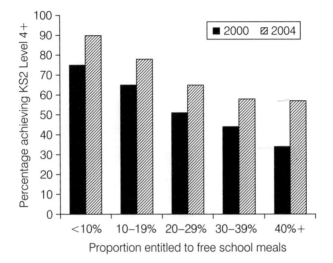

With reference to Figure 12.6, indicate whether the statements are true or false:

1   The percentage of pupils achieving KS2 Level 4 in
     English in 2004 was above that for 2000.   *Answer* ....

2   The schools with the highest proportion of pupils
     on free school meals showed the greatest improvements
     in KS2 performance from 2000 to 2004.   *Answer* ....

3   In 2004, fewer than 10% of the pupils achieved
     KS2 Level 4+ in schools where 90% were entitled to
     free school meals.   *Answer* ....

In a stacked (compound) bar chart each bar is split into two or more segments that represent different data sets. The data is easier to compare than would be the case if the segments were shown as individual bars placed side by side. The stacked bar chart shown in Figure 12.7 compares pupils at Key Stage 2 achieving Levels 2 to 5 in maths in two schools, A and B.

Figure 12.7 Stacked bar chart showing performance at Key Stage 2

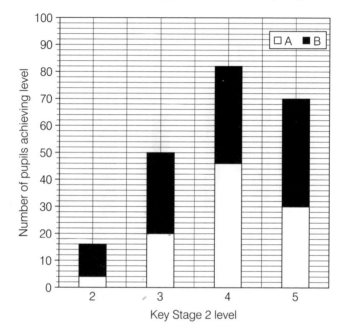

7 Easy question

With reference to Figure 12.7:

1   At which level did school A outperform school B?   *Answer* ....

2   The stacked bar chart shows that the number of pupils achieving Level 2 at school B was three times that of school A (3:1 ratio). What was the B:A ratio for pupils achieving Level 3?

                                                     Answer ....

8 Easy question

Figure 12.8 GCSE grade C achievement by subject and gender

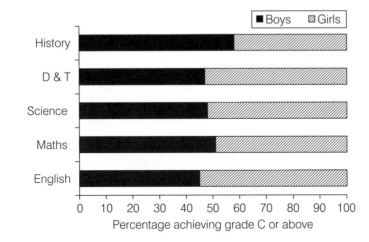

The bar chart in Figure 12.8 shows the percentage of pupils in a school who achieved GCSE grade C or above in five subjects by gender. What proportion of the pupils who achieved grade C or above in English are boys? Give your answer as a fraction.

Answer ....

Line graphs

With these graphs the data is plotted as a series of points joined by a line. Figure 12.9 shows a travel graph for a coach trip where the distance travelled in miles is plotted against the time in hours. The controlling quantity (time) is plotted on the x-axis and the quantity it controls (distance travelled) is plotted on the y-axis. The data table for the graph is as follows:

Time (hours)	0	0.5	1.0	1.5	2.0	2.5	3.0	3.5
Dist. (miles)	0	20	40	50	60	90	120	140

Figure 12.9 Distance time graph for a coach trip

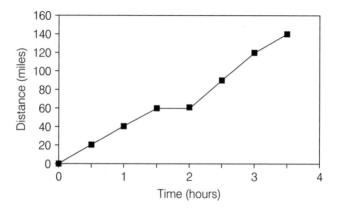

9 Easy question

With reference to Figure 12.9:

1   What was the average speed for the journey?   Answer ....

2   For how many minutes was the coach stationary?   Answer ....

3   If the coach set out at 1000 hrs, what was the average speed between midday and 1330 hrs, to the nearest mile per hour?
                                                                              Answer ....

4   What are the x and y coordinates of the point at 1300 hrs?
                                                                              Answer ....

Multiple line graphs

Line graphs are useful for showing trends. Two or more lines can be shown together on the same axes to facilitate comparisons. The line graph shown in Figure 12.10 compares a local authority's A-level passes in maths, physics, chemistry and biology.

Figure 12.10 A-level passes for a local authority

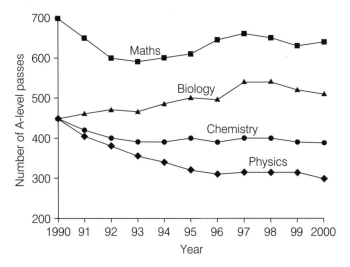

10 Warm-up exercise

With reference to Figure 12.10:

1   Which subject showed the least variation in passes from 1990 to 2000?
    (least change)   *Answer* ....

2   What was the range of the passes for physics between 1990 and 2000?
    (maximum minus minimum)   *Answer* ....

3   In 1995, how many more passes were there in biology than in chemistry?
                                                        Answer ....

4   Assuming the rate of decline in maths passes from 1990 to 1992 had
    continued, how many maths passes would have been predicted for the year
    2000? (extend the line downwards or calculate the common difference)
                                                        Answer ....

11 Easy question

Figure 12.11 shows the percentage of pupils in a school achieving Levels 5 to 8 and Levels 3 to 8 in maths at Key Stage 3.

Figure 12.11 Pupil achievement at Key Stage 3 maths

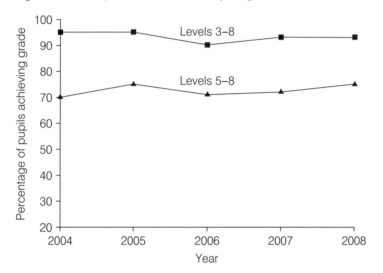

With reference to Figure 12.11:

1   What percentage of the pupils achieved Levels 5 to 8 in 2004?

Answer ....

2   What percentage of the pupils achieved less than Level 5 in 2004?
(hint: Levels 3–8 = 3, 4, 5, 6, 7, 8; Levels 5–8 = 5, 6, 7, 8).

Answer ....

3   What fraction of the pupils achieved Levels 5 to 8 in 2005?
Give your answer in its lowest terms.   *Answer* ....

4   What fraction of the pupils achieved less than Levels 5 in 2005?
(hint: Levels 3–8 = 3, 4, 5, 6, 7, 8; Levels 5–8 = 5, 6, 7, 8).

Answer ....

12 Easy question

Figure 12.12 Percentage of pupils at KS1 for a school and its LA

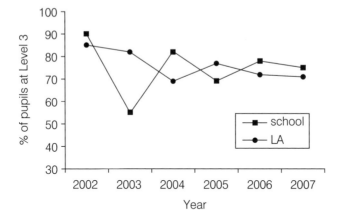

Figure 12.12 shows the percentage of pupils at Key Stage 1 maths Level 3 from 2002 to 2007 for a school and its local authority. In which year did the school's performance exceed that of the local authority by more than 10 per cent?

Answer ....

Scatter graphs

These are similar to line graphs in that points are plotted and a line can be drawn. However, the line is not drawn from point to point but is a 'line of best fit' through all of the points. This 'regression line' can be judged by eye or it can be calculated. The line identifies any relationship (correlation) between the x and y values, as shown in the following examples:

a)   Strong positive correlation; points lie close to a straight line (x and y increase in proportion to each other).

Figure 12.13 Strong positive correlation

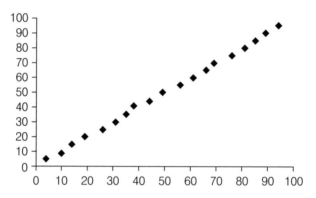

b)   Weak positive correlation; points are not close to a line. As x increases, y generally increases but not always and y sometimes decreases.

Figure 12.14 Weak positive correlation

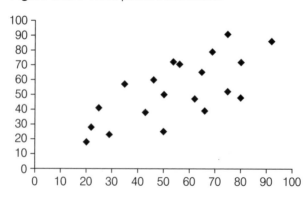

c)   No correlation; random (unable to predict x from y).

Figure 12.15 No correlation

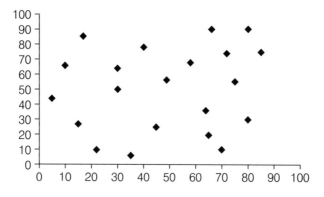

13 More difficult question

The scatter graph in Figure 12.16 shows a strong negative correlation between pupil performance and days of absence. As absence increases, percentage achieving Level 4 decreases.

Figure 12.16 Scatter graph to show how pupil performance at KS2 decreases with increasing absenteeism

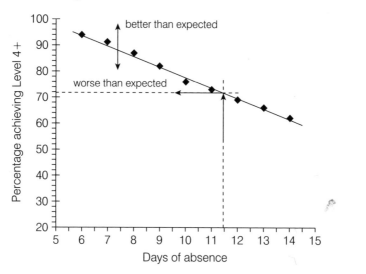

With reference to Figure 12.16:

1   What percentage of pupils would be expected to achieve Level 4+ if they had 23 half-days of absence?   *Answer* ....

2   Pupils in a school have on average 10 days of absence each. If 70% achieve Level 4 or above, is this better or worse than expected?
                    Answer ....

3   Pupils in a school have on average 8 days of absence each. If 90% achieve Level 4 or above, is this better or worse than expected?
                    Answer ....

The strong negative correlation shows how pupil performance decreases as days of absence increases.

14 More difficult question

Figure 12.17 Scatter graph comparing results in an arithmetic test with results in a writing test

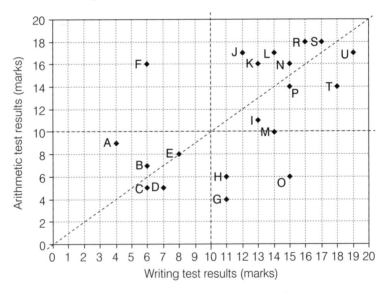

With reference to Figure 12.17, and using the three dashed lines to help you, determine:

1   Which pupil did equally well in both tests?   *Answer* ....

2   How many pupils did better in writing than in arithmetic?
                                                          Answer ....

3   How many pupils did better in arithmetic than in writing?
                                                          Answer ....

4   How many pupils gained 10 or more marks in arithmetic?
                                                          Answer ....

5   How many pupils gained 10 or more marks in writing?
                                                          Answer ....

6   How many pupils gained 10 or more marks in both writing and arithmetic?
                                                          Answer ....

7   How many pupils gained 10 or fewer marks in both writing and arithmetic?
                                                          Answer ....

8   Which two pupils had the largest difference in arithmetic and writing test
        results?   *Answer* ....

9   Calculate the average writing test result for all 20 pupils.
                                                          Answer ....

10 Calculate the average arithmetic result for all 20 pupils.
                                                          Answer ....

11 Use your answers in question 9 (x-coordinate) and 10 (y-coordinate) to
        locate the x and y coordinates of the 'average point'. *Answer* ....

12 A line drawn from the origin (0,0) through the average point is the line of
        best fit (line of regression). Is the line of best fit above or below the dashed
        diagonal line?   *Answer* ....

Tables

With tables you need to look along a row and down a column to find the answer. Table 12.1 has 8 columns and 10 rows.

15 Warm-up exercise

Table 12.1 shows temperatures in degrees Celsius (°C) of holiday resorts in Switzerland, from April to October.

Table 12.1 Temperature versus resort

	Apr	May	Jun	Jul	Aug	Sep	Oct
Interlaken	11	15	19	21	21	17	12
Adelboden	8	13	14	16	19	17	10
Central Reg.	12	17	20	22	21	17	12
Lake Geneva	11	16	19	22	21	17	13
Zermatt	8	13	17	19	19	16	10
Verbier	14	19	22	24	23	19	14
Davos	6	11	14	16	16	13	7
St Moritz	1	6	9	11	10	5	1
Lake Lugano	14	19	23	26	26	22	16

With reference to the table:

1   Which is the coldest resort?   Answer ....

2   Which is the warmest month for most of the resorts? Answer ....

3   Which two resorts have the same temperature in June?
                                                             Answer ....

4   In which month are four of the resorts at the same temperature?
                                                             Answer ....

5   How many resorts achieved 20 °C or more in July?   Answer ....

6   In how many resorts does the temperature drop below 10 °C?
                                                             Answer ....

7   In how many resorts does the temperature rise above 10 °C?
                                                             Answer ....

8   What is the difference in temperature between Interlaken
and St Moritz in July?   *Answer* ....

9   Which resort shows the largest increase in temperature, April to July?
Answer ....

10 In which month is Davos four degrees cooler than Lake Geneva?
Answer ....

11 What is the average temperature in Verbier for June, July and August?
Answer ....

12 What is the average temperature in St Moritz for all seven months?
Answer ....

13 What is the average temperature of all the resorts in October?
Answer ....

14 Which resort has the highest 'mean' (ie average) temperature over the
seven months? (hint: no calculation necessary)   *Answer* ....

15 Which resort offers the least variation (ie change) in temperature between
May and July?   *Answer* ....

16 What is the range of temperature (ie highest minus lowest) in Zermatt over
the seven months?   *Answer* ....

16 Easy question

Pupils are taken on a field trip to Ireland via the Holyhead–Dublin ferry. The ferry
timetable is shown in Table 12.2. What is the latest check-in time if the pupils are
to arrive back in Holyhead before midday?

Table 12.2 Ferry timetable

Vessel	Holyhead to Dublin		Dublin to Holyhead	
	Departs	Arrives	Departs	Arrives
Cruise	0240	0555	0805	1130
Swift	1200	1355	0845	1045
Cruise	1410	1525	1430	1630
Swift	1715	1915	2055	0020
	Latest check-in time is 30 minutes before departure			

17 Easy question

Table 12.3 Points score versus GCSE grade (old system)

GCSE Grade	Points
A*	8
A	7
B	6
C	5
D	4
E	3
F	2
G	1

Example:

Pupil with 8 GCSEs

2 As = 2 × 7 = 14 points

3 Bs = 3 × 6 = 18 points

2 Cs = 2 × 5 = 10 points

1 D = 4 points

Total = 46 points

Average score = 46 ÷ 8 = 5.75

With reference to Table 12.3:

1   What is the total score for a pupil with an A grade in English, Bs in sociology and psychology, and Cs in maths, history and economics?

Answer ....

2   What is the average points score for the pupil in question 1? Give your answer to 2 decimal places.   *Answer* ....

Table 12.4 looks very different from Table 12.3 but presents similar data in the form of nine columns and two rows instead of two columns and nine rows.

Table 12.4 Points score versus GCSE grade (new system)

Grade	G	F	E	D	C	B	A	A*
Points	16	22	28	34	40	46	52	58

18 More difficult question

A school can predict a pupil's GCSE grade in core subjects based on the level achieved at Key Stage 3 using the formula:

Point score = 6 × KS3 Level +3

With reference to the Table 12.4 and the above formula:

1   How many points would be expected for a pupil with a Level 7 in maths at Key Stage 3?   *Answer* ....

2   What would be the most likely GCSE grade for the pupil in question 1?
                                                            Answer ....

3   A pupil gains a Level 5 in English at Key Stage 3. What GCSE grade would be predicted?   *Answer* ....

4   A pupil is awarded GCSE grade B in science. What level would you have expected at Key Stage 3?   *Answer* ....

5   A pupil gained Level 7 in English and science and Level 6 in maths. What were the pupil's average points?   *Answer* ....

6   What are the total points for a pupil achieving Level 7 in eight subjects?
                                                            Answer ....

7   What are average points for a pupil with two Bs, four Cs and two Ds?
                                                            Answer ....

8   A pupil has a total of 8 GCSEs, including five Cs and two Bs. If the points totalled 314, what was the other grade?   *Answer* ....

19 More difficult question

Table 12.5 shows the percentage of pupils achieving Level 4 and above at Key Stage 2 English, maths and science between 2001 and 2005.

Table 12.5 Pupil achievement versus year

| Year | Pupils achieving Level 4+ at Key Stage 2 (%) | | |
	English	Maths	Science
2001	75	71	87
2002	75	73	86
2003	75		87
2004	77	74	86
2005	79	75	86
Mean		73.2	86.4

Indicate all the true statements:

1   The mean for English for the five-year period was 76.2%.
                                                          Answer ....

2   Seventy-two per cent of maths pupils achieved Level 4 or above in 2003.
                                                          Answer ....

3   For science for the five-year period the mode was 86%
     and the median was 86.5%.   *Answer* ....

20 More difficult question

Referring to Table 12.6, which test had the highest percentage mark and the smallest range?

Table 12.6 Test scores in reading, writing and arithmetic

	Reading score (out of 40)	Writing score (out of 50)	Arithmetic score (out of 60)
Lowest	15	18	25
Median	29	36	47
Highest	36	43	54

21 More difficult question

Table 12.7 shows pupil performance in end of Key Stage 3 English, maths and science.

Table 12.7 Pupil performance in three subjects

Name	English KS3 Level	Maths KS3 Level	Science KS3 Level
Aziz	6	5	5
Bethan	5	4	5
Carl	5	5	6
Eleri	4	6	4
Harry	5	5	6
Josh	5	4	5
Phoebe	7	7	7
Ruby	5	5	6
Yasmin	4	4	5
Zak	6	6	5
% at level 5 or above		70	90
% at level 6 or above	50	60	30

1   What percentage of the pupils achieved Level 5 or above in English?

Answer ....

2   What proportion of the pupils who achieved Level 5 or above in science also achieved Level 5 or above in maths? Give your answer as a fraction in its lowest terms.   *Answer* ....

3   What proportion of the pupils achieved Level 5 or above in all three subjects? Give your answer as a percentage.   *Answer* ....

Two-way tables

These are useful for comparing pupil performance in two subjects (or in two different years). One subject occupies the columns and the other subject occupies the rows. The cells show the number of times the subjects are paired at each grade or level; all the combinations possible can be recorded. The table may also include the total number (summation) of the combinations across each row and column.

22 Warm-up exercise

Table 12.8 compares the GCSE results of pupils who took both French (vertical column) and Spanish (horizontal row). Where a cell is empty, the number of pupils obtaining that combination of grades is zero.

Table 12.8 Two-way table for GCSE French and Spanish

GCSE grade in Spanish	GCSE grade in French								Total
	A*	A	B	C	D	E	F	G	
A*	1	2	1						4
A	1	2	1	1					5
B	1	2	3	2	1				9
C		1	2	4	2				9
D				2	1	1	1		5
E					1	1		1	3
F									0
G									0
Total	3	7	7	9	5	2	1	1	35

With reference to Table 12.8:

1 How many pupils achieved a grade C in
both French and Spanish?   *Answer* ....

2 How many pupils gained a grade C in Spanish?   *Answer* ....

3 How many pupils achieved a grade A in French? *Answer* ....

4 How many pupils in total took both
French and Spanish?   *Answer* ....

5 What was the modal grade for French?   *Answer* ....

6 How many pupils achieved
grade C or above in Spanish?   *Answer* ....

7 What percentage of pupils achieved grade C or
above in Spanish (to 1 d.p.)?   *Answer* ....

8   How many pupils achieved a lower grade in Spanish than in French (those left of a diagonal line from A*A* to GG)?   *Answer* ....

Tally charts, frequency tables and histograms

A tally chart is used to group and count data. The results are presented in a frequency table, and a frequency histogram (a bar chart of frequency distributions) is drawn. The histogram provides a mental picture of the spread of the marks, with the most frequent marks normally centred on the middle. For example:

Fifty-one pupils achieved the following GCSE grades:

B C D E A B D C B A C C D C A* C E B A C B D C B C E D C F D B C D B C D C F E C
D B C D C D B C D C C B

Figure 12.18 Tally chart

A*	I	1
A	III	3
B	HHT HHT I	11
C	HHT HHT HHT III	18
D	HHT HHT II	12
E	IIII	4
F	II	2

Table 12.9 Frequency table

Grade	F	E	D	C	B	A	A*
Frequency	2	4	12	18	11	3	1

Figure 12.19 Histogram

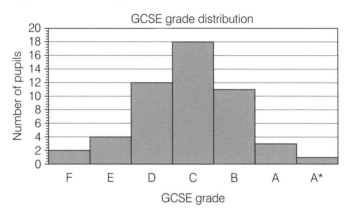

The performance of a school can be assessed by allocating points to GCSE grades as described earlier and shown in Table 12.10. The frequency of the grades enables the total number of points to be calculated (points multiplied by frequency for every grade).

Table 12.10

Grade	F	E	D	C	B	A	A*
GCSE points	22	28	34	40	46	52	58
Frequency	2	4	12	18	11	3	1

The mean value of all the points in the table is given by the total number of points divided by the total number of frequencies (total number of pupils):

$$\text{mean} = \frac{\text{'total of' [points multiplied by frequencies]}}{\text{'total number of frequencies'}}$$

$$= \frac{(58\times1) + (52\times3) + (46\times11) + (40\times18) + (34\times12) + (28\times4) + (22\times2)}{1 + 3 + 11 + 18 + 12 + 3 + 2}$$

$$= \frac{58 + 156 + 506 + 720 + 408 + 112 + 44}{51}$$

$$= 2004 \div 51 = 39.29 \text{ points}$$

The mean points per pupil are 39.29 or just below grade C (40).

The median points are those of the 26th pupil (middle of 51 is given by $(n + 1) \div 2 = 52 \div 2 = 26$th), found in the grade C group, ie median = 40 points.

The modal points = 40 (most frequent points, 18 times).

The mode and median can be read from the histogram whereas the mean requires a calculation.

23 More difficult question

Figure 12.20 Histogram of GCSE grades for A-level students

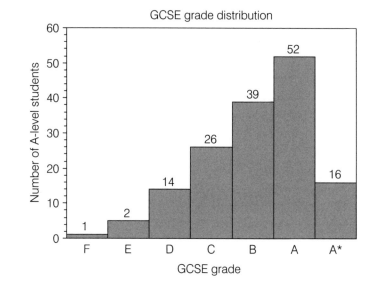

Referring to the histogram in Figure 12.20:

1   How many students achieved GCSE grades A* to F?

                                                                    Answer ....

2   What percentage of the A*–F students achieved grade C or above?
(Give your answer to 1 decimal place.)   *Answer* ....

3   What is the modal GCSE grade?   *Answer* ....

4   What is the median GCSE grade?   *Answer* ....

5   If 96% of the A-level students went on to higher
education, how many students was this?   *Answer* ....

Histograms often group the marks into intervals, for example 10–19; 20–29; 30–39 etc. to provide a clearer picture of the distribution of the marks; the bars should be touching because the data intervals are continuous.

The intervals can be described using less than ($<$) and less than or equal to symbols ($\leq$) to identify the boundaries of the marks:

symbol:	$n \leq 9$	$9 < n \leq 19$	$19 < n \leq 29$	$29 < n \leq 39$
interval:	0–9	10–19	20–29	30–39

Example: a sixth form college converted the GCSE grades of 120 students to points (Table 12.11). The points were averaged for each student to obtain a mean GCSE score (X).

Table 12.11

Mean GCSE score (X)	Frequency
$4.1 < X \leq 4.5$	5
$4.5 < X \leq 5.5$	13
$5.5 < X \leq 6.0$	27
$6.0 < X \leq 6.5$	43
$6.5 < X \leq 7.0$	25
$7.0 < X \leq 7.5$	8
$7.5 < X \leq 8.0$	4

24 More difficult question

Figure 12.21 Histogram of GCSE points scores

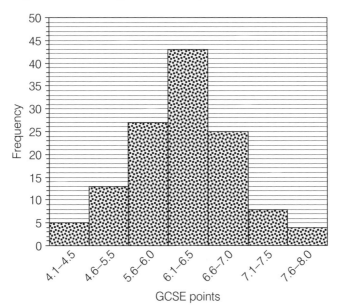

Referring to the histogram in Figure 12.21:

1   What percentage of the students scored more than 6 points?

Answer ....

2   What is the ratio of students scoring more than 6 points to students scoring 6 points or fewer?   Answer ....

3   What percentage of the students scored in the range shown by $5.5 < X \leq 7.0$?

Answer ....

Cumulative frequency graphs

These are 'S'-shaped graphs that show how many pupils achieved a *particular grade and below*. The running total of frequencies (not the actual frequency) is plotted against the grade. The *final* running total always equals the total number of pupils.

The cumulative frequencies in Table 12.12 have been charted in Figure 12.22.

Table 12.12

Grade	F	E	D	C	B	A	A*
Frequency	2	3	12	18	11	4	1
Cumulative frequency	2	5	17	35	46	50	51
	2	2+3	5+12	17+18	35+11	46+4	50+1

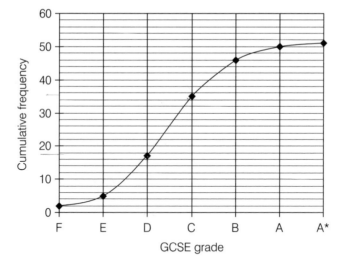

Figure 12.22 Cumulative frequency graph of GCSE grades

25 More difficult question

With reference to Figure 12.22, how many pupils achieved:

1   Grade C and below? (ie up to grade C)   *Answer* ....

2   Grade B and below? (ie up to grade B)   *Answer* ....

3   Grade A and below? (ie up to grade A)   *Answer* ....

There were 51 pupils in total. Refer to your answers in 1, 2 and 3 respectively to answer questions 4, 5 and 6.
    How many pupils achieved:

4   Grade B and above?   *Answer* ....

5   Grade A and above?   *Answer* ....

6   Grade A*?   *Answer* ....

7   Grade C or above? (hint: 51 minus grade D and below;
       or read from the table 18 + 11 + 4 + 1.)   *Answer* ....

8   Grade D or above?   *Answer* ....

9   What fraction of the pupils achieved grade C or above?
                                                       Answer ....

10 What percentage of the pupils achieved grade D or above?
       (Give your answer to 1 decimal place.)   *Answer* ....

11 What proportion of the pupils achieved grade B and above?
       (Give your answer to 1 decimal place.)   *Answer* ....

26 More difficult question

In the cumulative frequency graph shown in Figure 12.23 the GCSE grades have been converted to points as shown in Table 12.13.

Table 12.13

Grade	F	E	D	C	B	A	A*
GCSE points	22	28	34	40	46	52	58
Frequency	1	2	9	26	42	60	20
Cumulative freq.	1	3	12	38	80	140	160

Figure 12.23 Cumulative frequency graph of GCSE points

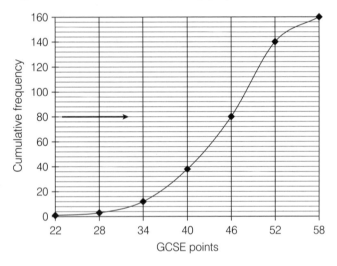

The median is the points score of the middle student (80th) located halfway up the cumulative frequency axis. With reference to Figure 12.23:

1 What is the highest GCSE points score?   *Answer* ....

2 What is the lowest GCSE points score?   *Answer* ....

3 What is the range of the GCSE points scores?   *Answer* ....

4 What is the median GCSE points score?   *Answer* ....

5 How many students achieved 52 points and below? *Answer* ....

6   How many students achieved more than 52 points?   *Answer* ....

7   How many students achieved more than 34 points?
(Read the y-axis scale carefully.)   *Answer* ....

27 More difficult question

One hundred students took a numeracy test. The cumulative frequency graph in Figure 12.24 shows the percentage of pupils achieving a given mark or less.

Figure 12.24 Cumulative frequency graph of numeracy marks

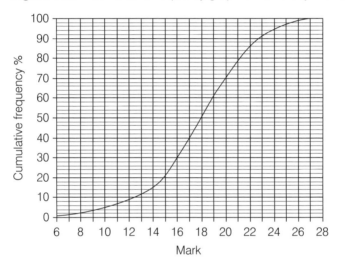

With reference to Figure 12.24:

1   The median mark can be read from the 50th percentile*
(50% cumulative frequency). What mark does this correspond to?
                                                              Answer ....

2   Which mark did 70% of the students fall below?   *Answer* ....

3   Which mark did 12% of the students fall below?   *Answer* ....

4   How many students achieved 16 marks or lower?   *Answer* ....

5   The pass mark is 17 out of 28. How many students passed?
                                                              Answer ....

  * percentiles dividing the data (marks) into 100 equal parts

Box and whisker plots

These plots provide a method of visualizing several key pieces of statistical information, including the maximum and minimum values, the median and the spread (distribution) of the values.

Figure 12.25 shows a box and whisker plot drawn on the cumulative frequency chart shown in Figure 12.24.

Figure 12.25 Cumulative frequency graph with box and whisker plot

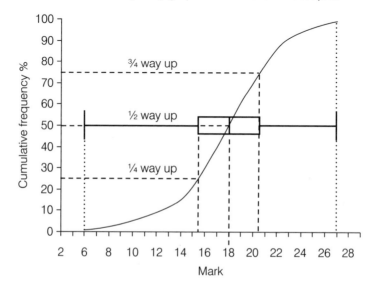

The box and whisker plot summarizes seven key values based on splitting the data into four quarters:

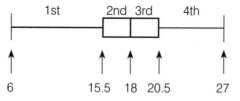

6 – the lowest mark (end of whisker);

15.5 – the lower quartile mark at the 25th percentile;

18 – the median mark at the 50th percentile;

20.5 – the upper quartile mark at the 75th percentile;

27 – highest mark (end of whisker);

20.5 – 15.5 = the inter-quartile range;

27 – 6 = the range (end of one whisker to the end of the other).

Box and whisker plots can also be drawn vertically as shown in Figure 12.26. The plots compare pupil performance in three subjects. The following points should be considered when answering the questions:

● The lower quartile is the mark below which one-quarter of the marks lie, and three-quarters of the marks lie above it.

● The upper quartile is the mark above which one-quarter of the marks lie, and three-quarters of the marks lie below it.

● The spread of the first and last quarters is shown by the length of the two whiskers drawn to the end points (the lowest mark and the highest mark).

● The spread of the two middle quarters is shown by the two boxes (each plot has two boxes and two whiskers) and represents the inter-quartile range.

● Half of the marks (50%) fall into the inter-quartile range.

28 Easy question

A teacher summarized the marks in a maths test using the box and whisker plot shown below:

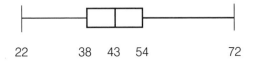

Indicate whether the statements are true or false:

1   At least one pupil achieved 72 marks.

2   The inter-quartile range was 16.

3   One-quarter of the pupils scored more than 38 marks.

29 More difficult question

Figure 12.26 Box and whisker plot for key subject exam results

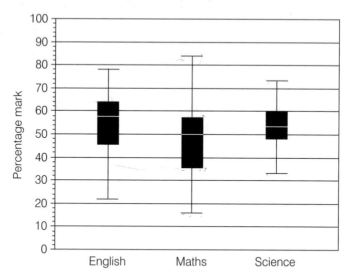

With reference to Figure 12.26:

1   Which subject has the lowest mark?   *Answer* ....

2   Which subject had the highest median mark?   *Answer* ....

3   Which subject had the smallest inter-quartile range?   *Answer* ....

4   In which subject was the range of marks the highest?

    Answer ....

5   In which subject did half the marks lie above 58%
    and half the marks lie below 58%?   *Answer* ....

6   Which subject had a similar number of marks in
    the upper and lower quartiles?   *Answer* ....

7   Above what mark did one-quarter of
    the science marks lie?   *Answer* ....

8   Which subject had the widest range of
    marks for the top 25%?   *Answer* ....

9   If 80 pupils took the English test, how many
    were in the inter-quartile range?   *Answer* ....

10 Which subject had the highest proportion of
    pupils achieving 60% or more of the marks?   *Answer* ....

Chapter 13

....

Probability

Probability is concerned with possibility and chance. When an event (e) takes place, for example a coin is flipped, the probability (P) of a given outcome occurring (eg a head or a tail) can be calculated. For a coin, the chance of the outcome being favourable (eg 'heads') is often described as 50:50 or 50 per cent. However, in probability terms we would say that it is a half (½) or 0.5. Most probability questions use fractions rather than decimals to express probabilities. Fractions are often easier to work with than decimals, especially if there are recurring numbers like 0.333333 (one-third) and 0.16666 (one-sixth).

Probabilities *always* range from 0 (the event is impossible) to 1 (the event is certain to take place). All probabilities must fall inside this range. We can express this range of probabilities mathematically as $0 \leq P(e) \leq 1$, meaning that the probability of an event taking place is greater than or equal to zero and less than or equal to one.

Looking at the probability for 'heads', we know that it is 0.5 or ½ or 1 out of 2. The general case is described by

$$P(e) = \frac{\text{number of favourable outcomes}}{\text{number of possible outcomes}}$$

When rolling dice, the number of possible outcomes is six (1, 2, 3, 4, 5, 6). The probability of throwing any chosen number, for example a 2, is one favourable outcome.

$$P(2) = \frac{\text{number of favourable outcomes}}{\text{number of possible outcomes}} = \frac{1}{6}$$

The chance of *not* getting a two is much higher than the chance of getting a two because there are five numbers that are not a two (1, 3, 4, 5, 6), so if we did not want to throw a two then

$$P(\text{NOT 2}) = \frac{\text{number of favourable outcomes}}{\text{number of possible outcomes}} = \frac{5}{6}$$

If we add the chances of getting a two to the chances of not getting a two we have

$$P(2) + P(\text{not } 2) = \frac{1}{6} + \frac{5}{6} = \frac{6}{6} = 1 = \text{a certainty.}$$

We can rearrange this expression to say $P(\text{not } 2) = 1 - P(2)$, or in the general case of an event (e) not taking place we have:

$$P(\text{NOT } e) = 1 - P(e)$$

If we consider the weather, for example, then if there is an 80 per cent chance of rain today (P = 0.8) then there must be a 20 per cent (P = 0.2) chance of no rain today, because $0.8 = 1 - 0.2$.

The general expression can be arranged another way to give

$$P(e) + P(\text{NOT } e) = 1$$

meaning that the probability of an event occurring added to the probability of the same event not occurring = 1. Considering the weather again, there is a 100 per cent chance (P = 1 = absolute certainty) that it will either rain or not rain today (0.8 + 0.2 = 1). Rain and NOT rain are *complementary* events.

Chances increase with increasing numbers of favourable outcomes, so when rolling a die the chance of getting a two *or* another number, for example a four, is given by

$$P(2 \text{ or } 4) = \frac{\text{number of favourable outcomes}}{\text{number of possible outcomes}}$$

$$= \frac{2}{6} = \frac{1}{3}$$

The chance of *not* getting a two or a four can be found by subtracting the above probability from one:

$$P(\text{NOT } 2 \text{ or } 4) = 1 - \frac{1}{3} = \frac{2}{3} \quad \text{(the four NOT outcomes are 1, 3, 5 and 6)}$$

The chance of getting a two *or* a four *or* a six are given by

$$P(2 \text{ or } 4 \text{ or } 6) = \frac{\text{number of favourable outcomes}}{\text{number of possible outcomes}}$$

$$= \frac{3}{6} = \frac{1}{2}$$

Similarly, the chance of *not* getting a two or a four or a six can be found by subtracting the above probability from one:

$$P(\text{NOT } 2 \text{ or } 4 \text{ or } 6) = 1 - \frac{1}{2} = \frac{1}{2} \quad \text{(the three NOT outcomes are 1, 3 and 5)}$$

Key point: find the NOT outcome by subtracting the favourable outcome (or favourable outcomes, if there are others) from one, rather than by counting the NOT outcomes; or simply remember that the probability of two complementary events = 1; P(e) + P(NOT e) = 1.

When rolling a die it is not possible to get a two and a four at the same time with *one* roll. In probability terms, these two events are described as 'mutually exclusive'. With *mutually exclusive events* the chances of a favourable outcome increase when the outcomes are combined because *the probabilities are added together*, as we have already seen. The general case for mutually exclusive events A and B is as follows:

For mutually exclusive events: P(A or B) = P(A) + P(B)

So when rolling an unbiased die *once*:

$$P(2) = \frac{1}{6} \text{ (or 0.167)}$$

$$P(2 \text{ or } 4) = \frac{1}{6} + \frac{1}{6} = \frac{2}{6} = \frac{1}{3} \text{ (or 0.333)}$$

$$P(2 \text{ or } 4 \text{ or } 6) = \frac{1}{6} + \frac{1}{6} + \frac{1}{6} = \frac{3}{6} = \frac{1}{2} \text{ (or 0.5)}$$

$$P(2 \text{ or } 3 \text{ or } 4 \text{ or } 6) = \frac{1}{6} + \frac{1}{6} + \frac{1}{6} + \frac{1}{6} = \frac{4}{6} = \frac{2}{3} \text{ (or 0.667)}$$

$$P(2 \text{ or } 3 \text{ or } 4 \text{ or } 5 \text{ or } 6) = \frac{1}{6} + \frac{1}{6} + \frac{1}{6} + \frac{1}{6} + \frac{1}{6} = \frac{5}{6} \text{ (or 0.833)}$$

$$P(1 \text{ or } 2 \text{ or } 3 \text{ or } 4 \text{ or } 5 \text{ or } 6) = \frac{1}{6} + \frac{1}{6} + \frac{1}{6} + \frac{1}{6} + \frac{1}{6} + \frac{1}{6} = \frac{6}{6} = 1 \text{ (a certainty)}$$

$$P(7) = \frac{0}{6} = 0 \text{ (impossible)}$$

You need to be competent with fractions, in particular equivalent fractions, for the following warm-up exercise.

1 Warm-up exercise

1   At a secondary school pupils arrive either on foot, by bus, by car or by bicycle. The probabilities of pupils arriving by foot, bus and car are:

walk $\frac{2}{5}$, bus $\frac{3}{10}$ and car $\frac{4}{15}$

What is the probability that the first pupil to arrive at school:

a)   does not walk to school?   *Answer* ....

b)   does not come by bus?   *Answer* ....

c)   does not come by car?   *Answer* ....

d)   walks or catches the bus or comes
     by car?   *Answer* ....

e)   cycles?*   *Answer* ....

f)   neither walks nor catches a bus?   *Answer* ....

(* hint: the same as not walking or not by bus or not by car)

2 Easy questions

1   A biased die does not land on each number with equal probability. The probabilities are shown below.

Number	1	2	3	4	5	6
Probability	0.1	0.15	x	$2x$	0.2	0.25

a)   What is the probability of getting a 3 or a 4?   *Answer* ....

b)   What is the value of x?   *Answer* ....

2   A bag contains red, green and blue balls. A ball is taken out of the bag at random and put back. The probability that the ball is red is 0.3 and the probability that it is green is 0.25.

a)   Calculate the probability that the ball drawn out:

    i)   is blue;   *Answer* ....

    ii) is either red or blue;   *Answer* ....

    iii) is not blue.   *Answer* ....

b)   If there are 12 red balls in the bag,
     how many balls are there in the bag?   *Answer* ....

Possibility space table

Probability calculations can become complicated when there is more than one way of obtaining an event. The correct calculations are made more obvious with the help of a possibility space table.

The possibility space table shown in Figure 13.1 shows all the possible scores that can be achieved when two dice are thrown. There are 36 possible scores (6 × 6).

Figure 13.1 Possibility space table for throwing two dice

		_1_	_2_	_3_	_4_	_5_	_6_
				1st die			
	_1_	2	3	4	5	6	7
	_2_	3	4	5	6	7	8
2nd	_3_	4	5	6	7	8	9
die	_4_	5	6	7	8	9	10
	_5_	6	7	8	9	10	11
	_6_	7	8	9	10	11	12

The table shows, for example, that there is only one way of obtaining a score of 12 ('double six') and there are six ways of obtaining a score of seven. In which case we can say P(6,6) = 1/36 and P(7) = 6/36 = one-sixth. The diagonal line separates scores of 7 or below from scores of 8 and above.

3 Easy question

1   With reference to the two-dice possibility table, and giving your answers as fractions in their lowest terms:

   a)   What is the probability of throwing two dice and obtaining a score of:

      i)   2?   *Answer* ....

      ii)   4?   *Answer* ....

      iii) 6?   *Answer* ....

      iv) 9?   *Answer* ....

   b)   What is the probability of throwing two dice and obtaining a score that is:

      i))   8 or below?   *Answer* ....

      ii)   7 or below?   *Answer* ....

      iii) 4 or below?   *Answer* ....

      iv) more than 4?   *Answer* ....

c) What is the probability of throwing two dice and obtaining a score:

   i)   that is *not* 5?   *Answer* ....

   ii) that is *not* 7?   *Answer* ....

d) What is the probability of throwing two dice and getting:

   i)   two identical numbers?   *Answer* ....

   ii) *not* two identical numbers?   *Answer* ....

   iii) a score that is a prime number?   *Answer* ....

   iv) a six on one die only?   *Answer* ....

4 More difficult question

1   A bag contains six balls, numbered 1, 2, 3, 4, 5 and 6. A second bag contains
    four balls, numbered 1, 2, 3 and 4. One ball is drawn out at random from each
    bag. Draw a possibility space table and find the probability that:

   a) the sum of the numbers on the two balls is 6;   *Answer* ....

   b) the sum of the numbers on the two balls is
       greater than 6;   *Answer* ....

   c) both balls have the same number;   *Answer* ....

   d) both balls have an even number;   *Answer* ....

   e) both balls have a number 3;   *Answer* ....

   f) one ball is 3 and the other ball is 2
       (two possibilities = 2/24 = 1/12).   *Answer* ....

We have seen that the probability of correctly guessing a head or a tail is a half or
0.5 when a coin is flipped, but what are the chances of guessing correctly twice in
succession? One solution is to look at all the possible outcomes by drawing up a
table of possibilities. We can use H to represent heads and T for tails (Figure 13.2).

Figure 13.2 Possibility space table for tossing a coin twice

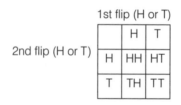

The figure shows that we can get a head on the first flip and a head on the second flip (HH); a head on the first flip and a tail on the second flip (HT); a tail on the first flip and a head on the second flip (TH); or a tail on the first flip and a tail on the second flip (TT). There are four possibilities and we want one (HH), so the probability is ¼ or 0.25.

The calculation is $P(HH) = P(H) \times P(H) = \frac{1}{2} \times \frac{1}{2} = \frac{1}{4}$

We have only a one in four chance of getting two heads in succession. Where two (or more) events take place separately from each other, as in flipping a coin twice, the outcome of one event has no influence on the outcome of the other event, and the probabilities are multiplied together.

The general case for *independent events* is:

$P(A \text{ and } B) = P(A) \times P(B)$

For example: when flipping a coin several times in succession, the probability of continuing to get a head becomes progressively smaller through *multiplication of a fraction*:

1st: $P(H) = \frac{1}{2}$

2nd: $P(HH) = \frac{1}{2} \times \frac{1}{2} = \frac{1}{4}$

3rd: $P(HHH) = \frac{1}{2} \times \frac{1}{2} \times \frac{1}{2} = \frac{1}{8}$

4th: $P(HHHH) = \frac{1}{2} \times \frac{1}{2} \times \frac{1}{2} \times \frac{1}{2} = \frac{1}{16}$

5th: $P(HHHHH) = \frac{1}{2} \times \frac{1}{2} \times \frac{1}{2} \times \frac{1}{2} \times \frac{1}{2} = \frac{1}{32}$

6th: $P(HHHHHH) = \frac{1}{2} \times \frac{1}{2} \times \frac{1}{2} \times \frac{1}{2} \times \frac{1}{2} \times \frac{1}{2} = \frac{1}{64}$

7th: $P(HHHHHHH) = \frac{1}{2} \times \frac{1}{2} \times \frac{1}{2} \times \frac{1}{2} \times \frac{1}{2} \times \frac{1}{2} \times \frac{1}{2} = \frac{1}{128}$

You have a 1 in 128 chance of getting seven heads in succession (a less than 1 per cent chance). The probability reduces by a power of two with each flip of the coin. Taking five flips as an example, $P(5th) = 1/32 = 1/2^5$, and for the general case of n flips, $P(n) = (0.5)^n$, so the chances of 20 heads one after the other is 0.5^{20} which is 0.000000954 or just over 1 in a million.

> **Key point**: Independent events are multiplied and the probability is reduced, whereas mutually exclusive events are added and the probability is increased.

5 Easy question

1   A bag contains 8 white balls and 4 black balls.

   a) Two balls are drawn out one at a time and then <u>replaced</u> (the first ball is put back before the second ball is drawn out). Giving your answer as a fraction in its lowest terms, what is the probability that:

      i)   the first ball drawn out is white?   *Answer* ....

      ii) the first ball drawn out is white and
           the second ball drawn out is white?   *Answer* ....

      iii) the first ball drawn out is black?   *Answer* ....

      iv) the first ball drawn out is black and
           the second ball drawn out is black?   *Answer* ....

      v) the first ball drawn out is white and
           the second ball drawn out is black?   *Answer* ....

      vi) the first ball drawn out is black and
           the second ball drawn out is white?   *Answer* ....

   b) Three balls are drawn out one at a time and <u>replaced</u> one at a time. What is the probability that:

      i)   all three balls are white?   *Answer* ....

      ii) the first two balls are white and the third
           is black?   *Answer* ....

      iii) the first ball is black and the second and
           third balls are white?   *Answer* ....

      iv) all three balls are black?   *Answer* ....

      v) only one ball is white?   *Answer* ....

If a ball is taken out of a bag and *not replaced* then the first draw affects the second and any subsequent draws. The events are no longer independent but have become *dependent* on the outcome of previous draws. When a ball is taken out and not replaced, the number of possible outcomes is reduced by one and the number of favourable outcomes (for the colour of ball taken out) is also reduced by one.

    If we have 8 white balls and 4 black balls (12 balls in total), the probability of drawing out a white ball on the first draw is 8 out of 12 or 8/12 (eight twelfths). If the white ball is not replaced the probability of drawing out a second white ball is $(8 - 1)$ out of $(12 - 1)$ which is 7 out of 11 or 7/11 (seven elevenths).

6 Warm-up exercise

1   A bag contains 6 red balls and 2 black balls. Three balls are drawn out one at a time and *not* replaced. Giving your answer as a fraction in its lowest terms, what is the probability that:

a)   the first ball drawn out is red?   *Answer* ....

b)   the second ball drawn out is red?   *Answer* ....

c)   the third ball drawn out is red?   *Answer* ....

d)   all three balls are red?   *Answer* ....

e)   the first ball drawn out is red and the second
ball drawn out is black?   *Answer* ....

In the last exercise, it is possible to calculate the probability of drawing out, say, two red (R) balls and one black (B) ball, without indicating the sequence. There are three possibilities: RRB, RBR and BRR.

The probabilities are:

$$P(RRB) = \frac{6}{8}\text{red} \times \frac{5}{7}\text{red} \times \frac{2}{5}\text{black} = \frac{3}{4} \times \frac{5}{7} \times \frac{2}{5} = \frac{6}{28} = \frac{3}{14}$$

$$P(RBR) = \frac{6}{8}\text{red} \times \frac{2}{7}\text{black} \times \frac{5}{6}\text{red} = \frac{3}{4} \times \frac{2}{7} \times \frac{5}{6} = \frac{5}{28}$$

$$P(BRR) = \frac{3}{9}\text{black} \times \frac{6}{8}\text{red} \times \frac{5}{7}\text{red} = \frac{5}{28}$$

Adding these three probabilities gives $\frac{16}{28} = \frac{4}{7}$.

7 More difficult question

1   There were 15 boys and 6 girls in a group of children. One child was chosen at random to leave the group. Another child was chosen at random to leave the group. Giving your answer as a fraction in its simplest form, calculate the probability that:

a)   the first child chosen was a girl;   *Answer* ....

b)   the first child chosen was a boy;   *Answer* ....

c)   both children were girls;   *Answer* ....

d)   a boy and a girl were chosen.   *Answer* ....

Tree diagrams

Sometimes it can be hard to decide whether to multiply or add probabilities. This is where a *tree diagram* can help.

Tree diagrams are drawn from left to right, starting at a single node with a pair of branches extending to the right, one branch up and one branch down. At the end of the first two branches two further pairs of branches extend up and down to give four branches. The way tree diagrams work is best explained by example. A very simple tree diagram can be used to show all the possible outcomes of tossing a coin twice (Figure 13.3). There are four possibilities as set out in the possibility space chart earlier.

Figure 13.3 Tree diagram for a coin flipped twice

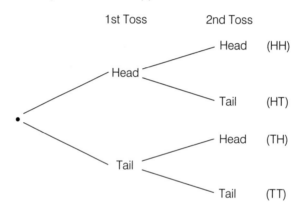

Example: a bag contains 4 red and 2 blue balls. Two balls are taken from the bag at random and *not replaced*. By drawing a tree diagram, calculate the probability that:

a) both balls are red;

b) both balls are blue;

c) at least one ball is red;

d) both balls are the same colour.

We draw the first two legs for the first ball and label these R (red) and B (blue) and continue the process for the second ball.

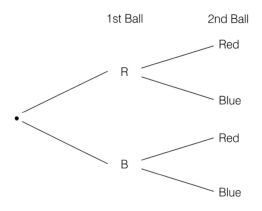

The diagram has to be completed before the questions can be tackled. We have six balls in total: four red balls and two blue balls. The probability of the first ball being a red ball is 4 out of 6 or four-sixths; this fraction is entered on the first upper leg (R). We have two blue balls, so the probability that the first ball is a blue ball is 2 out of 6 or two-sixths. However, the best way of finding the probability on the complementary leg of a tree diagram is to subtract the first probability from 1.

In our example $P(B) = 1 - P(R)$ so $P(B) = 1.0 - \dfrac{4}{6} = \dfrac{2}{6}$

Key point: to find the probability on the complementary leg of a tree diagram, subtract the known probability from 1.

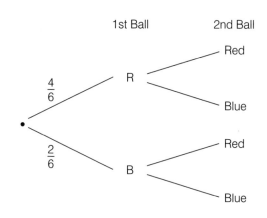

Key point: do not cancel fractions on the branches of tree diagrams.

For a red ball drawn out first, the probability of the second ball being red is: $(4-1)/(6-1)$ = three-fifths.

For a blue ball drawn out first, the probability of the second ball being blue is $(2-1)/(6-1)$ = one-fifth.

This information can be entered on the second sets of branches, with the three-fifths going on the uppermost branch and the one-fifth going on the lowermost branch.

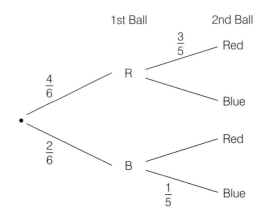

Key point: The probabilities in a tree diagram should add up to 1 in the vertical alignment for complementary events and are multiplied to combine probabilities when moving along branches.

Noting the above key point, we can complete the tree diagram as follows:

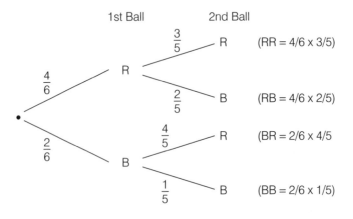

Key point: the four combined probabilities in the final vertical row must add up to 1.

Check: $RR = \dfrac{12}{30}$; $RB = \dfrac{8}{30}$; $BR = \dfrac{8}{30}$; $BB = \dfrac{2}{30}$. Total $= \dfrac{30}{30} = 1$

The questions are completed as follows:

i)   both balls are red $= RR = \dfrac{4}{6} \times \dfrac{3}{5} = \dfrac{12}{30} = \dfrac{2}{5}$

ii) both balls are blue $= BB = \dfrac{2}{6} \times \dfrac{1}{5} = \dfrac{2}{30} = \dfrac{1}{15}$

iii) at least one ball is red $= RR + RB + BR$. However, from the tree diagram we can see that the probability that at least one ball is red is the same as 1 minus the probability of two blue balls:

$$1 - BB = 1 - \dfrac{2}{30} = 1 - \dfrac{1}{15} = \dfrac{14}{15}$$

8 Easy question

1   A bag contains 16 balls, 10 of which are black and 6 are white. Two balls are taken from the bag without replacement. The tree diagram that represents these events has been drawn below.

a)   Find the values of x and y.   *Answer* ....

b)   Giving your answers in their simplest form, find the probability that:

i)   the two balls have different colours;   *Answer* ....

ii) at least one ball is black.   *Answer* ....

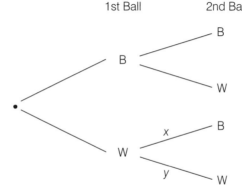

9 More difficult questions

1   Candidates sitting a numeracy and literacy test have a maximum of three attempts to pass. The probability of passing the test is 0.8 every time it is taken. By drawing a tree diagram, or otherwise, find the probability that a candidate will:

a)   fail the first attempt and fail the second attempt; *Answer* ....

b)   pass at either of the first two attempts, giving
       your answer as a percentage;   *Answer* ....

c)   pass at the third attempt after failing the first
       and second attempts;   *Answer* ....

d)   not pass any of the three attempts permitted.   *Answer* ....

2   The box and whisker plot summarizes the performance of 500 students in GCSE maths.

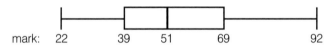

mark: 22   39   51   69   92

What is the probability that if two students are chosen at random, one will have achieved 40 marks or more and one will have achieved 70 marks or more?

Playing cards

Probability calculations involving playing cards are similar to those involving coloured balls or dice. However, some knowledge of playing cards is presumed, so it is worth familiarizing yourself with the following information:

Number of cards in a pack (standard deck): 52.

Number of suits: 4: clubs (black); diamonds (red); hearts (red); spades (black).

Number of cards per suit: 13, so there are 26 black cards and 26 red cards.

A suit consists of one ace, nine number cards (from 2 to 10) and three picture cards (also known as face or court cards), which are the Jack (also known as the Knave), the Queen and the King.

A suit of 13 cards: Ace, 2, 3, 4, 5, 6, 7, 8, 9, 10, J, Q, K.

10 Easy questions

1   You are dealt two cards from a shuffled pack of 52 playing cards. What is the probability that:

    a)   the first card will be black?   *Answer* ....

    b)   the first card will be a spade?   *Answer* ....

    c)   the first card will be a spade and the second card will be a club?   *Answer* ....

    d)   the first card will be a spade and the second card will be a spade?   *Answer* ....

2   Five cards are picked in turn from a shuffled pack of 52 playing cards. The first four cards are the Jack (Knave) of Spades, King of Hearts, Queen of Diamonds and Jack of Clubs. What is the probability that the fifth card will *not* be another face (court) card?   *Answer* ....

3   Five cards are picked in turn from a shuffled pack of 52 playing cards. The first four cards are all black. What is the probability that the fifth card will be:

    a)   black?   *Answer* ....

    b)   red?   *Answer* ....

    c)   a picture card if one has yet to be drawn?   *Answer* ....

4   A card is drawn from a shuffled pack of 52 playing cards and a die is thrown. What is the probability that both the die and the card will display the number six?   *Answer* ....

11 More difficult question

1   Two cards are drawn in turn from a shuffled pack of 52 playing cards and a die is thrown. What is the probability that the first card will be a picture card, the second card will not be a picture card, and the die will not display an even number?   *Answer* ....

Experimental probability

Earlier we showed that the probability of flipping a coin seven times in succession and obtaining a head every time was 1/128; this means that in a coin-flipping *experiment* we would expect to see seven heads in succession only once in every 128 flips (or *trials*), and it might not happen at all. Alternatively, it might, if we were 'lucky', happen two or three times. However, with a very large number of flips, for example 128000, the number of times we would achieve 'heads seven times' should approach the *theoretical* number of 1000. So, unless a coin is *biased* towards head or tails, the *experimental probability* should be very close to the *theoretical probability*, with a sufficiently large number of trials. The experimental probability (also known as the *relative frequency*) is given by:

$$\text{Experimental probability} = \frac{\text{frequency of outcome}}{\text{number of trials}}$$

Example: an unbiased coin is flipped 1000 times and 'heads' are recorded 485 times. For an outcome of 'heads', calculate:

a)   the theoretical probability;

b)   the experimental probability.

a)   The coin is unbiased, so the chances of getting a head are 1 in 2 or 0.5.

b)   The experimental probability is 458 ÷ 1000 = 0.485.

12 Easy question

1   A biased coin is flipped 250 times and 20 tails are recorded:

a)   What is the relative frequency of
obtaining a tail?   *Answer* ....

b)   What is the relative frequency of
obtaining a head?   *Answer* ....

c)   If the coin were flipped 1250 times,
how many heads might be expected?   *Answer* ....

d)   How many times more likely are you to obtain
a head than a tail with each flip of the coin?   *Answer* ....

Chapter 14

Venn diagrams and sets

Most Venn diagrams are drawn as two overlapping circles or ovals (*sets*) inside a rectangular box (the *Universal set*). The sets are usually described by capital letters, for example A and B, or P and Q. Each circle contains members (*elements*) that are characteristic of it, for example school subjects, different colours, shapes or particular numbers. The Universal set contains all the elements.

The Venn diagram below shows a Universal set (E) of 24 pupils where:

10 pupils study geography (set G) and 8 pupils study history (set H);

9 pupils study neither geography nor history (outside of both G and H);

3 pupils study both geography and history (the overlap of G and H);

7 pupils study geography but not history;

5 pupils study history but not geography.

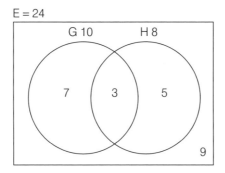

1   Set G (10) can be split into two subsets, namely those studying geography but not history (7), and those studying *both* geography and history (3) where: G = 7 + 3; and geography only (7) equals G minus the overlap: 7 = G − 3.

2   Set H (8) can be split into two subsets, namely those studying history but not geography (5) and those studying *both* history and geography (3) where: H = 5 + 3; and history only (5) equals H minus the overlap: 5 = H − 3. The overlap (3) is a subset common to both G and H.

3   The Universal set is the total of the elements inside the three subsets added to the elements outside of the three subsets (the overlap is counted only once). Adding the elements from left to right: E = 7 + 3 + 5 + 9 = 24.

Example question

The Venn diagram below shows a group of 40 pupils where: 15 pupils study art and design (set A); 20 pupils study business studies (set B). If 11 pupils study neither art and design nor business studies, how many pupils study a) only art and design; b) only business studies; c) both art and design and business studies?

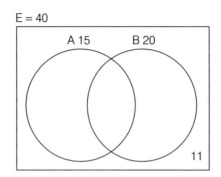

E = 40

A 15   B 20

11

Answer: **Key point**: start with the overlap (intersection) of A and B. There is no information about this, so label the overlap **x**. Then art and design *only* is given by A minus the overlap **x**, and business studies *only* is given by B minus the overlap **x**.

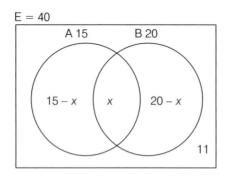

E = 40

A 15   B 20

15 − x   x   20 − x

11

Adding the elements from left to right:

$$E = 15 - x + x + 20 - x + 11 = 40$$

So 40 = 15 + 20 + 11− x; 40 = 46 − x; adding x to both sides gives

x + 40 = 46; subtracting 40 from both sides of the equation gives x = 6

a) Only art and design $= 15 - x = 9$.

b) Only business studies $= 20 - x = 14$.

c) Both art and design and business studies $= x = 6$.

The diagram shows the completed Venn diagram.

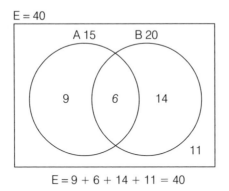

E = 40

A 15   B 20

9   6   14

11

$$E = 9 + 6 + 14 + 11 = 40$$

1 Easy question

In a group of 30 language students, 21 studied French, 16 studied Spanish and 6 studied neither French nor Spanish. Complete the Venn diagram and determine how many students studied:

a) both French and Spanish;

b) only French;

c) only Spanish.

Hint: start with the overlap (intersection).

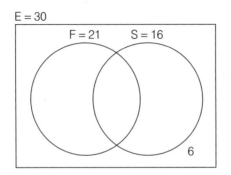

E = 30

F = 21   S = 16

6

2 More difficult question

The Venn diagram shows a group of A-level students (E), some taking biology (B) and some chemistry (C). The letters p, q, x and y represent the number of students in each subset.

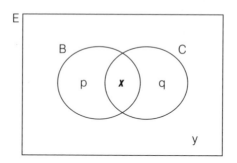

a) If B = 18 and C = 15, find:

    i)   an expression for **x** in terms of p;

    ii) an expression for **x** in terms of q;

    iii) **x** if p + q = 9;

    iv) p;

    v) the size of the group (E) if y = 3.

b) Expressing your answers in their lowest terms where appropriate, find:

    i)   the ratio of students taking biology to students taking chemistry;

    ii) the percentage of students who studied biology;

    iii) the ratio of students taking biology only to students taking biology;

    iv) the fraction of students who take chemistry only.

c) Expressing your answers as decimals, find:

    i)   the probability that one student picked at random will take chemistry;

    ii) the probability that one student picked at random will not take chemistry;

    iii) the probability that one student picked at random will take both biology and chemistry;

    iv) the probability that one student picked at random will take either biology or chemistry, or neither subject.

Set notation and terminology

Sets use their own symbols (*notation*) to describe areas and items (*elements*) in the set. These need to be remembered and understood for some Venn diagram questions. We have already looked at the Universal set (E), and the overlap, or intersection, of two sets A and B (which in set notation is A ∩ B). We have also seen how some elements can be outside a circle (set), for example not in set A (described as the *complement* of A, or in set notation as A').

Set notation

1. Universal set (all the elements inside the rectangle)	E or ξ
2. Set of elements inside Set A	A={eg 2,4,6,8}
3. Number of elements (n) in Set A	n(A) = 4
4. Intersection (overlap) of A and B	A ∩ B
5. Union (∪) of A and B (all the elements in A and in B)	A ∪ B
6. A is a proper subset of B (A is included in B)	A ⊂ B
7. Compliment of set A (all the elements <u>not</u> in Set A)	A'
8. Empty set	Ø
9. Is an element of	∈
10. Is not an element of	∉

Example (easy)

Given A = {2,4,6,8} and B = {1,2,3,4,5,6}:

    a)   Draw a Venn diagram placing the elements in the correct regions;

    b)   list the Universal set E;

    c)   identify, in terms of A and B, the set containing the elements 2, 4 and 6 only.

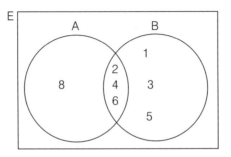

a) Draw two overlapping circles, A and B, inside the Universal set E. Start with the overlap: only 2, 4 and 6 are common to both A and B so these elements go in the intersection; 8 is only in Set A and 1, 3 and 5 are only in Set B.

b) The universal set is all the elements inside the rectangle:
E = {1,2,3,4,5,6,8}.

c) The elements 2, 4 and 6 only are in the intersection of A and B ie A ∩ B.

The Venn diagrams show the shaded regions of key set relationships for one or two sets inside the Universal set. Note especially how A complement (everything outside A) is the Universal set minus A, and how B complement (everything outside B) is the Universal set minus B.

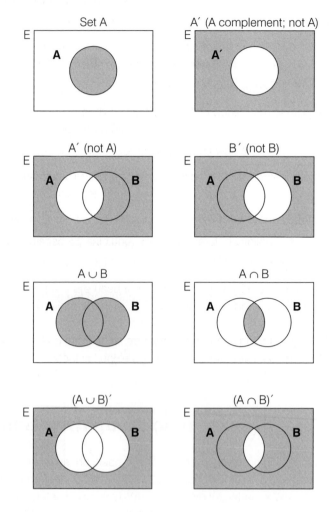

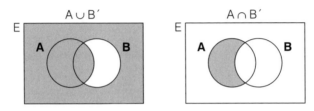

A ∪ B′ (A union not B) is everything in A *together with* everything not in B.

A ∩ B′ (A intersection not B) is A where it *overlaps* with everything not in B (shade in circle A and then everything outside B to see where they overlap).

The following Venn diagrams show the shaded regions of key set relationships for three sets inside the Universal set. In the final two diagrams the circles have been drawn disjoint to emphasize that 'union' does not require linked circles.

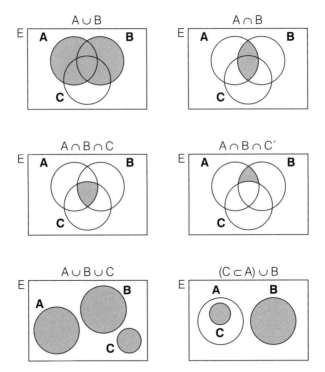

3 Warm-up exercise

Look at the Venn diagrams a) to j) and use set notation to describe them.

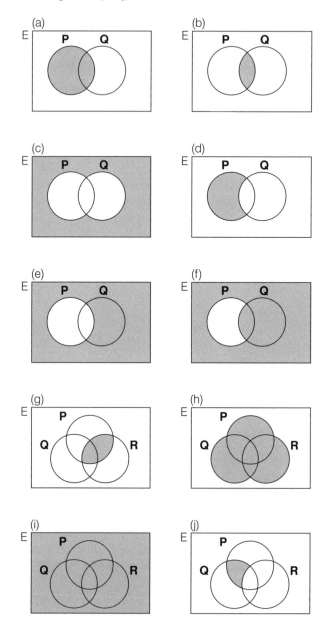

4 Warm-up exercise

Look at the Venn diagram and find the elements in the sets a) to l).
   List the elements in ascending order of size inside the curly brackets.
   Hint: if necessary, shade regions in order to find the overlap.

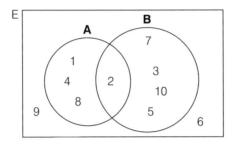

a)   E = {   }

b)   A = { }

c)   B = {   }

d)   A′ = {   }

e)   B′ = {   }

f)   A ∩ B = {   }

g)   A ∪ B = {   }

h)   (A ∪ B)′ = { }

i)   A ∪ B′ = {   }

j)   A ∩ B′ = {   }

k)   B ∪ A′ = {   }

l)   B ∩ A′ = {   }

5 Warm-up exercise

Look at the Venn diagram and find the elements in the sets a) to m).
List the elements in ascending order of size inside the curly brackets.

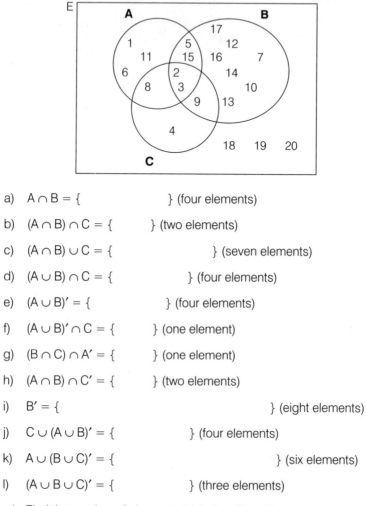

a) $A \cap B = \{$ $\}$ (four elements)

b) $(A \cap B) \cap C = \{$ $\}$ (two elements)

c) $(A \cap B) \cup C = \{$ $\}$ (seven elements)

d) $(A \cup B) \cap C = \{$ $\}$ (four elements)

e) $(A \cup B)' = \{$ $\}$ (four elements)

f) $(A \cup B)' \cap C = \{$ $\}$ (one element)

g) $(B \cap C) \cap A' = \{$ $\}$ (one element)

h) $(A \cap B) \cap C' = \{$ $\}$ (two elements)

i) $B' = \{$ $\}$ (eight elements)

j) $C \cup (A \cup B)' = \{$ $\}$ (four elements)

k) $A \cup (B \cup C)' = \{$ $\}$ (six elements)

l) $(A \cup B \cup C)' = \{$ $\}$ (three elements)

m) Find the number of elements (n) in $A \cup (B \cap C)$

6 Easy question

The results of a survey of 100 sixth-form students are shown in the Venn diagram:

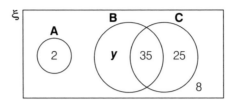

ξ = {students in the survey};

A = {students who study art and design};

B = {students who study biology};

C = {students who study chemistry};

n = number of members in a set.

a) Find:

   i) **y**;

   ii) n(B);

   iii) n(C′);

   iv) n(B ∪ C);

   v) (A ∪ B ∪ C)′.

b) Describe in words the set with 25 members.

c) What fraction of those students who studied biology also studied chemistry? Give your answer in its lowest terms.

d) How many students who studied biology also studied art and design?

e) What percentage of students surveyed studied both biology and chemistry?

f) What is the probability that one student selected at random from the survey will not have studied chemistry? Give your answer as a decimal.

g) What is the ratio of students taking biology only to students taking biology?

Example question

Given the following set information:

E = {x: x is an integer and $1 < x \le 10$}

A = {x: x is an odd number}

B = {x: x is a factor of 20}

C = {x: x is an integer and $3 < x \le 8$}

a)   Complete the Venn diagram, placing the elements in the correct regions.

b)   Describe in set notation the set containing no elements.

We need to find the integers in each of the four sets, E, A, B and C:

E =   {x: x is an integer and $1 < x \le 10$}. This means that the integers (whole numbers) in the Universal Set E are described by x, where x has any value that meets the requirements that '1 is less than x' (meaning x is greater than 1) and 'x is less than or equal to 10'. So x is every whole number between 2 and 10 inclusive. E = {2,3,4,5,6,7,8,9,10}.

A =   {x: x is an odd number}. This means that x can be any odd number. However, x cannot lie outside the Universal set of elements, so this limits the elements to A = {3,5,7,9}.

B =   {x: x is a factor of 20}. This means that x can be any number that will divide into 20 exactly. The factors of 20 can be found by in pairs as follows: 1 and 20, 2 and 10, 4 and 5 (ie 1, 2, 4, 5, 10 and 20). However, x cannot lie outside the Universal set of numbers, so this limits the elements to: C = {2,4,5,10}.

C =   {x: x is an integer and $3 < x \le 8$. This means that x can be any whole number that meets the requirements that '3 is less than x' (meaning x is greater than 3) and 'x is less than or equal to 8'. So x is every whole number between 4 and 8 inclusive: C = {4,5,6,7,8}.

The Venn diagram is completed by comparing the three sets, A, B and C to see where the elements overlap. We can see that 5 is common to all three sets (underlined); 7 is common to Sets A and C; and 4 is common to Sets B and C.

A = {3,5,7,9}

B = {2,4,5,10}

C = {4,5,6,7,8}

This leaves 3 and 9 in A only, 2 and 10 in B only, and 6 and 8 in C only.

a) The completed Venn diagram is shown below.

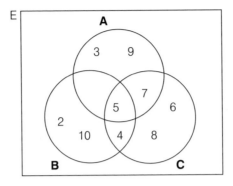

b) The set with no elements is the overlap of circles A and B, excluding those
    in the overlap with circle C (4, 5 and 7), which is $(A \cap B) \cap C'$.

7 Difficult question

a) On the Venn diagram shade the region $(P \cap R) \cap Q'$

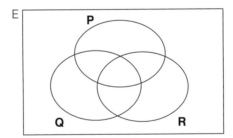

b) If $E = \{1,2,3,4,5,6,7,8,9,10,11,12\}$, $P = \{x: x \text{ is a prime number}\}$,
    $Q = \{x: 0 < x \leq 9\}$ and $R = \{x: x \text{ is an even number}\}$, find:

    i) $n(R \cup Q)$;

    ii) $n(R')$.

    iii) List the elements of $P \cup (Q \cap R)$.

    iv) List the elements of $P \cap (Q \cup R)$.

c) A number n is chosen at random from E. Find the probability that:

    i) $n \in Q$ (as a fraction);

    ii) $n \in R'$ (as a fraction).

Chapter 15

Flowcharts

At its simplest level, a flow chart or flow diagram is a list of instructions to be followed in sequence (an *algorithm*). Flowcharts frequently include questions with yes/no answers to ensure that correct procedures are followed. In maths, a flowchart can be used to solve a simple problem. The mathematical processes and instructions are written inside the boxes or symbols of the flowchart.

There are numerous flowchart symbols but basic flowcharts need only four symbols (Figure 15.1). These are: two lozenge-shaped boxes (or ovals) to show the *start* and *end* (stop) of the flowchart; rectangular *process boxes* that indicate the actions to be taken – the first process box contains the trigger event; and diamond-shaped *decision boxes* that contain a question that needs a yes/no answer. The fourth symbol is an arrow to show the *direction of flow*. Only one flow line should enter and leave a process box, whereas a decision box will have one flow line that enters the box and two flow lines that exit the box, depending on whether the answer is a 'yes' or a 'no'.

Figure 15.1 The four main flowchart symbols

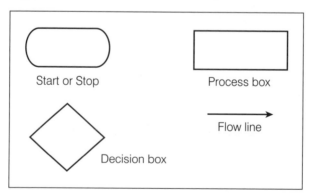

At its simplest, a flow chart consists of an input, a rule and an output. For example:

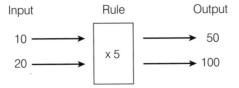

1 Warm-up exercise

1 Complete the following flow diagram:

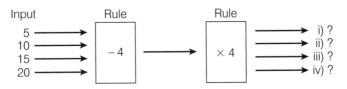

2 Find the rule that completes the following flow diagram:

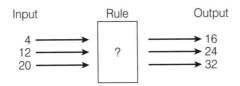

2 Easy question

1   To convert from °C to °F, the rule is multiply by 9, divide by 5 and add 32. Complete the following flowchart to convert °F to °C by the reverse process.

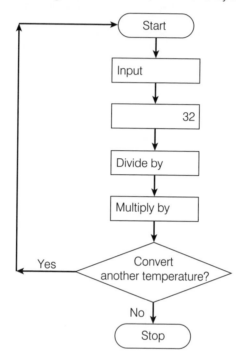

3 More difficult question

1 In a game where two dice are thrown, a player wins if the dice total 7 or 11; a player loses and stops playing if the dice total 2, 3 or 12; a player throws again if the dice total 4, 5, 6, 8, 9 or 10. Use the flow diagram to determine the probability (P) that a player will:

a) win with the first throw of the dice;

b) win with the second throw of the dice.

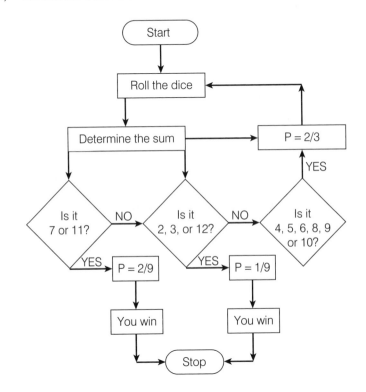

Part two
....
Literacy

Chapter 16

....

Spelling

Introduction

You will be tested on words that are part of everyday English as well as words found in a teacher's written vocabulary.

You might feel that spelling mistakes are not as important as content if the meaning remains clear. Spelling mistakes, though, serve as a focal point in a text and can distract the reader away from the message. Furthermore, if pupils, colleagues and parents spot a mistake it can create a negative impression of the writer. Spelling is either right or wrong and errors can dent your image as a professional.

Many students have trouble with spelling and rely on a computer's spell-checker function to expose misspellings and to suggest corrections. Although this may not diminish your spelling skills, you are more likely to repeat the errors instead of endeavouring to improve.

Rules of spelling

There are some simple rules that can help with spelling. If you know how to pronounce a word and are aware of the appropriate rule then it may be possible to work out how to spell a word rather than have to commit it to memory.

Mnemonics are short rhymes or verses that are intended to aid the spelling of words that are known to cause trouble; for example, when writing the word *necessary*, the correct number of <c's> and <s's> can be remembered from the mnemonic <one coffee with two sugars>. Unfortunately, many mnemonics are more difficult to remember than the spelling itself, so these will not be considered further beyond the well-known rule <i before e except after c>, and even this has its exceptions.

1 *Problems with vowel sounds*

Except for short words such as <my> and <by>, every word in the English language must contain one or more of the five vowels <a>, <e>, <i>, <o> and <u>; the remaining letters are consonants. Choosing between the vowel sounds <a>, <e> and <i> can prove troublesome. The following spellings are best learnt by heart:

admissible (<i> not <a>)
appearance (<a> not <e>)
cemetery (<e> not <a>)
definitely (<i> not <e> or <a>)
difference (<e> not <a>)
existence (<e> not <a>)
experience (<e> not <a>)
grammar (<a> not <e>)
grievance (<a> not <e>)
illegible (<i> not <a>)
irresistible (<i> not <a>)
maintenance (<a> not <e>)
occurrence (<e> not <a>)
permissible (<i> not <a>)
reference (<e> not <a>)
relevant (<a> not <e>)
respondent (<e> not <a>)

2 *Problems with consonants*

Spelling mistakes arise when the consonants <l>, <m>, <r>, <s> and <t> are unnecessarily doubled or when a double consonant is omitted. These mistakes arise because, unlike languages such as Welsh and Spanish, the single and double consonants are pronounced the same in English and the meaning is unchanged. The following words are commonly misspelt when the double consonant is omitted:

accommodate (not accomodate)
exaggerate (not exagerate)
excellent (not excelent)
generally (not generaly)
misspell (not mispell)
occurrence (not occurence)
referring (not refering)

In the following words a double consonant is frequently added where it is not needed:

disapprove (not dissapprove)
fulfil (not fulfill or fullfil)
harass (not harrass)
helpful (helpfully but not helpfull)
largely (not largelly)
until (not untill)

The following rules are helpful when adding suffixes, for example <-er>, <-est>, <-ing> and <-ed> to short words of one or two syllables. A syllable is the part of a word that has a single vowel sound, often with consonants, for example: be has one syllable, begin two syllables, and beginning three syllables:

● For one-syllable words, double the last consonant if the root word ends 'consonant–vowel–consonant' (CVC). Examples are shop and shopping; fit and fitted; big and biggest.

● For two-syllable words, double the last consonant if the spoken word is stressed on the last syllable rather than the first, as in begin and beginning; admit and admitting; or if the word ends in <l> as in travel and travelling; jewel and jeweller. The doubling rule only applies if the root word ends CVC, so, for example, wide (VCV) and wider, clear (VVC) and clearest, fail (VVC) and failing all use single consonants when adding a suffix.

1 Warm-up exercise: double consonants (rules apply)

Choose either the single consonant spelling (A) or the double consonant spelling (B). Half the answers are As and half are Bs.

	Root	A	B
1	run	runing	running
2	bag	baged	bagged
3	hot	hoter	hotter
4	hard	harder	hardder
5	enrol	enroled	enrolled
6	excel	exceled	excelled
7	cancel	canceling	cancelling

	Root	A	B
8	defer	defered	deferred
9	enter	entered	enterred
10	ruin	ruining	ruinning
11	appear	appearing	appearring
12	diet	dieting	dietting
13	stoop	stooping	stoopping
14	wear	wearing	wearring
15	commit	commiting	committing
16	occur	occured	occurred
17	panel	paneling	panelling
18	happen	happened	happenned
19	open	opening	openning
20	benefit	benefited	benefitted

The spellings in the following test fall outside the categories described earlier and are best learnt by heart. In some cases the wrong consonant has been doubled.

2 Warm-up exercise: double consonants (learn by heart)

Choose the correct spelling (A) or (B). Half the answers are As and half are Bs:

	A	B
1	abreviate	abbreviate
2	acept	accept
3	agressive	aggressive
4	alowed	allowed
5	aproach	approach
6	cigarete	cigarette
7	elicit	ellicit
8	family	familly
9	imediatley	immediately
10	inoculate	innoculate

	A	**B**
11	mispelled	misspelled
12	mistakes	misstakes
13	normaly	normally
14	occasions	occassions
15	professional	proffessional
16	quarelling	quarrelling
17	recommend	reccommend
18	sincerely	sincerelly
19	tomorrow	tommorrow
20	vacuum	vaccuum

3 Problems with words ending in ‹ie›, ‹y› and ‹e›

● For words ending in <ie>, drop the <e> and change the <i> to a <y> when adding the suffix <-ing>; for example, lie and lying, die and dying.

● For words ending in <y>, change the <y> to an <i> when adding the suffixes <ed>, <er> or <able> if the <y> is preceded by a consonant, but retain the <y> if it is preceded by a vowel or when adding the suffix <-ing>. For example, carry, carried, carrier and carriable, but enjoy, enjoyed, enjoyable and enjoying. When adding the suffix <ly>, change the <y> to an <i>; for example, necessary and necessarily, happy and happily (exceptions: shyly and coyly).

● For words ending in <e>, retain the <e> if the suffix begins with a consonant but drop it if it begins with a vowel. Examples: use and useful, but usable (no <e>); care and careful, but caring (no <e>); hope and hopeless, but hoping (no <e>). Exceptions to dropping the <e> occur when the root word ends in <-ee>, <-ce> and <-le>, for example: agree and agreeable, peace and peaceable, sale and saleable; exceptions to retaining the <e> include argue and argument, whole and wholly, true and truly.

4 Problems with ‹ie› and ‹ei› transposition

The mnemonic <i before e except after c> applies to most words where the vowel sound is <ee>. Examples are:

● before <e>: field, piece, tier, believe, hygiene, thief, yield, niece, siege, yield;

● except after <c>: receive, ceiling, conceive, perceive.

Exceptions to the rule are: seize, caffeine, either, forfeit, heinous, neither, weird, protein and species.

5 Problems with prefixes

- Add one <s> with <mis-> or <dis-> prefixes, as in heard and misheard, agree and disagree, appear and disappear; spell and misspell (add one s).

- Add one <n> with <un-> or <in-> prefixes, as in usual and unusual, discreet and indiscreet; necessary and unnecessary (add one n).

6 Problems with homophones

These are pairs of words (and sometimes three words) that sound similar but are spelt differently and have different meanings (examples in brackets). The following list includes pairs of words that sound different but still give trouble.

Homophones and similar sounding words to learn by heart:

accept and except (receive something and exclude it)
adverse and averse (weather conditions and feelings against)
affect and having an effect (alter something and the result of it)
allot and a lot (to allocate and many)
aloud and allowed (out loud and permitted)
amoral and immoral (without morals and morally wrong)
ascent and assent (to 10,000 feet and agree to)
assure, insure and ensure (guarantee, against theft, the safety of)

baring and bearing (one's arm and bearing north west)
bated and baited (enthusiasm and a trap)
been and bean (there and baked bean)
born and borne (native born and costs borne by)
breach and breech (terms of an agreement and a birth)
broach and brooch (a topic and a jewellery item)

callus and callous (growth on skin and unfeeling)
check and cheque (the spelling of and pay money)
complacent and complaisant (after previous success and obliging)
compliment and complement (say nice things and go well together)
conscience and conscious (moral sense and awareness)
council and counsel (estate and guidance)
course and coarse (college and grit paper)
cue and queue (to action and in a line)
currant and current (bun and right now, also electric)

defuse and diffuse (a bomb and spreading out)
dependent and dependant (-child is a dependant (noun))
decent, dissent and descent (respectable, disagree and downhill)
discreet and discrete (tactful and separate from each other)
dough and doe (for bread and a female deer)
draft and draught (a letter and an excluder)
dual and duel (two of and a fight)

elicit and illicit (obtain and illegal)

guilt and gilt (ashamed and gold covered)

heel and heal (of shoe and cure)

into and in to (looked into the jar and looked in to see)
its and it's (belonging to it; and a contraction of it is or it has)

licence and license (noun/verb; driving licence and to permit)
lose and loose (verb/adjective; one's licence and slack fitting)

maybe and may be (perhaps and could be)
moral and morale (dilemma (good/bad); low (state of mind))

oral and aural (speaking test and listening test)

palate, palette and pallet (taste, paint and wooden)
passed and past (the test and the previous week)
personal and personnel (lives and colleagues)
piece and peace (portion and harmonious)
plain and plane (cooking and a vertical)
practice and practise (noun/verb; use practice tests to practise)
principal and principle (college head and of freedom of speech)
proceed and precede (to the checkout and lightening to thunder)
program and programme (computer and television)

raise and raze (a family and a building to the ground)

shoot and chute (a video and a playground slide)
scene and seen (scene of an accident and as seen on TV)
slight and sleight (small; and crafty as in sleight of hand)
stair and stare (climb up and through the keyhole)
stationary and stationery (stopped and paper)

there, their and they're (look in (place); home (belonging); they are)
through and threw (a doorway and a ball)
to, too and two (we went to; too much or also; and 2)

waist and waste (measurement and rubbish)
wave and waive (your hand and your rights)

wait and weight (a long time and kilograms)
weather and whether (forecast and if)
whole and hole (all of it and in the ground)
write and right (a letter and correct)

your and you're (belonging to and a contraction of you are)

3 Warm-up exercise: 100 words to spell correctly

	A	B	C	D
1	absence	absensce	abscence	abcense
2	accidently	accidentaly	accidantly	accidentally
3	accessable	accessible	accescible	acessibel
4	accomodate	accommodate	acommodate	accommadate
5	acheive	achieve	acheave	acheve
6	addresses	adressess	addreses	addresess
7	agresive	aggresive	agrassive	aggressive
8	allwrite	allright	all right	alright
9	announcment	anouncement	announcement	anouncment
10	annonymous	anonymous	anonimous	annonimous
11	argument	arguement	argumeant	arguemeant
12	auxillary	auxilliary	auxillairy	auxiliary
13	appealling	appealing	apealing	apealling
14	begginning	begginning	begining	beginning
15	beleaved	beleived	believed	bellieved
16	believable	beleivable	beleavable	believible
17	benifitted	bennefitted	benefited	benefitted
18	britain	Britain	britan	Brittain
19	business	buisness	bisiness	businness
20	carefull	carful	carfull	careful
21	cemetery	cematery	cemetary	semetery
22	chargable	chargeable	chargible	chargiable
23	colleages	colegues	colleuges	colleagues

	A	B	C	D
24	comittee	commitee	committee	committy
25	conscientous	conscientious	consientous	concientous
26	contraversial	controversial	contravesal	controvesal
27	copys	copyies	copies	coppies
28	decesive	disisive	desesive	decisive
29	definitely	definetly	deffinitely	definately
30	detterrent	detterent	deterent	deterrent
31	diference	difference	differance	diferance
32	dissernible	discenrable	discennible	discernible
33	disappoint	dissappoint	disapoint	dissapoint
34	dissappear	disappear	dissapear	disapeare
35	disscretely	discretley	disscreetly	discreetly
36	endevour	endeavour	endeavor	endeavore
37	embarress	embarras	embarrass	emmbarras
38	existance	existence	existense	existanse
39	exstacy	exstasy	ecstacy	ecstasy
40	ennrolment	enrolement	enrollment	enrolment
41	fulfill	fullfill	fulfil	fullfil
42	forgetable	forgettable	forgetible	forgettible
43	gratefull	greatful	grateful	greatfull
44	greivence	grievance	grievence	greavence
45	harass	harrass	haras	harras
46	humouress	homourous	humoress	humorous
47	illegable	illegibel	ilegable	illegible
48	immediatley	immediatly	immediately	immedietly
49	innoculate	inoculate	inocculate	innocculate
50	irresistable	irrisistible	irresistible	iresistable
51	jepordy	jepardy	jeperdy	jeopardy
52	jewelery	jewellery	jewellry	jewellerey
53	laboratory	labratory	laborotory	laboratary
54	livleyhood	livelyhood	livlihood	livelihood

	A	**B**	**C**	**D**
55	maintenance	maintainence	maintainence	maintenence
56	millenium	milenium	milennium	millennium
57	karioke	karaoke	karoake	karaoki
58	liase	liaize	liaise	leaise
59	manoeuvre	manouver	manouvre	manouever
60	michievoeus	mischevous	mischievous	mischeavous
61	neccessary	necessary	necesary	neccesary
62	occasionally	occasionly	ocasionally	occasionaly
63	occurance	occurrence	occurence	occurrance
64	opulence	opulensce	opulescence	oppulence
65	parallel	parallell	parrallel	paralell
66	pavillion	parvillion	parvilion	pavilion
67	pedlar	pedaler	peddlar	pedler
68	permisable	permissible	permisseable	pemissable
69	prescence	precence	presence	presense
70	precede	preceed	preeced	presede
71	proffession	proffesion	profession	profesion
72	privileged	priviledged	privilidged	priviliged
73	questionaire	questionnare	questionnaire	questionare
74	receit	reciept	reciet	receipt
75	recognise	recognize	reccognise	reccognize
76	recommend	reccomend	reccommend	recomend
77	recooperate	recuperate	recouperate	recuprate
78	rediculous	riddiculous	ridicullous	ridiculous
79	refferring	reffering	referring	refering
80	reference	refference	referrence	referance
81	rellevance	rellevence	relevance	rellevance
82	rythm	rythym	rhythym	rhythm
83	shedule	schedual	schedule	schedul
84	seperately	separately	sepperately	seperatly
85	successfull	succesful	successful	succesfull

	A	B	C	D
86	supercede	superceed	supersede	superseed
87	susceptible	susceptable	susseptable	susseptible
88	temperary	temporary	temparary	temperery
89	tolerent	tollerent	tolerant	tollerant
90	tomorrow	tomorow	tommorow	tommorrow
91	umberella	umbrella	umberela	umberrela
92	unneccessary	unnecesary	unecessary	unnecessary
93	vaccum	vaccuum	vacuum	vacum
94	vanderlism	vandalism	vandelism	vandallism
95	vetnary	vetinary	vettinary	veterinary
96	wholly	wholey	wholley	wholy
97	xylofone	xylophone	zylophone	xylophon
98	yaught	yaucht	yauht	yacht
99	yoghurtt	yoghert	yoghurt	yoggurt
100	zellot	zealott	zealot	zeallot

4 Easy questions (circle choice)

1   Disruptive behaviour may be _____ by poor classroom management.
     aggravated, agravated, agrivated, aggrivated

2   We have a green, yellow and red card system for dealing with insolent, rude
     or _____ behaviour.
     beligerent, belligerent, belligerant, beligerant

3   Both student teachers and pupils have _____ from lessons in citizenship.
     benefitted, benifited, benifitted, benefited

4   Our football team lost the match because we had become too _____ and
     underestimated the opposition.
     complaicent, complaisant, complacent, complaisent

5   Many schools are making a _____ effort to offset their carbon-footprint.
     consious, conscious, consciouse, concious

6 There has been much _____ over school selection policies.
controversey, contraversy, controvercy, controversy

7 Higher education workers took part in a 'day of _____'.
descent, discent, dissent, disent

8 Classroom _____ is essential for efficient teaching and learning.
disipline, dicipline, disciplin, discipline

9 My two Bs and a C were mildly _____.
dissappointing, dissapointing, disappointing, disapointing

10 It would be _____ to make a simple spelling mistake.
embarrassing, embarassing, embarrasing, embarasing

11 The debt crisis could _____ teacher shortages.
ecsacerbate, exsacerbate, exaserbate, exacerbate

12 I sprained my ankle playing five-a-side football and it was _____ painful.
extremely, extremelly, extreamly, extremley

13 The x-axis is used to plot the _____ variable.
independent, independant, indipendent, indapendent

14 Unhealthy snack foods have become _____ for some pupils.
irrisistible, irresistible, irrisistable, irresistable

15 There will be a meeting of the parents' _____ committee on Friday week.
liason, liaison, liasion, liaision

16 Some university students may be eligible for a non-refundable _____ grant.
maintainance, maintenence, maintenance, maintainence

17 A temporary post led to a _____ position.
permenant, permanant, permanent, permenent

18 Her story stressed the virtues of hard work and _____.
perseverence, perseverance, persaverance, persaverence

19 Our tutor spoke _____ about his own problems with maths.

poiniantly, poingnantly, poignantly, poynantly

20 Their sixth form college has a careers _____ library where resources may be viewed but not borrowed.

reference, refrence, referance, refference

21 Should teachers dress more _____ or at least appropriately?

professionaly, proffesionally, profesionally, professionally

22 It is _____ that pupils with packed lunches are seated separately from those having hot dinners.

regrettable, regretable, reggretable, reggrettable

23 Prejudice and discrimination are part of _____ education.

religous, religious, relligious, religouis

24 A letter starting Dear Mr or Mrs should end Yours _____

sincerly, sinserely, sincerely, sincerley

25 Old technology has been _____ by interactive whiteboards.

superseded, superceded, superceeded, superseeded

26 The group booking was an _____ good deal.

unbelievabley, unbelievably, unbelieveably, unbellievably

27 Children who behave _____ at school may find themselves being sent home.

unacceptably, unacceptabley, unnacceptabley, unaceptably

28 Excessive testing can cause _____ stress for pupils and teachers alike.

uneccesary, unneccessary, unnecesary, unnecessary

29 OFSTED stated _____ that teaching was better in small schools with proportionately more good teachers.

unequivicolly, uniquivacally, unequivocally, uniquivacolly

30 The teacher proved that sound does not travel in a _____ by pumping the air out of a bell-jar with the bell ringing.

vaccuum, vacuum, vaccum, vacume

Chapter 17

Punctuation

Introduction

You will be given short passages of text that have had some of their punctuation marks removed, for example commas, semi-colons, colons, apostrophes and full stops. To find the errors you need to look for natural breaks, lack of clear meaning, or inconsistencies in the punctuation. When you add punctuation, it must be consistent with the punctuation already in the passage.

The emphasis on correct punctuation reflects that careless mistakes or omissions can distort the meaning of text, as in:

> <Today's school menu: Meat pie with mixed vegetables or baked beans, and potato wedges.>

which looks like one meal unless the menu meant:

> <Today's school meal: Meat pie with mixed vegetables, or baked beans and potato wedges.>

A misplaced comma can introduce ambiguities into your written work and make it difficult to understand.

Problems with paragraphs

To help with reading and comprehension, a piece of prose (text) should be split into manageable chunks or paragraphs that deal with a distinct theme or aspect of the work. Each paragraph covers a single topic or expresses an argument within a few sentences. Every sentence in a paragraph should be relevant to its topic, with the first sentence (topic sentence) outlining the main thrust of the paragraph.

A new theme or topic begins with a new paragraph. If you have to subdivide text, it should be done on the basis of content rather than length; if the topic changes after only one sentence then you need a new paragraph. Long paragraphs (eg more than half a page) can be off-putting to readers, so you can split a single topic into two or more paragraphs to make it more readable.

Problems with capital letters and full stops

A capital letter is used at the start of a sentence or any text. The pronoun <I> is always capitalized, as is the first letter of a proper noun, for example <Mr Roberts>, <London> and <Private Peaceful>. Common nouns, for example <teacher>, <school> and <book>, are only capitalized when they start a sentence or when they are linked to a title or an individual person's name:

> I wish to appeal against my son's failed application for a transfer to a new <secondary school>. Josh was baptized as an infant and attended a <catholic primary school>. I accept that he was never guaranteed a place at <St Peter's Catholic Secondary School>. However, I feel that his social and emotional development will improve at a <catholic school>. Josh's <headteacher>, Mr Collins, supported my application for Josh's transfer. It was <Headteacher> Collins who first said, 'He needs more pastoral support than we provide at this school'.

Problems with commas

A comma cannot be used to splice two sentences together. However, two mini-sentences (clauses) can be joined by a conjunction (connecting word) preceded by a comma. In the following example, two clauses have been joined with a comma instead of using the conjunctions <so> or <and>. Notice that the comma must be placed before the connecting word and not after it for the punctuation to be correct.

> The girl enjoyed art, she looked forward to art classes. ✗

> The girl enjoyed art, so she looked forward to art classes.

> The girl enjoyed art, and she looked forward to art classes.

A comma is not required with the conjunction <because>. One valuable tip when inserting a phrase into a clause is to remember that commas come in pairs, ie one before the phrase and one after it. The sentence will still read correctly if the phrase is taken out. Phrases and clauses are covered in the grammar section.

> The girl enjoyed art, but she did not enjoy art lessons.

> The girl enjoyed ICT, and she looked forward to ICT classes.

The girl enjoyed music, yet she did not enjoy music lessons.

The girl did not enjoy maths, nor did she enjoy maths classes.

The girl looked forward to art classes because she enjoyed art.

The pupils, who are not allowed into the classroom before the lesson begins, have to line up quietly in the corridor.

Commas are used to set off some opening words and phrases, such as <However,> <Therefore,> <Nevertheless,> <Meanwhile,> <In the first instance,> <On the other hand,> <All the same,>. They also are used to separate a string of items (three or more) in a sentence. There is no need to use a comma before the final <and>, except when it is necessary to clarify the meaning.

The teacher entered the classroom carrying a mixing palette, paints, brushes and a foam roller.

The teacher entered the classroom carrying a mixing palette, paints, brushes and a foam roller to wet the canvas. ✗

The teacher entered the classroom carrying a mixing palette, paints, brushes, and a foam roller to wet the canvas.

You may be unsure about whether a sentence needs a comma. The alternative would be to omit the comma and use a full stop followed by a new sentence. If you are in any doubt, then use a full stop and a new sentence. If the sentence is very short simply omit the comma.

Problems with semi-colons and colons

As a pause in a sentence, a semi-colon falls midway between a full stop and a comma. Unlike a comma, a semi-colon can be used to hold two linked sentences (clauses) together.

The girl enjoyed art; she looked forward to art classes.

The girl entered the room with glee; she enjoyed art classes and was looking forward to completing her final piece of coursework.

Semi-colons are also used to list information that has been introduced following a colon.

The teacher entered the classroom carrying the following items: an easel and canvas; an assortment of paints, together with a tin of thinners; a palette to mix

the paints on; a palette knife to mix the paints and to scrape the palette clean;
four artists' brushes in incremental sizes.

Problems with the apostrophe and possession

The apostrophe is probably the most misused punctuation mark as it is often
inserted where it is not needed. The most common error is to pluralize a noun with
<'s> as in potatoe's. An apostrophe should only be used to show possession
(ownership). If there is one owner (singular) then add <'s> to the end of the owner's
name and if there is more than one owner (plural) add <'>. If a plural noun does
not end in <s> then you need to add <'s>.

There are five maths books left in the library.

There are five maths book's left in the library. ✗

The keen pupil's arrive early for the class. ✗

The keen pupils arrive early for the class.

I have the boy's books (the books belonging to one boy).

I have the two boys' books (the books belonging to the two boys).

It is the children's school.

It is the childrens' school. ✗

Problems with contractions

When speaking we tend to contract two words to make a single, short version.
These contractions use an apostrophe mark placed above the position of the
missing letter or letters; the second word loses a letter or letters and the first word
remains unchanged.

didn't and haven't instead of did not and have not (missing <o>);

he's instead of he is (missing <i>);

it's instead of it is (missing <i>) or it has (missing <ha>);

they'll instead of they will (missing <wi>);

might've instead of might have (missing <ha>); not might of.

who's instead of who is (this is different from whose, which is the possessive
form of who, as in 'Whose is this book?').

Problems with speech marks and quotation marks

Speech marks ('---') are used to indicate the actual words spoken by someone (direct speech). A comma is placed inside the speech marks to separate the actual words spoken from the rest of the sentence. Alternatively, the sentence can be written in such a way that the comma comes before the speech marks and the direct speech starts with a capital letter.

> 'You took your time getting here,' said Bond.
>
> 'Take a seat please James,' Felix said.
>
> Bond said, 'You took your time coming.'
>
> Felix said, 'Take a seat please James.'

Any number of sentences can be included inside the direct speech without having to close the quotation marks and start new ones.

> Evans frowned. 'Sorry, I can't allow it. It's against the rules.'
>
> 'Have you finished already?' said Evans. 'Well done. I am pleased with your progress. You've earned more golden time.'
>
> 'Hey, you there!' he yelled. 'Come here. I can't wait all day.'

Full stops, questions marks and exclamation marks come before the closing speech marks and not after them.

> Joe frowned. 'Sorry, I can't allow it.'
>
> 'Have you finished it?' said Joe. 'Hey you there!' he yelled.
>
> 'Lord of the Flies' and 'Of Mice and Men' are GCSE favourites.

Quotation marks ('---') are used to indicate a title; to quote a phrase from another source; and to highlight an unusual or questionable choice of word.

> My teacher asked me to think about the 'different types of prejudice' in the novel. To what extent is Lennie a victim of the prejudices of the 1930s 'depression era'?

Problems with question marks

A question mark takes the place of a full stop when a sentence asks a direct question; a question mark cannot take the place of a comma. Sentences that end with a question mark often begin How, Why, What, Where, When or Who. A question mark is not used with indirect (reported) questions but is part of direct speech.

Was the numeracy test difficult?

I asked, 'Was the numeracy test difficult?'

I asked if the numeracy test was difficult? ✗

Problems with brackets (parentheses)

Brackets are used to insert more information in a sentence without interrupting its flow; the sentence must read correctly after the words in brackets have been removed. The information in brackets often clarifies what has just been said or describes it in more detail.

Gifted and talented students (those above the 90th percentile) must not lose their motivation between key stages.

Our school's lessons cater for the more able pupils (the top 10%) who need to maintain their motivation between key stages.

Our school's lessons cater for the more able pupils (the top 10%) need to maintain their motivation between key stages. ✗

1 Easy questions

Half the questions are punctuated correctly (✓) and half are not (✗)

1   Boys do better in maths, girls in English and languages.
Answer .... ✗

2   The Labour Government of 1964, and subsequent governments, supported the phasing out of grammar schools.
Answer ....

3   However there are still more than 150 grammar schools in England, and they remain popular with parents and young people.
Answer .... ✗

4   To be certain of being seen, all pupils should wear clothing with yellow, orange, or light green fluorescent strips.
Answer .... ✗

5   Semi-colons have several uses in punctuation, one of them is to hold two linked sentences together.

Answer ...X...

6   Pupil behaviour will improve by adopting the following
  – a consistent, whole-school approach to classroom discipline;
  – an interactive style of teaching designed to increase motivation;
  – the inclusion of social skills training to improve self-awareness;
  – an incentive scheme that encourages positive behaviour.

Answer ...X...

7   A student's expectations of the course can be unrealistic.

Answer ...✓...

8   Students' expectations of the course can be unrealistic.

Answer ...✓...

9   Our school's rating was comparable with the average schools' rating for the Local Authority.   Answer ...✓...

10   Parents expressed concerns about their children's safety, which meant that the school's annual trip had to be cancelled.

Answer ...✓...

11   Most library's allow books to be renewed online.   Answer ...X...

12   Twelve books' can be taken out on your card at any one time.   Answer ...X...

13   If I had foreseen my low mark I might of studied harder.   Answer ...X...

14   It's not easy working with mixed ability classes.   Answer ...✓...

15   The school has achieved its LEA targets.   Answer ...✓...

16   "I'm not surprised that foreign language teaching is in decline," said the head teacher. "Languages are no longer compulsory for 14 to 16 year olds, and there aren't enough jobs to go around."

Answer ...✓...

2 Easy questions

The following passage has 12 pieces of punctuation missing. Insert the missing punctuation in the correct places.

Should calculators be banned from the classroom?
    Calculators were invented to increase the speed of basic arithmetic calculations; they were not intended to replace mental agility with numbers. However, if too much time is spent on basic calculations, then maths becomes tedious and pupils have less time to develop more advanced mathematical skills.
    Problems involving fractions can rarely be solved with a calculator, even though addition, subtraction, multiplication and division remain as key elements. On the other hand, problems involving; trigonometry, calculus and graphs are greatly assisted by calculators.
    Pupils' dependency on calculators can impair number skills that require rough checks, such as rounding, approximation and estimation. In these situations, calculators need only be used when precision and accuracy are essential. Calculators should be allowed into the classroom, but not at the expense of paper and pencil skills. After all, speed is not everything, and what happens in the real world when a calculator is not available.

3 Punctuation test

The following passage has 13 pieces of punctuation missing. Insert the missing punctuation in the correct places.

Working children.
If you're under 13 then apart from a few exceptions you cannot do paid work. At age 14, you can be employed in a wide range of jobs, but these must not harm your health and development or affect your attendance at school.
    By law, young people aged 14 to 16 can only do light work. It is illegal to work on a building site or with heavy machinery. You must not drive vehicles (including tractors on farms) and you cannot work in kitchens and chip shops, or serve alcohol, cigarettes and medicines.
    It is illegal for 14 to 16 year olds to work for more than:

    two hours on any school day;

    one hour before school starts;

    twelve hours in any school week.

Chapter 18

Grammar

Introduction

In this section, the questions are based on a passage of prose split into half-finished sentences, each with a choice of four possible endings (clauses or phrases), only one of which uses the correct grammar. If you read back through the completed passage it should:

be grammatically acceptable and conform to the conventions of standard English;

make sense as a whole, with appropriate links between sentences;

be grammatically consistent from sentence to sentence;

avoid any ambiguity of meaning or any lack of clarity.

Teachers need a full grasp of the rules of formal written English. In the test you will have to spot mistakes in relation to:

inconsistent tense/wrong or incomplete verb forms;

lack of agreement between subject and verb; noun and pronoun;

particles unrelated to a noun; incorrect or missing adverbial forms;

problems with comparatives and superlatives;

wrong or missing prepositions (eg different from/to);

errors from speech, linked to contractions and the apostrophe;

failure to observe where one sentence should end and another sentence should start;

faulty sentence constructions with fragments left out;

lack of cohesion between sentences when grammatical links are missed.

Review of grammar

Problems with verb forms and tense

Verbs are words that express action or a state of being, for example to run, to speak, to work, to feel, to laugh, to be and to have. Regular present tense verbs can be changed into the simple past tense by adding the letters <ed> to the end. For example: walk becomes walked, and help becomes helped. Irregular verbs follow no such pattern. There are over two hundred irregular verbs. Some examples are:

awake/awoke; become/became; begin/began; break/broke; build/built; buy/bought; choose/chose; do/did; draw/drew; eat/ate; forget/forgot; freeze/froze; give/gave; get/got; go/went; have/had; hear/heard; hold/held; know/knew; leave/left; make/made; meet/met; read/read; ride/rode; send/sent; sing/sang; sink/sank; sit/sat; shake/shook; spell/spelt/ spelled; swear/swore; swim/swam; take/took; wake/woke; wet/wet/wetted; write/wrote.

The verb <to be> takes the following forms in the present tense:

I am (first person singular; yourself)

you are (second person singular or plural; someone else)

we are (first person plural)

he is, she is, it is, Jack is (third person singular)

they are, Jack and Lucy are (third person plural)

All verbs must have a subject, eg Jack and Lucy (the subject) <are>. Plural verbs (unlike plural nouns) are not made by adding an <s> to the end; the <s> is some-times removed to make a singular verb plural, for example <he walks> and they <walk>. The verb <to be> takes the singular form <was> in the past tense and the plural form <were> in the past tense. The verb <to have> takes the form <had> in the past tense.

I am late. You are late. He is late.

Jack and Lucy are early.

He walks, she walks and it walks.

I walk, we walk, they walk and you walk.

I was, he was, she was, it was.

You were, they were, we were.

I had, he had, she had, it had, you had, they had and we had.

Future tense is expressed using the auxiliary verb <will> followed by another verb as in: I <will be> late for school. Sometimes <will> becomes separated from the other verb in the sentence as in: What time <will> you <leave> school? <Will> can also be combined with two other verbs to complete the sentence verb as in: English lessons <will be presented> in the library tomorrow. <Would> is used instead of <will> to express the future from some time in the past: I think class <will> finish early today (relates to now); I thought class <would> finish early yesterday (relates to earlier).

Past, present and future tenses with <to be> and <to have> are shown in the following table.

Tense	To be	To have
Present	I am, you are	I have, you have
	He is, she is, it is	He has, she has, it has
	We are, they are	We have, they have
	You are	You have
Past	I was, you were	I had, you had
	He was, she was, it was	He had, she had, it had
	We were, they were	We had, they had
	You were	You had
Future	I will be, you will be	I will have, you will have
	We will be, they will be	We will have, they will have

Example: Jack has tried hard to improve his English skills this term but still needs to improve. He knows the rules of English grammar and how to construct a sentence but not:

a)   what clear and precise expression are.

b)   what clear and precise expression was.

c)   what clear and precise expression were.

d)   what clear and precise expression is.

All four choices are the same apart from the verb <to be> in the forms of <are> (plural present tense), <were> (plural past tense), <was> (singular past tense) and <is> (singular present tense). The correct answer is d):

He knows the rules of English grammar and how to construct a sentence but not what clear and precise expression is.

Verb tenses must be consistent in a sentence, so <knows> in the example's question stem requires the present tense verb <is> in the answer text and not the past tense verbs <was> or <were>.

Verb–noun agreement is required, so the singular noun <expression> takes the singular verb <is> and not the plural verbs <are> or <were>.

The two adjectives <clear> and <precise> serve as distracters, tempting the reader into choosing <are>. You can remove these adjectives from the sentence to see the solution more clearly. Another trap finds a plural pronoun (eg they) used at the start of a sentence and attempts to link it with a plural verb at the end:

He knows what <clear and precise> expression is.

They know what <clear and precise> expression are.

They know what <clear and precise> expression is.

They know what <clear and precise> expressions are.

Problems with participles

These are the <ing> form and the <ed> form of verbs. The <ing> form is the present participle and describes continuous action, as in: I am eating. It can be combined with all three tenses (past, present and future) to give the complete verb for the sentence, telling you what is, was or will be happening. For example: I am eating, was eating, will be eating. The <ed> form is the past participle and describes completed action. Participles can be combined with all three tenses to tell you what is, has or will be finished, as in: <I have helped>, <I had helped> and <I will have helped>. Past participles are often used with 'had' and many have irregular verbs.

Present tense	Past tense	Past participle
am	was	been
break	broke	broken
drink	drank	drunk
eat	ate	eaten
freeze	froze	frozen
give	gave	given
ring	rang	rung
shake	shook	shaken
swim	swam	swum
tear	tore	torn

Problems with nouns

A noun is the name of a person, place or thing and is often the subject of a sentence. Proper nouns are names of people, days of the week, titles of books etc, and are capitalized; some words can be both nouns and proper nouns as in: the British Government believes in small government. Collective nouns denote many individuals, for example family, government, team, audience. Pronouns are used instead of nouns. They can have different forms depending on whether they form the subject or the object of the sentence as shown in the table below.

Subject	Object	Subject	Object
I	me	we	us
you	you	they	them
he	him	it	it
she	her		

A personal pronoun always uses the subjective case when it follows the verb 'to be' at the start of a sentence. In spoken English the subjective case sounds stilted so the objective case is often used. In written work the objective cases should only be used at the end of a sentence or with a preposition (in, at, on, with, between, after, before, from).

> It was I. It was he. It was they. (all subject)
>
> It was he (subject) and not her (object).
>
> It was I (subject) and not them (object).
>
> She and Jack (subject) can go with Lucy and me (object).
>
> We (subject) are quicker than them (object) but they (subject) are slower than us (object).
>
> Jack (subject) will leave before her and me (object).
>
> You and I (subject) will leave together.
>
> Between you and me; after them; before us; with me; from him.

Problems with adjectives: comparatives and superlatives

These modify nouns; they come in front of a noun and tell you more about it, for example: quick worker, clever pupil, careful teacher, two coins. An adjective that describes one noun or pronoun is known as a positive; comparatives compare two nouns and superlatives compare three or more nouns. For example <Lucy is tall> (positive), <Jack is taller> (comparative) and <James is the tallest (superlative) of

all>. Usually we add <er> and <est> to make the two different comparisons, but there are exceptions. Examples are given in the following table.

Positive (1 noun)	Comparative (2 nouns)	Superlative (3 or more)
tall	taller	tallest
brave	braver	bravest
hard	harder	hardest
small	smaller	smallest
good	better	best
many/much	more	most
little	less	least
bad	worse	worst

Problems with adverbial forms

These words describe verbs. Adverbs are usually placed after the verb and many are made by adding <ly> to an adjective, for example quick and quickly, careful and carefully, easy and easily. Other adverbs include today, soon, now, before and immediately. Some 'doing' words can act as adjectives, verbs and adverbs as in <the careful nurse cared carefully for her patients>.

She spoke loudly (adverb) in a loud (adjective) voice.

I made a sudden (adjective) decision to leave suddenly (adverb).

Josh is a happy (adjective) pupil and acts happily (adverb).

Problems with prepositions

These are usually placed before a noun or pronoun and show its relationship to something, for example <The exam is next year>. Some commonly used prepositions are: in, on, of, off, by, at, with, for, from, after, before, through, between, about, away and around. Choosing between prepositions is sometimes difficult because there are no hard and fast rules so the correct preposition has to be memorized. The most difficult choice is often whether to use <to>, <with>, <for> or <from>, as in the following cases:

It corresponds to (not with) the first chapter.

I will correspond with (not to) the headmaster.

We disagreed with the headmaster but agreed to differ.

I have grown accustomed to it (not with it).

The second edition was similar to (not with) the first edition.

Results had improved compared with (not to) last year.

We were disgusted with Jack and disgusted at his behaviour.

Problems with subject (noun) and verb agreement

The main subject noun and its verb should agree, ie either both are singular or both are plural. Collective nouns denoting many individuals are usually singular, whereas two singular subjects joined by <and> always take a plural verb:

The pupil was ready to board the coach (he/she was ready).

The team was ready for the kick-off (it was ready).

The team were ready for the kick-off (it were ready). ✗

Jack and the remaining pupil were leaving (they were leaving).

The pupils were leaving (they were leaving).

Jack and Lucy were leaving (they were leaving).

Jack or Lucy was leaving (Jack was or Lucy was).

Jack or Lucy were leaving (Jack were or Lucy were). ✗

Jack, together with the other pupils, was leaving (he was leaving).

Confusion arises when the subject noun and the verb become separated:

The results for the worst performing school is the most improved (the results is the most improved). ✗

The results for the worst performing school are the most improved.

Problems with who and whom

Use <who> for the subject and <whom> for the object:

I questioned the lecturer who I thought had made a mistake.

I questioned the lecturer whom I thought had made a mistake. ✗

I thought I had made a mistake so I questioned the lecturer whom I knew.

I thought I had made a mistake so I questioned the lecturer who I knew. ✗

Problems with which and who

Use which (or that) with objects and who (or whom) with people:

> This classroom, which is larger, will accommodate the students.
>
> These are the students who need extra help.
>
> These are the students which need extra help. ✗

Problems with this, that, these and those

These is the plural of this and those is the plural of that:

> This is the new textbook. These are the new textbooks.
>
> That was the new edition. Those were the new editions.
>
> These is the new textbooks. ✗ That was the new editions. ✗

1 Warm-up exercise

Half the sentences are correct (✓) and half are incorrect (✗):

1	Is the team ready?	Answer ✓
2	We are happy if she is.	Answer ✓
3	We was ill after he was. *were*	Answer *were*
4	It were faster than he was. *was*	Answer *was*
5	Either you are right or I am.	Answer ✓
6	I were late and left alone. *was*	Answer *was*
7	It was you who was last.	Answer ✓
8	The choir are singing.	Answer ✓
9	The teacher was late and so misses his train.	Answer
10	It was extremely cold and the pipes had froze.	Answer
11	They shook hands and made up.	Answer
12	Carl speaks too loud in class.	Answer
13	Josh writes slowly and carefully.	Answer

14   Lucy and me are friends.   *Answer* ....

15   Emma can go with you and me.   *Answer* ....

16   It was they all along.   *Answer* ....

17   Jack, Ben and Steve are tall, but Steve is the tallest.   *Answer* ....

18   Neither Moira nor Jane bring lunch.   *Answer* ....

19   Twenty per cent of the class are missing.   *Answer* ....

20   No pupils are ready.   *Answer* ....

21   Our team is ready so they will bat first.   *Answer* ....

22   Our pupils are ready so they will leave first.   *Answer* ....

23   The head teacher, along with the other teachers,
         are in class.   *Answer* ....

24   Homework compliance for the worst performing
         classes are the most improved.   *Answer* ....

25   The improvement in results for the schools with the highest proportion of
         pupils on free school meals was the greatest.   *Answer* ....

26   Every child, including those with special needs, have a fundamental right
         to education.   *Answer* ....

Sentence construction

The easiest sentences to understand are those that contain a single idea. When a sentence is crammed with too many ideas it becomes confusing and its thread is lost. If you introduce a second idea then make sure that it is properly linked with the main idea. Failure to link in the second idea leads to a run-on sentence that sounds disjointed. Sentence boundaries need to be observed, but a long sentence can be grammatically correct, if it is punctuated well and there are clear links between the ideas. If a sentence becomes too long or complex then it may be made clearer by splitting it in two; if you have any doubts then use a full stop to split it.

> The girl enjoyed art. She looked forward to art classes.
>
> The girl enjoyed art she looked forward to art classes. ✗
>
> The girl entered the room with glee because she enjoyed art classes and looked forward to completing her coursework.
>
> The girl entered the room with glee. She enjoyed art classes and looked forward to completing her coursework.

Problems with subject and object

In a sentence, the words are grouped together in a logical order that the person reading it can understand. Students with English as their first language will have no difficulty spotting faulty constructions, though it is worth recapping the basics.

All sentences must start with a capital letter and end with a full stop. They always contain a verb in the middle. A sentence begins with a subject, which is often a noun (person or place), and is often finished by adding an object; the object is the person or thing (a noun) at which the action (verb) is aimed. Not all sentences have an object, but they all have a subject. To give the sentence more meaning the last object is often joined to another noun to complete the picture. For example:

The lecturer gave the students additional resources
(subject)   (verb)   (object)   (adjective) (noun)

Problems with clauses and phrases

These are the main components of a sentence. A clause is a group of words that contain both a subject and an object. A main clause is a mini-sentence and most sentences contain one or more clauses. A phrase is a group of words that forms part of a sentence but it does not contain both a subject and a verb, which are necessary for a sentence. If a phrase is removed from a sentence the remaining words still make sense (the clause is left). A subordinate clause contains both a subject and a verb but, like a phrase, it does not make sense without a main clause:

The bell rang (clause) and the pupils entered the room (clause).

The students, who are not allowed into the room (phrase), had to wait outside. (The students had to wait outside (main clause).)

The students had to wait outside (main clause) until the bell rang. (main clause with subordinate clause)

Until the bell rang. (subordinate clause on its own) ✗

If a phrase or a subordinate clause is added incorrectly to a main clause it can create grammatical ambiguities:

The school can hire the coach (main clause).

When it is ready, the school can hire the coach. ✗
(When the school is ready or when the coach is ready?)

The school can hire the coach when it is ready. ✗
(Probably 'when the coach is ready' but the ambiguity remains).

The meaning can be made clear by replacing the pronoun <it> with the appropriate noun:

> The school can hire the coach when the coach is ready. OR

> The school can hire the coach when the school is ready.

Alternatively, the word <to> can be added to either clause:

> When the school is ready to, it can hire the coach. OR

> When it is ready to, the school can hire the coach.

Problems with participles: related (✔) and unrelated (✗)

A participle (eg <ing> or <ed> forms of the verb) in an opening phrase should relate to the noun in a clause that follows. If the noun becomes separated from the participle to which it relates then the meaning can become unclear.

> TIP: look for the answer that keeps the participle nearest to the noun.

> Arriving late for school, the teacher saw the children. ✗
> (Who arrived late, the teacher or the children?)

> Arriving late for school, the children were seen by the teacher. ✓

In some cases it is better to recast the sentence:

> The teacher saw the children arriving late for school.

> Behaving inappropriately, the teacher asked the pupil to leave the class. ✗
> (Whose behaviour was inappropriate, the teacher's or the pupil's?)

> Behaving inappropriately, the pupil was asked by the teacher to leave the class. ✓

Alternatively, recast the sentence: The pupil, who was behaving inappropriately, was asked by the teacher to leave the class.

> Increasingly expensive, some parents cannot afford school trips. ✗

> Increasingly expensive, school trips are unaffordable for some parents. ✓

Alternatively, recast the sentence: School trips are becoming more expensive and some parents cannot afford them.

2 Warm-up exercise

Half the sentences are constructed correctly (✓) and half are not (✗):

1 How many pupils are at grade C or above?   *Answer* ....

2 Are school dinners still unhealthy?   *Answer* ....

3 A well-balanced, healthy diet, low in saturated fat.

Answer ....

4 It's now or never.   *Answer* ....

Assessing

5 Assessed by the popularity of A-level subjects last year,
maths and science are making a comeback.   *Answer* ....

6 Seen as a candidate for A* grades at A-level, the teacher thought
she had every chance of a place at medical school.   *Answer* ....

7 Having acquired the skills of self-assessment and self-evaluation, teaching
will benefit from reflective practitioners.   *Answer* ....

8 Recognizing the possibility of plagiarism, students must use the Harvard
system of referencing for information taken off the internet.

Answer ....

9 Widely acknowledged as a seminal work on classroom management,
the many facets of poor pupil behaviour were explored by Kounin (1970).

Answer ....

10 Shaken by the breach in confidentiality, changes were implemented by
the head to prevent any more disclosures from taking place.

Answer ....

11 Between you and me.   *Answer* ....

12 That's all right then.   *Answer* ....

13 Between you and me, that's all right then.   *Answer* ....

14 Even though I had not expected to be on the winning team, it was
disappointing for us to have lost the match.   *Answer* ....

15 Sarah went outside the library building to use
the phone, to avoid disrupting other users.   *Answer* ....

16 Jackson states that the traditional method of teaching mathematics
has failed pupils of low ability, believing that a whole-class interactive
approach is the best way to reduce ability gaps.

Answer ....

3 Easy questions

Complete the following sentence by choosing the best of the four alternatives.

1   Our school trip to France

   a)   because of the falling value of the pound against the euro will cost £15 more per pupil this year.

   b)   because of the falling value of the pound against the euro will cost £15 more this year per pupil.

   c)   will cost £15 per pupil more this year because of the falling value of the pound against the euro.

   d)   will cost £15 more per pupil this year because of the falling value of the pound against the euro.

   Answer ....

2   Judged by their evaluation forms,

   a)   it was not found that larger classes were detrimental to the students' learning experiences.

   b)   students did not find that larger class sizes were detrimental to their learning experiences.

   c)   there was no detriment to students' learning experiences in larger classes.

   d)   larger classes were not found to be detrimental to the students' learning experiences.

   Answer ....

3   GCSE results were very good again this year. The percentage that gained grades A* and A

   a)   has risen to 35%.

   b)   will rise to 35%.

   c)   rose to 35%.

   d)   rising to 35%.

   Answer ....

Chapter 19

Writing task

Teachers need to be able to write school reports, lesson plans, and questions for their pupils. The writing task will test your ability to compose a piece of prose, write clearly, and pay attention to spelling, punctuation and grammar. Topic questions can relate to teaching issues in a general way or any subject matter with socio-cultural, philosophical or ethical components. No specialist teaching knowledge is expected. Where a choice of question is offered you should read through *all* the questions quickly but carefully, before making a decision. Grade each question after you have read it. If you like the question then give it a tick; if you are uncertain but it seems possible then give it a question mark; if it is definitely not the question for you then give it a cross. Do not assume automatically that the question you have ticked is the best choice. Look again at the more challenging question; it may offer the better-prepared candidate the chance to excel. Note well: before you make your final decision, make sure that you can see both sides of the argument so that you can develop a well-rounded essay.

Thorough planning is an essential part of your answer. It needs a beginning, a middle and an end that cover all parts of the question. This hints at three paragraphs; however, an additional paragraph at the start serves as an introduction when the questions ask you to explain what you think the author means or is trying to imply. Adopt a three- or four-paragraph approach:

i) **Paragraphs**: each paragraph informs the examiner that you are covering a new aspect of the question and each sentence in the paragraph carries a single idea related to the theme of the paragraph.

ii) **Sentences**: your sentences can (and should) vary in length from the short, for example 14 words or fewer, to the long, for example 26 words or more. Shorter sentences are easy to read and understand, but if there are too many they make your work sound choppy and your ideas fragmented. Longer sentences make your ideas sound *unified* but they are more difficult to read and if a sentence carries too much detail the meaning becomes obscure. By way of example, the sentences on this page average 24 words.

iii)   **Layout**: taking an average sentence length of 20 words, for every 300 words (one A4 page) you will need to write 15 sentences in four paragraphs. A 300- to 400-word limit would suggest a 2–3–4–4-sentence plan, consisting of two sentences for the introduction, three arguments that support the statement, four that counter it, and two examples (one for each point of view) followed by a four-sentence conclusion.

The 4-paragraph approach: introduction, arguments for, arguments against and conclusion. Each paragraph relates to one part of the question:

i)   **First paragraph** (eg two sentences): at the preparatory stage you need to *identify the task* and jot down what it entails. The introduction usually involves paraphrasing, ie re-stating in *your own words* what the question is asking or what points the author is trying to make. If the question contains a hidden assumption then you may wish to highlight it here, but not to excess. Explain what the statement means to you in two or three sentences at most. If the question can be paraphrased in a single sentence, you can run it into the main body of the text and use one paragraph fewer.

ii)   **Second and third paragraphs**: use *brainstorming* as a first step to generate any ideas without judging their value; it is the quantity rather than the quality of the ideas at this stage. Even so, it is worthwhile classifying the ideas as either for or against the argument. You can do this by placing key words or phrases in two opposing columns, for or against the argument/statement, as shown in the table below.

Arguments **FOR** (eg 2nd paragraph) (choose three or four ideas in support of the argument)	Arguments **AGAINST** (3rd paragraph) (choose your four best ideas counter to the argument)
Hints and tips when choosing ideas:	Hints and tips when choosing ideas:
Avoid including too many examples; one may suffice. An example is not a substitute for a well-crafted argument.	Avoid including too many examples; one example that counters the argument may suffice.
Do not leave your best ideas until the last in an attempt to build a crescendo. Get to the heart of the matter straight away; you have limited time.	Do not get drawn in to an emotional response even if you disagree strongly with what is being asserted. Be dispassionate; do not set yourself against the argument. Maintain a balanced view and avoid unnecessary bias.
Use arrows to link brainstorming ideas that are counter to each other.	

iii) **Fourth paragraph**: *evaluate and synthesize* your arguments (discuss strengths and weaknesses) to formulate a coherent conclusion that takes a clear position or reconciles the differences (you can introduce your own opinions).

Composing the essay

The following points are worth remembering:

i) Do not deviate from your chosen topic and answer all the components. Make a confident start, for example:

'I believe that the statement implies that…'
'The statement argues that…'
'The author makes the point that…'

ii) Remember to keep your handwriting legible.

iii) Be careful with your grammar, spelling and syntax to avoid losing marks; avoid jargon or abbreviations. If you were to use the words 'information and communications technology', put ICT in brackets after it; now you can use ICT if you need it again.

iv) Follow your plan, keeping to one theme per paragraph; use linking words and phrases to facilitate a smooth transition from one paragraph to the next and to inform the examiner that you are starting a new theme, for example:

'On the other hand…'
'To counter these assertions…'
'However, it might also be said…'

v) Vary the length of your sentences while keeping to one idea per sentence; short sentences make your work easier to understand.

vi) Use bullet points/roman numerals to make sequential points clearly (as per this list), but you must write a *unified* essay.

vii) The final paragraph: here you can take a clear position as long as you have weighed up the arguments for and against to reach an informed decision. Do not just give your own views or show unnecessary bias.

The final check

Spend a few minutes reading though your essay to check your punctuation, spelling and grammar. Look for missed-out words or repetition of words. Have you avoided clichés, or presented assumptions as facts? Are the sentences well constructed, and do they communicate a clear message using sufficient vocabulary? Does the

essay flow, with good transitions between paragraphs? Have you started con-
fidently and finished with a strong conclusion? Most importantly, have you covered
all parts of the questions and kept to the stated length?

If you haven't done any writing since you left school, and that could well be
several years ago, try writing short simple passages to begin with. Describe one of
your children, your journey to work, your feelings when everyone has left the house
– don't bother at this stage about paragraphs or punctuation, just write as you feel
– you will be surprised how much you can do. For a warm-up exercise you could
write about someone or something that has been important to you, or how a book
or a film has influenced you.

The following writing task questions range from the very simple to the more
challenging. There are no right or wrong answers.

1 Example (easy level)

Some people believe that schoolchildren should be made to wear a uniform. Others
feel that the children should be free to choose their own clothes.

Discuss both sides of the argument.

Do you agree or disagree with pupils wearing uniforms?

Write at least 250 words.

There are arguments both for and against children having to wear a school uniform.
Some people favour uniforms simply because they look smart. However, uniforms
do more than this because they identify you with a particular school, which can
help to maintain discipline and reduce truancy. Uniforms also promote safety and
security by making it easier to identify intruders in the school. On a practical note,
a uniform makes choosing clothes straightforward and problem-free for parents.
Contrast this with the difficulties faced by parents with limited means (for example,
living off state benefits) when a child wants to wear expensive designer clothes,
mainly to impress friends. In this circumstance, children from poorer backgrounds
can find themselves disadvantaged.

On the other hand, some people would argue that wearing a school uniform is
an unnecessary restriction on personal freedoms and expression. Instead, pupils
should be allowed to choose their own clothes as suits them as individuals, rather
than having to conform to a fixed dress code. Many pupils do not like a school
uniform, which means wearing the same clothes every day.

Personally, I see nothing wrong with wearing a uniform to school because there
is plenty of opportunity to wear your own clothes outside the school gates. Also,
some restrictions are always necessary to stop people from dressing inappropriately while at school. There are strict dress codes and uniforms for adults in certain

occupations, so children might as well get used to the idea of having to wear a uniform of some type. I do not think it is a good idea to let young people have everything their own way too soon, otherwise they will have problems with authority later on.

Method

In the first paragraph, the author introduces the topic without copying from the question and then continues by explaining the benefits of wearing a school uniform. The second paragraph describes some disadvantages of wearing uniforms. The third paragraph covers the author's personal opinion on the topic, as required by the question, and includes more reasons to support the author's conclusion.

2 Example (easy level)

Some people believe that electronic calculators should not be allowed in school until the pupils have mastered mental arithmetic. Others believe that calculators save pupils time, especially with complicated calculations.

Discuss both these views and give your own opinion.

Write at least 250 words.

The electronic calculator is a very useful tool for carrying out basic calculations and it is hard to imagine anyone never having used one. Calculators are ideal for adding up large columns of numbers quickly and reduce the chances of making a mistake. This does not mean that calculators should be used for making every calculation. In some maths problems, for example fractions, it is not possible to find the solution with a calculator. For this reason, pupils should be able to solve arithmetic problems either in their head or by writing the calculation down on paper.

If calculators are introduced in school too early, the pupils will not have developed their mental arithmetic skills. In a situation where a calculator is not available, the pupils will find that they are unable to solve the problem. Calculators can save time but this is not always more important than being able to work out the right answer unaided. In the real world it is important to have a good grasp of numbers, even for simple things like money.

I believe that calculators should be allowed in schools but only after the pupils can remember their multiplication tables and work out basic arithmetic problems. It is very important that pupils have competent number skills so that they can solve a wide range of mathematical problems. Calculators are not the answer to every problem and it is still possible to make a mistake if you press the wrong button. Mental arithmetic is particularly useful for checking if an answer makes sense. A calculator is not an alternative to pupils using their brains.

Method

The first paragraph expands on what has been said in the question and includes the advantages of calculators and also some limitations. The second paragraph focuses on why calculators should not be allowed in school before number skills have been mastered. The third paragraph is used for the writer's own opinion as expressed by the words 'I believe'. It also brings together the advantages and disadvantages of calculator use so as to create a balanced argument.

3 Example (easy level)

Opinions vary on whether students should take a gap year before going into higher education.

Discuss the possible advantages and disadvantages of taking a year out.

Do you believe that taking a gap year is a good idea?

Give reasons for your answer and include any relevant experience or knowledge.

Write at least 250 words.

Many students choose to take a year out before going to university. To do so can be a positive and rewarding experience but there are also downsides to consider.

Some people will spend their time travelling while others will seek work experience. Travelling, especially to foreign countries, is advantageous because it broadens your outlook on life and its possibilities. It will make you more aware of different cultures and people and should increase your confidence, especially in social situations.

If you choose to spend your year out working, this can also bring benefits. Work experience can help you to confirm that you have made the right degree choice. Working in an area related to your degree can also be helpful when it comes to finding a permanent job at the end of your course. A job can also improve your financial situation.

However, there are downsides to delaying your entry into university. One obvious problem is that you will have grown out of the habit of studying. There is a risk that the lure of paid employment will sway you from going to university altogether. If you spent your year out travelling then a future employer might look less favourably on you than a candidate who spent their time working.

I believe that a gap year can be a good idea as long as you do something productive that will be to your advantage in the future. Taking a year out can give you a better feel for life in the world in general and also in the workplace. You may never have the opportunity to take time out again so I would recommend it, but only if you choose carefully what to do or where to go.

4 Example (easy level)

Do good exam results at school or college guarantee success in life?

Discuss the advantages that a good education can have on your future.

Do you believe that studying hard will bring a better life?

Give reasons for your answer; include any relevant experience or knowledge.

Write 300 to 350 words.

I do not believe that academic achievement equates with a successful life. Obtaining good grades at school is a separate issue to making the most of your life. However, it is hard to see how a person can have a rewarding career without a sound education and appropriate qualifications, for example a degree.

Well-educated, well-qualified people have more opportunities in the workplace and are more likely to find a well-paid job or be promoted. The result is often more job satisfaction and a better lifestyle compared with people who lack qualifications. On the downside there can be more responsibility and stress.

It is still possible to do well in life without good qualifications. Not everybody is academically inclined. Many successful people left school at an early age and went on to achieve great things, often in the world of business. What is clear, though, is that most people had to work hard to achieve success, so failure to do well at school is not a good sign if it means that you were lazy.

There is more to life than work and money, so it is important to strike an appropriate work–life balance. Too much time spent working can harm people's social lives and relationships. Young people can lose out if they spend too much time studying rather than engaging in social activities and acquiring life skills.

I am not certain that by studying hard I will definitely improve my chances in life, but I am sure that I need to study if I am serious about wanting to improve myself. Good results in my examination alone will not bring success. I will have to make the most of my education and any opportunities that present themselves if I am to succeed.

Method

The author starts with his own opinion, while being careful to mention the other side of the argument so as not to appear biased (balanced view). The second paragraph looks at the advantages of having a good education (second part of the question) and also mentions a downside. The third paragraph explains that qualifications are not always needed to achieve success. The fourth paragraph explains some disadvantages of working too hard. The fifth paragraph deals with the last part of the question, pulling together strands from earlier paragraphs to provide a well-thought-out conclusion.

5 Example (more difficult)

'Every teacher is a teacher of English.' (George Sampson, 1922)

What does the author mean by this statement?

Develop arguments for and against.

Do you believe that it is true whatever the subject lesson?

Write about 300 to 350 words.

The essence of the above statement is that teachers need to be reminded that literacy is a component of every lesson and that all teachers, regardless of their subjects, must not neglect English in their classroom. The statement appears to be as relevant today as it was in 1922.

When a student writes an essay for a subject such as history, the historical content may be fine but the essay can suffer from poor spelling, punctuation and syntax. These deficits will create a negative impression of the author and could lead to the work being downgraded. Furthermore, students occasionally have to write essays and research papers, whatever the subject. It does not matter if the school is primary, secondary or higher educational; being able to communicate your ideas effectively in English is crucial. Teachers who refuse to accept poor English skills among their students are acting in their best interests in preparing them for life after school. Indeed, after graduation, those most successful in their careers will be those who have the best command of English when speaking or writing.

On the other hand, there are some teachers who would argue that teaching of their subjects would suffer as a result of having to focus too much on English. These teachers might feel that teaching English is best left for the English department and that the system is more efficient when teachers stick to their areas of expertise. They would argue that precious time is taken away from teaching a particular subject when teachers have to correct their students' English.

I would say that every teacher should be, to a certain extent, a teacher of English. However, an educational balance must be struck between teaching the particular subject at hand and improving English communication skills among students. English must not be neglected in any classroom. Only then can teachers prepare their students for the highly competitive world they will soon venture into.

6 Example (more difficult)

'Learning is the discovery that something is possible.' (Frits Peris)

Write a unified essay in which you discuss whether or not it is more effective for learners to discover facts and solve problems for themselves, rather than being taught. Start by discussing what you understand by the word effective.

Write 300 to 350 words.

For something to be effective it must be successful in producing the desired outcome or intended results. Education is effective if it has succeeded in imparting knowledge to students and those students are capable of applying that knowledge to the world around them.

Consider the topics of mathematics and algebra. The goal may be to teach students mental arithmetic, solve simple equations, work with money and handle basic maths in everyday life. If students can do this when they leave school, then the education they received has been effective.

Students could very well learn the same mathematical information by themselves through discovery; they can read books and study maths online. Solving problems and discovering facts independently is a great way to learn. It increases confidence and encourages self-reliance. Memory and recollection can be enhanced when the information has been discovered rather than being handed to you by someone else.

On the other hand, people who try to learn through discovery might find the topic harder to learn than if they had been taught at school. Important points may be learnt out of order, or missed out altogether. Frustration may set in when a problem appears insurmountable. You cannot just put up your hand to ask a question! Worse yet, the learner may become so discouraged by the process that he or she stops seeking that knowledge.

Arguably, teaching is a more effective form of education than learning by discovery. When an educator is teaching, he or she is typically following a well-planned process designed to help students absorb information with the least amount of confusion. Each lesson is built on the knowledge gained from the lessons before. This ensures a solid foundation on which students can continue to expand their knowledge in a given time frame. While the usefulness and value of learning by discovery should not be discounted, being taught will always be the more efficient way to learn.

7 Easy questions

1   Is fast-food to blame for obesity in society or is gaining too much weight the responsibility of the individual?

 What factors contribute to obesity?

 Why do you think that children are becoming obese?

 Give reasons for your answer; include any relevant experience or knowledge.

 Write at least 250 words.

2   Some people believe that unemployed people should be made to work for their welfare/benefit payments. Others, however, see this as cheap labour.

Discuss the possible advantages and disadvantages of making unemployed people take any job.

Do you believe that making unemployed people work is a good idea?

Write at least 250 words.

8 More difficult questions

1   'Education is what remains after one has forgotten everything he learned in school.' (Albert Einstein)

What do you think Albert Einstein meant by this statement?

Do you think that life experiences are more important than academic qualifications?

Write 300 to 350 words.

2   'Success is a journey, not a destination. The doing is often more important than the outcome.' (Arthur Ashe)

Write a unified essay that argues for and against the statement.

Do you believe that 'the doing' is more important than the outcome?

Write about 300 to 350 words.

3   'So long as we learn it doesn't matter who teaches us, does it?' (ER Braithwaite)

What do you understand by the above statement?

Develop arguments for and against.

Do you believe that the teacher matters?

Write about 300 to 350 words.

4   'A teacher is one who makes himself progressively unnecessary.' (Thomas Carruthers)

What does the author mean by this statement?

Discuss the implications of the question in the classroom.

Write about 300 to 350 words.

Part three

Reasoning

Chapter 20

Numerical, verbal and abstract reasoning tests

Introduction

The questions in this last chapter are typical of those found in psychometric test batteries. While standardized tests can help to identify strengths and weakness in numeracy and literacy in children, tests of these abilities in adults are an established part of selection and recruitment processes. Candidates may be graduates invited to a job interview, university applicants for popular courses such as medicine, dentistry, nursing, law and teaching, or people applying for non-graduate positions in organizations both large and small. Psychometric tests routinely check applicants' maths and English skills, in addition to any specific job skills (eg keyboard skills). Some tests include personality questionnaires, but these are not part of the ITT tests.

Numerical reasoning tests are rarely above CGSE maths standard (higher level) and almost all the number work necessary for the ITT tests has been covered in earlier chapters. However, emphasis is placed on logical thinking and sound reasoning. For these reasons, number sequences have been included as a new topic because they develop critical thinking skills, and increase candidates' confidence when faced with problems in different formats.

Verbal reasoning tests are similar to comprehension exercises in that you have a passage of text to read, but instead of a question you are given a statement that is either true or false; these tests have not been covered in earlier chapters. A wide range of word-based aptitude tests have been included as warm-up exercises to increase candidates' mental strategies with decision making.

Abstract reasoning tests, also known as diagrammatic reasoning or non-verbal reasoning tests, are a popular selection test because they look at your ability to think laterally and solve problems from different perspectives. You cannot rely on your existing knowledge to find the solution, but instead you need to 'think outside the box'. Questions of this type are comprised of diagrams that have an association or follow a pattern, similar to IQ tests. The learning in this chapter is new and includes warm-up exercises that will improve your analytical skills with diagrams. The chapter concludes with a set of exercises at a more difficult level to build confidence in tackling more complex abstract reasoning questions.

Number sequences

This section covers most of the different types of sequence (or pattern) you are likely to meet, including those using letters in place of numbers. You may be asked to predict the next number in a sequence of numbers or identify a missing number. The data series may involve an arithmetic or geometric progression, as explained below.

The arithmetic progression (AP)

This is a sequence of numbers where the difference between consecutive terms is constant. In an *arithmetic series* there is a *common difference* between the consecutive terms, as in the following examples:

Write down the next number in the following sequences:

i)   1, 2, 3, 4, 5, 6, 7, _____   (common difference = 1)   *Answer*   8

ii)   2, 4, 6, 8, 10, _____   (common difference = 2)   *Answer*   12

iii)   30, 35, 40, 45 _____   (common difference = 5)   *Answer*   50

In each case, the *common difference* between the numbers is found by subtracting any term from the following term. So, in the third example, $35 - 30$, $40 - 35$ and $45 - 40$ give a common difference of 5. We can then predict that the next term in the sequence is 45 plus the common difference of 5 equals 50.

Arithmetic progressions can involve fractions and decimals. Example: what is the next number in the following sequence?

$$\frac{1}{8} \ \frac{1}{4} \ \frac{3}{8} \ \frac{1}{2} - \qquad Answer \quad \frac{5}{8}$$

Here the numbers increase in steps of $\frac{1}{8}$.

For example: Write down the next number in the sequence:

0.9, 1.5, 2.1, 2.7 ___   *Answer*   3.3

Here the numbers increase by 0.6.

A variation on the basic arithmetic progression occurs when two patterns are combined; for example, 2, 3, 4, 5 and 25, 30, 35, 40 can be combined to give:

2, 25, 3, 30, 4, 35, 5, 45, ___ ___

In this example, the next two numbers are 6 and 50.

In another type of sequence, the difference between consecutive numbers no longer remains common, but increases (or decreases) for each change. For example:

1   2   4   7   11   16   _?   *Answer*   22
+1   +2   +3   +4   +5   +6

The same sequence can be represented in alphabetical form. Here, the question asks for the next letter in the sequence, as opposed to the next number. The alphabet is printed to help you:

ABCDEFGHIJKLMNOPQRSTUVWXYZ

For example, complete the sequence:

A   B   D   G   K   P   *Answer* V
(1   2   4   7   11   16)   (22)

The geometric progression (GP)

In a *geometric series* the *ratio* of consecutive numbers is constant; for example, the numbers double or halve in value:

1   2   4   8   16   32   64   128   256   512   ___?
(common ratio = 2 so multiply by 2 or double it)

96   48   24   12   6   _?   (common ratio = 0.50 = halve it)

20000   4000   800   160   32   __? (common ratio = 0.2 = multiply by 1/5)

1 Warm-up exercise: numerical reasoning

Calculate the common difference (check that your answer fits each pair of numbers in the sequence):

1   200   400   600   800   1000   *Answer* ....

2   300   350   400   450   *Answer* ....

3   65   59   53   47   41   *Answer* ....

4   7.8   6.1   4.4   2.7   *Answer* ....

Find the next number in the sequence:

5   3   5   7   9   11   *Answer* ....

6   1   4   7   10   13   *Answer* ....

7   12   18   24   30   *Answer* ....

8   55   49   43   37   *Answer* ....

9   40   30   21   13   *Answer* ....

10   2   14   4   16   6   18   *Answer* ....

11   10   16   21   27   32   *Answer* ....

12   22   19   20   17   18   15   *Answer* ....

13   2.8   3.4   4.0   *Answer* ....

ABCDEFGHIJKLMNOPQRSTUVWXYZ

In each of the following questions, find the next letter in the sequence:

14   A D G J __

15   Y W U S __

16   D I M P __

Find the missing number:

17   4   7   __   13   16   **19**   64   16   4   __ $\frac{1}{4}$

18   110   __   106   104   **20**   3.25   2.9   __   2.2

The geometrical progression (GP)

In this sequence, the *ratio* of consecutive numbers is constant, as per the examples described below. You need to multiply by this common ratio to find the next number in the sequence:

i)   2   4   8   16   32   64   128   __   (common ratio = 2; double)

ii)   48   24   12   6   3   1.5   __   (common ratio = 0.5; half)

iii)   5000   1000   200   40   8   __   (common ratio = 0.2; $\frac{1}{5}$)

As with arithmetic progressions, two geometric progressions can be combined. For example:

    2   48 4 24 8 12 16 6 32   ___

In another type of series the numbers increase by a constantly increasing ratio, rather than a constant ratio. For example:

    1 2 6 24 120   ___
    (ratio = ×2, ×3, ×4, ×5 etc)

In a variation of the above, the numbers are increased (or decreased) by a common ratio plus a constant number. For example:

    2   5   11   23   ___   (ie double and add 1)
    (2×2+1) (5×2+1) (11×2+1)

In the following example the numbers follow a sequence of squares:

    1   4 9 16 25   __
    (1^2 2^2 3^2 4^2 5^2)

In the following example the numbers appear random at first sight; however, pairs of numbers can be combined to give a pattern:

    12 13 12 14 11 16 10 __   (*Answer* 18)
    (25)   (26)   (27)   (28)

2 Easy questions: numerical reasoning

In each of the following questions, find the next number in the sequence:

1   1 3 9 27   *Answer* ....

2   1024 256 64 16   *Answer* ....

3   0.1 0.4 1.6   *Answer* ....

4   3 $\dfrac{1}{2}$ $\dfrac{1}{12}$ *Answer* ....

5   1 8 27 64   *Answer* ....

In each of the following questions find the missing number:

6   1 2 __ 8 16

7   1 3 7 __ 31

8   32 8 __ 0.5

9   2 6 12 __ 72

10   9 12 9 11 9 __

11   5 __ 45 135

12   12.15 __ 1.35 0.45

In each of the following questions find the two missing answers:

13   1 3 5 7 9 11 ___ ___

14   0.5 2 8 32 ___ ___

15   100 ___ ___ 73 66 60

16   1 10 28 55 ___ ___

17   90 60 30 0 ___ ___

18   55 45 35 25 35 ___ ___

19 $\dfrac{1}{4}$ $\dfrac{7}{32}$ $\dfrac{3}{16}$ ___ ___

20   10 $8\dfrac{3}{4}$ $7\dfrac{1}{2}$ ___ ___

21 $\dfrac{1}{16}$ $\dfrac{1}{4}$ $\dfrac{1}{12}$ $\dfrac{1}{3}$ ___ ___

22   4.25 3 2 1.25 ___ ___

23   BA DC FE HG ___ ___

24   ZYX WVU ___ ___

3 Easy questions: numerical reasoning

Find the next value in the following series:

1   10   8.75   7.5   6.25   *Answer* ....

2 $5\dfrac{1}{8}$ $3\dfrac{3}{4}$ $2\dfrac{3}{8}$ *Answer* ....

What are the next *two* answers in the following series?

3   −1 5 10 14 17 19   *Answer* ....

4   1 12 34 78   *Answer* ....

5   A D H M   *Answer* ....

6   PO NM LK   *Answer* ....

7   A C B D C E   *Answer* ....

What are the next *three* answers in the following series?

8   ZYX   WVU ____ ____ ____

9   A   C   B   D   F   E ____ ____ ____

10   A   D   G   J   M ____ ____ ____

11 $\frac{1}{32}$ is to $\frac{1}{8}$ as $\frac{1}{16}$ is to:

$\frac{1}{2}$	$\frac{1}{3}$	$\frac{1}{4}$	$\frac{1}{6}$	$\frac{1}{12}$
1	2	3	4	5

12   Write 400 mg as a fraction of 1 gram in its lowest terms.

13   Express 1100 ml in litres.

14   Work out 0.0214×400.

15   Work out $25.4 \div 0.04$.

16   What is 1 kg − 10 g − 100 mg in grams?

17   Divide 15 by 9 giving your answer to three decimal places.

18   There are 12 male students and 16 female students in a class. What is the ratio of males to females expressed as a fraction in its lowest terms?

4 More difficult questions: numerical reasoning

1   60 kg is to 100 kg as 18 kg is to: 10 kg   15 kg   24 kg   30 kg   36 kg
                                                             1   2   3   4   5

2   Water drips from a tap at a rate of 1 drop every 3 seconds. If the volume of water in each drop is 0.1 ml, calculate:

   a) how many drops there are per ml of water;

   b) how many drops there are per minute;

   c) the amount of water in litres going to waste if the tap is left to drip for 25 hours.

3   Multiply the following mixed number fractions:

   $3\frac{3}{16} \times 1\frac{7}{17} \times 1\frac{1}{3}$

4   Find x if $\frac{5x}{8} = \frac{x+1}{3}$

5   Find x if $\frac{2}{3} = \sqrt{4x}$

Related words

These questions test your ability to recognize words that are related in some way. There are several possibilities, including synonyms (similar meaning), antonyms (opposite meaning), analogous words (different but related) and classification (in the same group).

Antonyms are pairs of words that have opposite meanings. Examples are:

full   and   empty

entrance   and   exit

cautious   and   impulsive

optimistic   and   pessimistic

arrive   and   depart

often   and   seldom.

Synonyms are pair of words that have very similar meanings. Examples are:

circular   and   round

leave   and   depart

affectionate   and   loving

amaze   and   wonder

hate   and   detest

nice   and   pleasant.

Analogous words have different meanings and are yet related in some way. Examples are:

petrol   and   diesel

car   and   van

road   and   street

water   and   ice

house   and   castle.

The relationship between one pair of words can be used to predict a similar relationship between another pair of words. So for example:

metres relates to height as kilograms relates to ?

The answer is found by realizing that metres are a measure of height and kilograms are a measure of weight.

When the answer is less obvious or you have to choose the correct answer from a set of answers, it is important to identify the exact relationship. For example:

> morning is to day   as   evening is to night
>
> BUT morning is to light   as   evening is to dark

Relationships can also exist between objects and between people. For example:

> cone is to pine as acorn is to oak
>
> teachers are to pupils as doctors are to patients

Words which have something in common can be brought together, or classified in a group. Examples are:

> petrol, diesel, coal, gas, paraffin (all fuels)
>
> tennis, football, cricket, golf, rugby (all sports)
>
> house, mansion, cottage, apartment (all abodes).

Actions and feelings can also have common themes. For example:

> glide, hover, swoop, flutter, soar (all aerial motions)
>
> smell, sight, sound, taste, touch (all senses).

The question may ask you to find the 'odd man out' in a group of words, for example: hat, helmet, tie, cap. Here, all except 'tie' are always worn on the head.

5 Warm-up exercise: verbal reasoning

Choose *one* word that is the *opposite* of the other words:

#				
1	permit	allow	grant	forbid
	1	2	3	4
2	leave	depart	meet	abandon
	1	2	3	4
3	estimate	determine	guess	judge
	1	2	3	4
4	conceal	reveal	display	exhibit
	1	2	3	4

Choose *one* word that is *most unlike* the other four:

5 puzzle expound perplex confuse bewilder
    1   2   3   4   5

6 discharge emit egest digest excrete
    1   2   3   4   5

7 reactive passive inert sluggish inactive
    1   2   3   4   5

Choose *two* words, one from each bracket, that are *similar* to each other:

8 (climb, jump, walk) (run, fall, leap)
    1   2   3   1   2   3

9 (fair, dark, strong) (tricky, weak, honest)
    1   2   3   1   2   3

10 (reveal, request, disguise) (explain, conceal, discuss)
    1   2   3   1   2   3

11 (sarcasm, humour, funny) (irony, helpful, critical)
    1   2   3   1   2   3

12 (require, repudiate, resent) (resolve, reject, retract)
    1   2   3   1   2   3

13 (foremost, prohibit, disclose) (entreat, impugn, forbid)
    1   2   3   1   2   3

Find the relationship between the first two words and hence identify the word that relates to the *key* word:

14 Bow is to arrow as gun is to:
    rifle   shoot   aim   fire   bullet
    1   2   3   4   5

15 Sap is to plants as blood is to:
    humans   oxygen   circulation   life   mammals
    1   2   3   4   5

16 Dilute is to concentrate as transparent is to:
    weak   clear   strong   opaque   potent
    1   2   3   4   5

17 Exercise is to fitness as study is to:

success	diet	health	work
1	2	3	4

18 Thermometer is to temperature as barometer is to:

weather	wind	heat	pressure
1	2	3	4

Choose *one* word that does *not belong* with the other four:

19

daffodil	daisy	tulip	cauliflower
1	2	3	4

20

pine	oak	tree	beech	elm
1	2	3	4	5

21

student	teacher	lecturer	tutor
1	2	3	4

22

waist	wrist	ankle	elbow	knee
1	2	3	4	5

23

chew	munch	masticate	digest
1	2	3	4

24

pen	pencil	ruler	crayon	chalk
1	2	3	4	5

25

defile	devout	debase	denigrate
1	2	3	4

26

metre	mile	centimetre	inch	kilogram
1	2	3	4	5

27

carbohydrates	calories	fats	proteins	fibre
1	2	3	4	5

Rules and codes

Here, one word will be related to another word by a rule. The rule has then to be applied to another word to find the missing word. For example:

TAB, TABLE; CAB ?

The missing word is CABLE, because TABLE is formed by adding LE to the end of TAB, ie the rule is 'add LE' to the first word to make the second word.
   Another example is:

MEAN, MEAL; TRIED, TRIAL; DIET, ?

The rule to replace the last two letters at the end of the first word with AL, to give the second word of the pair, so the answer is DIAL.

Codes

Here you 'break the code' in order to find the word. Letters of the alphabet can be replaced by numbers or by other letters. For example:

If 1234 stands for PEAL, what does 4231 stand for?

To answer this type of question, you can write the letters of the word beneath the code, ie

	1	2	3	4	so:	4	2	3	1
gives:	P	E	A	L	gives:	L	E	A	P

Similarly, if FZVXQVK stands for BRITAIN, what does FQVX stand for?

	F Z V X Q V K	so:	F Q V X
gives:	B R I T A I N	gives:	B A I T

Similarly:

If OIJDL is HOUSE written backwards, what does ILDO stand for?

	O I J D L	so:	I L D O
gives:	E S U O H	gives:	S H O E

Any combination of letters or numbers can be used in the code. For example:

If XZ56 stands for TEAM, what does 6Z5X stand for?

Answer:	X Z 5 6	so:	6 Z 5 X
gives:	T E A M	gives:	M E A T

The code can be contained within two or more words. For example:

If UTP5 stands for DICE, and 7JY2 stands for LOAF,
what does 2T57U stand for?

Answer:	U T P 5	7 J Y 2
gives:	D I C E	L O A F

so: 2 T 5 7 U gives: F(2), I(T), E(5), L(7), D(U) = FIELD

Writing in code

This process is the reverse of solving a code. For example:

If PEAL is written as 1234, then PALE is written as 1342.

P E A L	so:	P A L E
1 2 3 4	is:	1 3 4 2 in code

Example: If BRILLIANT is written as 245775936, what is the code for BRAIN?

BRILLIANT	so:	BRAIN
245775936	is:	24953 in code

Other codes

If a code appears more difficult to solve at first sight, it may be because a simple rule exists between the code and the word with it. For example:

If ABCD is written as BCDE, what does IPVTF stand for?

We compare the code and the given letters, ie

A B C D
B C D E

and see that each of the four letters, ABCD, is found one place earlier in the alphabet than in the code BCDE,

so:	I P V T F
gives:	H O U S E

Similarly, if: ALIBI is written as 1 12 9 2 9, what is BAY written as?

A L I B I
1 12 9 2 9

Here, each letter of the alphabet corresponds with a number from 1 to 26, ie A = 1, B = 2, C = 3, D = 4, E = 5, ... Z = 26, so: BAY is 2 1 25.

6 Easy questions: verbal reasoning

Each of the following questions has a different rule or code. You must find the rule or solve the code. Complete the third pair:

1	SAP, SLAP;	FOG, FLOG;	FIT,
2	CREW, CROWS;	PET, POTS;	TEN,
3	TAB, BAT;	PEAL, LEAP;	ROUT,

The same second letter is missing from the following sets of three words. Find the letter that completes all three words:

4   TAIN, FET, WAP

5   CIP, FOAT, SOT

Solve the code:

6   If COMPLETE is 74986252 then POLE is ____

7   If LIZZIVQJY is DIFFICULT, then JQVIL is ____

8   If LJP stands for HAT, and 1245 stands for RICE written backwards, what does P1J2L15 stand for?

ABCDEFGHIJKLMNOPQRSTUVWXYZ

9   If COMPUTER is AMKNSRCP when written in code, then decode BGUM.

10   If ABRADE is 26 25 9 26 23 22 then WAY is ____

Text comprehension passages

English comprehension exercises form the basis of the more difficult verbal reasoning questions. You need to elicit facts from a passage of text. Accuracy is important when answering questions. It is important to identify answers that appear likely but cannot be concluded from the evidence presented in the text. One hint for preparation is to try to improve your reading speed without detracting from the understanding. The faster you can read the more time you will have for answering the questions. Another tip is to read each question first before scanning the passage to find key words linked to the question; finally reread the crucial text slowly and carefully.

A set of statements follows each passage. You have to decide whether the statements are true, false, or if the information pertaining to the statement has not been given. Use the following guidance when deciding between true, false, or not given responses:

True: the statement is clearly true, implied, can be deduced, or a reasonable conclusion to draw.

False: the statement is clearly untrue, a distortion of the facts or an unreasonable conclusion to draw.

Not given: the statement lacks sufficient information to say true or false with certainty. The answer choice 'Not given' can also be expressed as 'Can't tell'.

Knowing when to choose 'Can't tell' ('Not given') often presents candidates with the greatest challenge. As a guide, the answer is likely to be 'Can't tell' if there is uncertainty arising from the passage, but less likely to be 'Can't tell' if the uncertainty is introduced in the question.

The following warm-up exercises include questions that check your comprehension of the passage first, followed by statements that require a 'True', 'False' or 'Not given' response.

7 Warm-up exercise: Oxbridge

Although more than 60 miles separates the English cities of Oxford and Cambridge, their universities are linked by the term 'Oxbridge'. It is a name that can be applied to either university or to both. Traditionally, a degree from Oxbridge symbolized the pinnacle of academic achievement. Cities like Birmingham, Liverpool, Bristol and Manchester had their own universities, but these were not as esteemed as Oxbridge and received the derogatory title of 'Red Brick' universities. In recent times, the name Oxbridge has also become a derogatory term. Some people believe that Oxbridge is part of a social class system that favours the privileged few, born into wealth or high social status, at the expense of the less well-off, socially disadvantaged, though equally talented students. While Oxford and Cambridge encourage applications from candidates living in deprived areas, only 1 in 100 of the poorest university students in England received an Oxbridge education in 2010, far lower than the percentage of poorer students at the 'Red Brick' universities.

It cannot be disputed that a disproportionate number of Oxbridge entrants went to a fee-paying private school rather than to a free, state school. Nationally, only 1 in 15 pupils receive a private education, but nearly half of the students at Oxbridge went to a private school. Fee-paying schools have higher staff to pupil ratios, so their pupils receive more tuition and achieve higher grades than pupils from state sector schools. It is surely no surprise that pupils with an education paid for by their parents are about twenty times more likely to be offered a place at Oxbridge. There is no reason to believe that the best pupils in the state sector are any less intelligent that those in the private sector. Given the same educational opportunities and life circumstance, state-sector pupils can achieve equally high grades. The failure of the best pupils to achieve their potential can often be linked to a difficult home life, lack of motivation or peer pressure from less academic pupils. The attainment gap between university applicants from fee-paying and state schools is maintained when Oxbridge graduates are rewarded with the best-paying jobs, affording them the opportunity to send their own children to the best schools.

Looked at from the perspective of life chances, Oxbridge helps to maintain the 'social divide' where the rich get richer and the poor remain poor. Some people would argue that this 'Oxbridge advantage' is a symptom of social stratification rather than a cause of it. After all, parents cannot be blamed for wanting the best education for their children and Oxbridge cannot be held responsible for the failure of state schools to achieve the necessary grades. There is no evidence to suggest that Oxbridge selects students on anything other than merit. Indeed, in some subjects the application process includes admissions and aptitude tests that help to ensure a level playing field. Perhaps then, the state sector needs to encourage and support more applications from their best pupils to the best universities. Alternatively, the low aspiration of some pupils' parents may fail to drive gifted pupils onwards and upwards, or it may be that some pupils from an ordinary background are not comfortable with the idea of attending Oxbridge. Students who do not feel that they will 'fit in' at Oxbridge can still make the most of their talents by attending one of the country's many other excellent universities.

Inequalities in our society do not begin and end with Oxbridge. The best state schools are usually found in the most affluent areas. Injustices can arise when parents move house to secure a child's place at a more desirable school and in doing so they force another child into an underperforming school. Other, better-off parents, though not necessarily wealthy, will pay for their children to be educated at a private school to avoid having to move home. Either way, the desire to furnish one's children with the best possible education outweighs any sense of social justice. Unless remedies can be found for the disparity in educational standards in the pre-university years, it is unrealistic to believe that Oxbridge contributes in any substantial way to a lack of a social mobility. A place at Oxbridge should be seen as an opportunity for self-improvement and learning at the highest standards whatever one's social background.

Questions 1 to 4

Choose the correct letter A, B, C or D for the questions based on passage 1:

1   In the past Oxbridge has been seen as
   A an education only for those who can afford to pay for it.
   B the best universities in the country.
   C an opportunity for learning and self-improvement.
   D a place that represents the highest educational standards.

2   Everybody agrees that
   A too many Oxbridge students have had a private education.
   B there are higher staff to student ratios at Oxbridge.
   C life at Oxbridge is for those with money and social status.
   D Oxbridge applicants are rewarded with the best degrees.

3   In the passage, there is an example of how Oxbridge
   A encourages applications from pupils living in deprived areas.
   B has made the application process fairer.
   C selects students based on their exam results.
   D maintains its advantage over other universities.

4   In the passage, a link is made between a degree at Oxbridge and
   A inequalities in state schools.
   B a pupil's aspiration.
   C a successful career.
   D underperforming schools.

Questions 5 to 10

Do the following statements agree with the information given in the passage? Write:

True   if the statement agrees with the information;

False   if the statement contradicts the information;

Not given if there is no information on this.

5   The 'Oxbridge advantage' refers to better prospects in life.

6   Some Oxbridge candidates are offered a place whether they deserve it or not.

7   A student from an ordinary background is unlikely to do well at Oxbridge.

8   A lack of applications from state schools is the only reason for the low number of state-school students at Oxbridge.

9   The author does not believe that Oxbridge is responsible for social inequalities.

10 There are few good schools in the state sector.

Questions 11 to 14

Complete the summary below using the list of words, **A to K**, below:

The best schools tend to be found in the most **11** ____ areas. This leads to a lack of **12** ____ in the state school system. For example, some parents will move closer to a better-performing state school, or failing this, pay for them to be educated **13** ____ Children from poorer families can lose out, but the desire for one's children do well at school is more **14** ____ than any sense of social justice.

A deprived	**B** essential	**C** quality
D fairness	**E** applicants	**F** advantaged
G important	**H** privately	**I** prosperous
J selectively	**K** preferentially	**I** expensive

8 Warm-up exercise: Home-schooling

A   Introduction
    In developed countries, compulsory education is the norm for children aged from around 6 to 16. Even so, in most cases this does not mean that the child has to attend a school. Increasing numbers of parents are choosing to educate their children at home. In the UK it is estimated that up to 100,000 pupils are being taught in this way, which equates to about 1 per cent of the UK school population. In the United States, home education, or home-schooling as it is known, has reached unprecedented levels with approximately two million children, or 4 per cent of the compulsory age group, now receiving tuition at home. Parents cite various reasons for keeping their children away from school, ranging from a lack of satisfaction with the school environment to a wish to provide their own religious instruction. Home-schooling is a controversial issue surrounded by misgivings, with supporters emphasizing its benefits and detractors pointing to its limitations and risks.

B   The reasons why parents elect to educate their children at home are often linked to emotionally charged issues rather than rational arguments that reflect the pros and cons of home-schooling. Typically, a child is removed from a school following negative experiences, for example bullying, or exposure to bad influences such as drugs, discrimination, bad language, or falling in with the wrong crowd. Consequently, home-schooling is ardently defended by its proponents, who are not necessarily best placed to consider its downsides dispassionately. While the popularity of home-education is on the increase, it remains an oddity, associated more with problems at school rather than a positive decision to provide a real alternative.

C   While home-schooling of a child is unusual, learning from parents is not, so formal teaching at home can be regarded as an extension of the parents' normal role. However, education in the home environment can have its limitations, for example when there are gaps in the parents' knowledge in key subject areas such as fractions or algebra. Moreover, teaching is not merely the dispensing of knowledge acquired, but rather a skill that has to be taught, practised and mastered. Parents are not professional teachers and if the outcomes are poor then the parents can only blame themselves. Home-schooling is both time-consuming and demanding. Parents can lose out financially and socially when they are obliged to spend the entire day at home.

D   Lack of socialization is perhaps the main criticism of home-schooling. When children are taken out of school they cannot interact with other pupils or engage in school activities, including team sports. Later, a young person may find it difficult to integrate in ordinary social settings or lack the coping skills to deal with the demands of everyday life. Socialization outside the home can negate some of these shortcomings, bearing in mind that the home-educated child is likely to have more free time to engage in recreational activities. Indeed, it might be argued that the socialization experienced in the natural setting of a community is preferable to that within the confines of a school.

E   While home-schooling has its shortcomings, it also offers several advantages. Tuition is on a one-to-one basis so it can be personalized to meet an individual child's needs. There is no strict curriculum so the teaching can be readily adapted for those with special educational needs or learning disabilities. Children are allowed to develop at their own rate, and attention can be focused on subjects that a child enjoys or has a particular aptitude for. Parents can provide religious education and impart moral values consistent with their own beliefs, and they can also include subjects that may not be available in their local schools, for example Latin or archaeology. The timetable is entirely flexible, with no time wasted travelling to and from school, no lack of educational continuity when moving home, and no restrictions on when to take family holidays. It should come as no surprise that with all these benefits, home-educated children usually outperform their schooled counterparts academically. However, this is not conclusive proof of the effectiveness of home-schooling. Parents who home-school their children tend to be well educated and in a higher than average income bracket. Consequently, these parents are more likely to show an interest in their child's education, encouraging compliance with homework and offering support, meaning that the child would probably have performed well had they remained within the school system.

F   Parents who educate their children at home may choose to shun school completely. Despite this, local schools should offer parents and children support and guidance, extending access to school trips, library resources, recreational facilities, syllabus information, assessments and examinations. The future of home-schooling and its position in the education system are uncertain. Nevertheless, it is the duty of the state and the parents to ensure that home-educated children are given an education that affords them opportunities in life and equips them for the world of work.

Questions 1 to 5
Reasoning passage 2 has six paragraphs, A to F. Choose the correct heading for the paragraphs B, C, D, E and F from the list of headings given:

List of headings

i) Disadvantages	ii) Range of benefits	iii) Problems at school
iv) Main advantage	v) Overcoming a weakness	vi) No bad influences
vii) Introduction	vii) Shared responsibility	ix) Parents as teachers

Example: paragraph **A** = vii (Introduction)

1   Paragraph B

2   Paragraph C

3   Paragraph D

4   Paragraph E

5   Paragraph F

Questions 6 to 12

Do the following statements agree with the information given in the passage?

Write:

True   if the statement agrees with the information;

False   if the statement contradicts the information;

Not given   if there is no information on this.

6   In the United States there are four times as many home-educated children as in the UK.

7   There is much disagreement about the merits of home-schooling.

8   School children with disabilities are the most discriminated against.

9   There is nothing unusual about children learning from their parents at home.

10   Only children who attend school can be favourably socialized.

11   Pupils in school achieve higher grades than home-school children.

12   Children from better-off homes are more likely to complete their homework.

9 Easy question: religious education

Read the following text from a *Department for Children, Schools and Families* news article, then answer the questions that follow.

The new non-statutory programme of learning for primary religious education (RE) will give local authorities and schools more ideas and support on how to develop their local RE curriculum. This will also make RE teaching consistent with the rest of the new primary curriculum.

The programme of learning covers the study of Christianity and the five other principal religions – Buddhism, Islam, Judaism, Sikhism and Hinduism. It also recommends that pupils should be given the chance to learn about other religious traditions such as the Bahà'i faith, Jainism and Zoroastrianism, along with secular world views, like humanism, where appropriate.

Suggested topics for learning in primary RE lessons include: teaching about important festivals like Christmas, Easter, Pesach, Eid-ul-Fitr or Diwali, and learning about different forms of religious expression, like music, dance and art; and thinking about responses to ethical questions.

The guidance to all schools was updated to take into account significant changes in types of schools and the curriculum, and to set out the Government's views on the importance of RE in the early 21st century. It reflects the multi-ethnic and multi-faith nature of our society and the Government's emphasis on community cohesion, which schools have a new duty to promote.

The guidance also includes a greater emphasis on personalizing learning to help pupils to better develop socially and emotionally as well as in their studies; information on how different types of schools should provide RE; more guidance on how to link RE to other subjects; and case studies on how teachers can work with local faith groups and use RE to support community cohesion.

Questions 1 to 5
Do the following statements agree with the information given in the passage?

True   if the statement agrees with the information;

False   if the statement contradicts the information;

Not given if there is no information on this.

1   The new RE curriculum will cover five main religions.

2   The new RE guidelines will not be set out in law.

3   Most students will have a religious faith.

4   Schools will be obligated to foster good community relations.

5   Students will not have to answer questions on moral issues.

10 Easy question: school uniforms

Read the following extract from a *Department for Children, Schools and Families* article, and then answer the questions that follow.

Ministers said that schools needed to publicize financial support available for parents, and do everything they can to keep school costs down.

A Cost of Schooling 2007 report looked at uniforms, PE kit, trips, lunch, travel, stationery, extra classes and voluntary contributions. The report found that the average total annual cost for primary schools was £684 and in secondary schools was £1195 – overall a rise of £34 or 4 per cent since the previous report in 2003 (after adjustment for inflation). Eight in ten parents were happy with the costs of school – down from 90 per cent in 2003, but almost four in ten found it very difficult or quite difficult to meet the overall costs, up from 27 per cent in 2003. Low income families, especially those not working, found it most difficult.

Ministers said they were concerned that one in six parents had to buy all items of uniform and PE kit from a designated sole supplier or their school itself – despite clear government guidance that setting up exclusive uniform deals with retailers disadvantages low income families. The mandatory Schools Admission Code (SAC) places a statutory duty on all schools to ensure that admissions policies do not disadvantage any children. One-third of parents who buy clothes from sole suppliers were unhappy with the costs compared to just 9 per cent of those who were free to buy clothes anywhere.

Ministers also said it was unacceptable and unlawful for any school to ask for compulsory contributions towards school trips which were part of the normal curriculum – as some schools admitted they do. Three-quarters of all parents said they were asked to pay for the entire cost of a school trip – over nine out of ten paid the full cost of the residential trips and 68 per cent for day trips. Only 38 per cent knew that they should not pay for trips during school hours.

Questions 1 to 5

Do the following statements agree with the information given in the passage?

True   if the statement agrees with the information;

False   if the statement contradicts the information;

Not given   if there is no information on this.

1   The cost of schooling has risen by 4 per cent in 4 years.

2   At least six in ten parents found it easy to meet the overall cost of school.

3   Uniform deals with sole suppliers disadvantage poorer families.

4   Parents should not have to contribute towards any school trips.

5   Over 90 per cent of parents paid the full cost of residential trips.

11 More difficult question: our guarantee

Read the following extract from a *Department for Children, Schools and Families* press notice, and then answer the questions that follow.

The 'Teachers' Guarantee' goes alongside the Government's pupil and parent guarantees. The 'Pupil Guarantee' sets out what every young person should get during their school careers, including one-to-one or small group tuition for pupils falling behind at primary and the first year in secondary school. The 'Parent Guarantee' includes tougher Home–School Agreements, so every family under-stands their responsibilities. For example, Heads can take action against parents who take their children on holidays in school time, or fail to address bad behaviour, and parents are entitled to have their views listened to about how their child's school is doing.

The 'Teachers' Guarantee' includes new powers for teachers to tackle bad behaviour and dispels the myth that schools should have 'no contact policies'. The 'guarantee' also ensures that teachers get dedicated time to plan and prepare lessons and time to assess pupils' progress so teachers can continue to deliver high quality lessons; support from the wider school workforce means that teachers are not tied up with photocopying and other administration tasks but in the class-room inspiring every child to learn.

The 'Pupil Guarantee' includes guaranteed one-on-one English and maths tuition for primary pupils starting Key Stage 2 below expectations and unlikely to make two levels of progress by age 11; statutory proper choice of high quality learning routes at 14; guaranteed education or training at 16 and 17; specialist outside help for health and social problems; and a clear say on how their school is doing and how it can be improved.

The 'Parent Guarantee' includes: clearer information about their child's school performance; help and advice on choosing schools; high quality advice about career and subject choices; closer involvement about their child's progress through access to a named personal tutor or teacher, with regular face-to-face and secure, online information about their child's attainment, progress, Special Educational Needs, attendance and behaviour in secondary schools.

Behaviour expert and headteacher Sir Alan Steer has been monitoring progress on improving behaviour in schools since 2008 and concludes in his latest report that behaviour in schools is still good and continues to improve. His reports have provided invaluable insight into behaviour policies in schools, which has led to stronger, clearer guidance for teachers on how they can make better use of their powers.

Questions 1 to 6

Do the following statements agree with the information given in the passage?

True   if the statement agrees with the information;

False   if the statement contradicts the information;

Not given   if there is no information on this.

1   All pupils who fall behind in secondary school should get personal or small-group tuition.

2   Parents are expected to comply with Home–School Agreements.

3   Pupils are expected to reach Key Stage 4 by age 11.

4   Teachers must not use physical force to stop disruptive behaviour.

5   Parents can expect clear information about university courses.

6   Pupils' behaviour in school was not improving before 2008.

12 More difficult question: world's language

The pre-eminence of English language globally may be under threat. Mandarin is the dominant language of China and there are one billion speakers of Mandarin in the world compared with 330 million English speakers. If economic trends continue then China is set to dominate world trade and quite possibly global communication with it. It is perhaps a surprising fact, then, that learning English is growing fast in China, which has more English Language teaching jobs than in any other country. The International English Language Testing System (IELTS) is taken by more than one million people worldwide and last year 300,000 tests were taken in China. This fact belies the notion that the number of speakers of a language determines its status. English is set to remain influential because it is seen as the language of academia, diplomacy and especially science, with 95 per cent of scientific publications worldwide written in English.

The language of English is robust because it has great literary heritage and prestige (though notably so did Latin, which has declined), and it is the main language of the prosperous and stable nations of the West. The use of English became widespread following the expansion of the British Empire and it remains the primary language of at least 45 countries and the official language of many international organizations. Above all else, it is the popularity of English as second and third language that confirms its status as the world's language. Globally there are almost three times as many non-native speakers of English as native speakers. The number of people who can speak English in India is second only to the number in the United States and more people can speak English (Pidgin) in Nigeria than in the UK.

Questions 1 to 7

Do the following statements agree with the information given in the passage?

> **True** if the statement agrees with the information;
>
> **False** if the statement contradicts the information;
>
> **Not given** if there is no information on this.

1 Globally, almost three times as many people speak Mandarin as speak English.

2 There is a vague conception that the status of a language increases in accordance with how many people speak it.

3 There are more English Language teaching jobs in the United States than in China.

4 The IELTS is more popular in China than in any other country.

5 The language of Latin was displaced by English in more affluent countries.

6 More people speak English outside the UK than in the UK.

7 In terms of English speakers, four countries are ranked as follows: United States, India, Nigeria, UK (highest number first).

Non-verbal reasoning (diagram tests)

We have already seen how words can be related to each other using analogies. For example:

> UP is to DOWN as LEFT is to RIGHT

Relationships of this type can also be depicted in diagrams, for example:

 is to ↓ as ← is to →

Relationships can also exist between shaded and unshaded shapes, for example:

 is to as is to

(fully shaded, half shaded; fully shaded, half shaded)

Questions involving diagrams may be designed to test your powers of observation, for example: Spot the odd man out in the following diagrams:

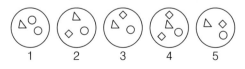

The answer is no. 4 because the other circles contain three shapes.

Shapes or objects can be rotated about a specific point (known as the centre of rotation) to produce an image. In the example shown below, a smiling face has been rotated about its centre. There are four main angles that you should be familiar with when rotating. These are as follows:

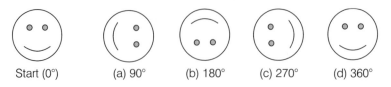

| Start (0°) | (a) 90° | (b) 180° | (c) 270° | (d) 360° |

a)   rotation through 90 degrees (90°) – also known as a right-angle rotation, or rotation through a quarter circle (clockwise);

b)   rotation through 180 degrees (180°) – through half a circle;

c)   rotation through 270° (three-quarter circle);

d)   rotation through 360° (full circle – back to the start).

Symmetry

A shape has rotational symmetry if it can be rotated about its centre and still looks the same. Some shapes can be rotated through several angles and still look the same, in which case they have more than one 'order of rotational symmetry'. Examples of rotational symmetry are shown below.

| 2 orders | 3 orders | 4 orders | 5 orders | 1 order |

A shape has reflection (or line) symmetry if it appears identical, or symmetrical, either side of a line, like a mirror image. Shapes can have one, two, or more lines of symmetry. For example:

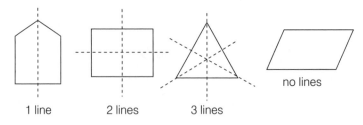

| 1 line | 2 lines | 3 lines | no lines |

Notice that a rectangle has two lines of reflection symmetry; the diagonals are not lines of symmetry (except for a square). If you are unclear about this, try folding an A4 sheet across the diagonal.

Example. Which shape does not belong with the other four?

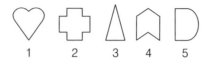

The shapes numbered 1, 2, 3, 4 and 5 have only one line of symmetry so the answer must be shape number two, the square cross, which has four lines of symmetry.

The following exercises will test your ability to see patterns, identify relationships, spot differences and complete sequences.

13 Warm-up exercise: abstract reasoning

One of the numbered drawings to the right of the first three completes the statement. Choose *one* drawing which best completes the statement:

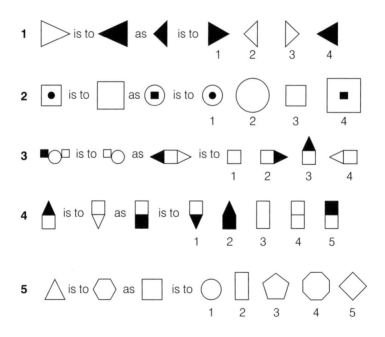

Find the *odd one out* in each group of shapes:

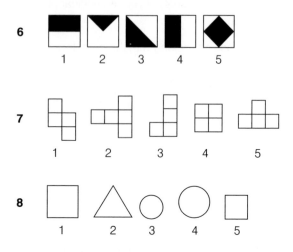

6
1   2   3   4   5

7
1   2   3   4   5

8
1   2   3   4   5

14 Easy questions: abstract reasoning

Identify the *odd one out* in each group of shapes:

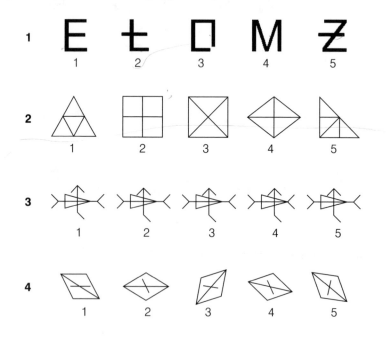

1
1   2   3   4   5

2
1   2   3   4   5

3
1   2   3   4   5

4
1   2   3   4   5

Choose *one* drawing that best completes the statement:

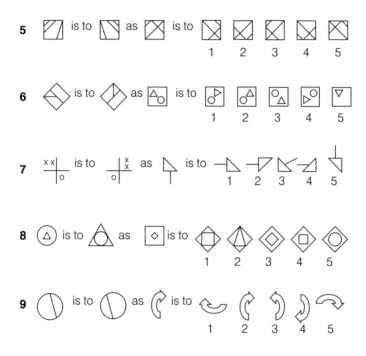

Which of the five numbered drawings comes next in the series?

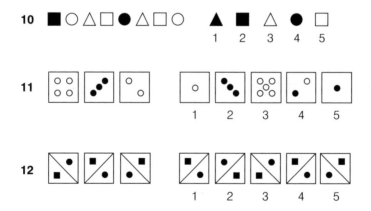

Choose *one* drawing that best completes the statement:

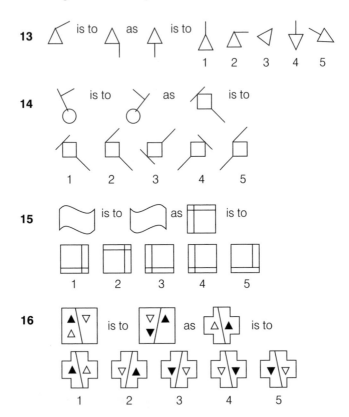

15 More difficult questions: abstract reasoning

In the following questions you are presented with two sets of shapes, set A and set B, followed by a series of five test shapes. Your goal is to identify whether the test shapes belong with Set A, Set B, or neither set. If a test shape belongs with both sets then the answer is neither set by definition. You have a one-in-three chance of choosing the correct answer (choose A, B or neither).

Your success depends on your ability to characterize the pair of sets as a first step; matching the test shapes is easy once you have understood the rationale for the choice. Each set contains six boxes of shapes which are sufficient to characterize the set. The distinguishing feature is normally straightforward. However, additional shapes can be included in the boxes to 'muddy the waters', slowing the process down. You need to be able to look beyond the extraneous shapes to identify the features in common.

Examples of Set A and Set B characteristics

Set A	Set B
White shapes	Black shapes
Solid lines	Broken lines
Squares	Circles
Straight lines	Curved lines
Straight and curved lines	Straight or curved lines
Right angles	Acute angles
Rotational symmetry	No rotational symmetry
Line of reflection	No line of reflection
Sequence	Altered sequence
Size	Altered size
Shaded shapes	Unshaded shapes
Diagonal pattern	Horizontal/vertical pattern
Shapes divided in two	Shapes divided in three
Shapes within shapes	Shapes outside of shapes
Same number of sides	Different number of sides
Divided into triangles	Divided into rectangles
Drawn without lifting the pen	Drawn by lifting the pen
Shapes with a right-angle	Shapes with no right angle

It is not possible to remember all the likely rationales. However, you can still adopt a methodical approach to finding the answer. This could include checking the set boxes for simple repeats, patterns and for symmetry between the shapes (reflections and rotations).

When answering questions of this type it is tempting to study the test shapes in the hope that these will provide additional insights. Unfortunately this is only likely to waste precious time. The candidate is urged to ignore the answer test shapes and to study the two sets, one at a time, in an attempt to characterize and distinguish between them. For example, one set may contain only rectangular shapes and the other set only circular shapes.

You should find the questions relatively easy to answer once you have identified the distinguishing features of each set correctly. If you have problems choosing an answer then look at the sets again to see if you need to change the rationale.

Examples

For the two examples that follow, the rationale is given below to clarify the process. Match each of the test shapes to Set A, Set B or neither set (if neither or both). Be careful, as marks are lost through careless mistakes.

Question 1:   Set A – shapes drawn with straight lines
                      Set B – shapes drawn with curved lines

Question 2:   Set A – shapes divided into triangles
                      Set B – shapes divided into squares/rectangles

Hint: the rationales for many of the following questions can be found in the list of characteristics on the previous page.

Example 1: straight lines and curved lines

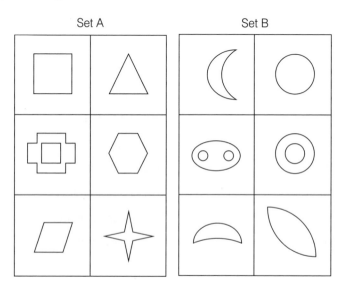

Text shapes 1 to 5:

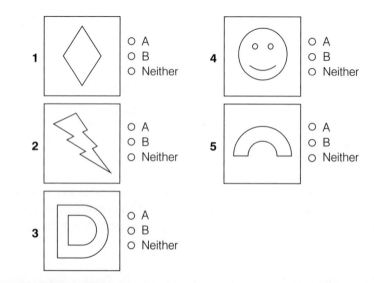

Example 2: divided into triangles; divided into squares/rectangles

Set A   Set B

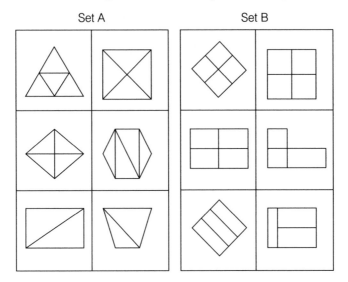

Text shapes 6 to 10:

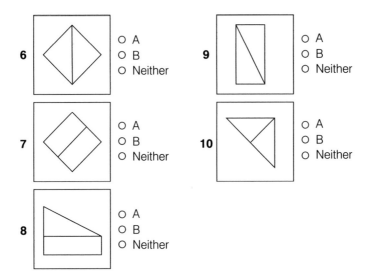

16 More difficult question

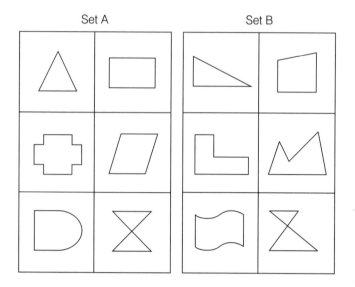

Set A   Set B

Text shapes 11 to 15:

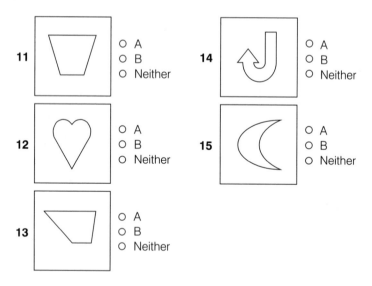

11
  ○ A
  ○ B
  ○ Neither

12
  ○ A
  ○ B
  ○ Neither

13
  ○ A
  ○ B
  ○ Neither

14
  ○ A
  ○ B
  ○ Neither

15
  ○ A
  ○ B
  ○ Neither

17 More difficult question

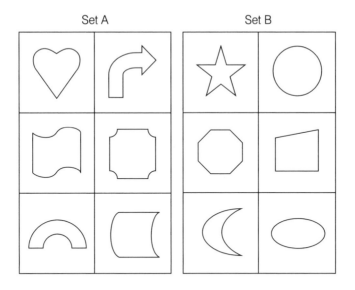

Set A   Set B

Text shapes 16 to 20:

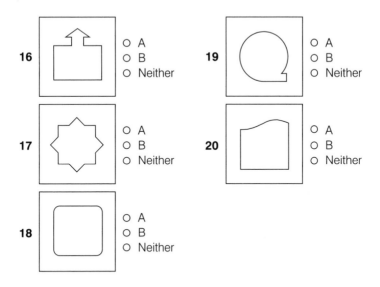

16
- ○ A
- ○ B
- ○ Neither

17
- ○ A
- ○ B
- ○ Neither

18
- ○ A
- ○ B
- ○ Neither

19
- ○ A
- ○ B
- ○ Neither

20
- ○ A
- ○ B
- ○ Neither

18 More difficult question

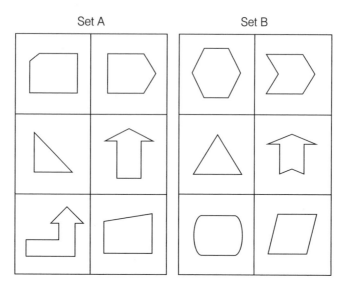

Set A   Set B

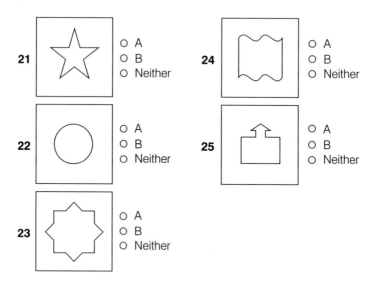

Text shapes 21 to 25:

21   ○ A   ○ B   ○ Neither

22   ○ A   ○ B   ○ Neither

23   ○ A   ○ B   ○ Neither

24   ○ A   ○ B   ○ Neither

25   ○ A   ○ B   ○ Neither

19 More difficult question

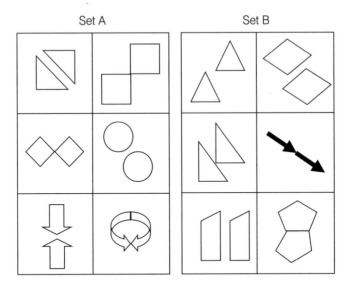

Set A   Set B

Text shapes 26 to 30:

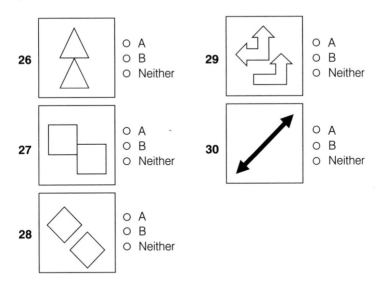

26   ○ A
      ○ B
      ○ Neither

27   ○ A
      ○ B
      ○ Neither

28   ○ A
      ○ B
      ○ Neither

29   ○ A
      ○ B
      ○ Neither

30   ○ A
      ○ B
      ○ Neither

20 More difficult question

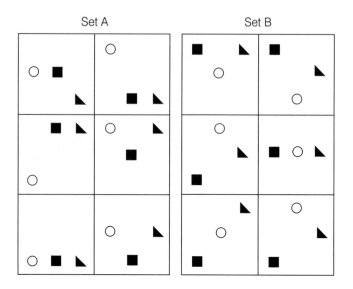

Text shapes 31 to 35:

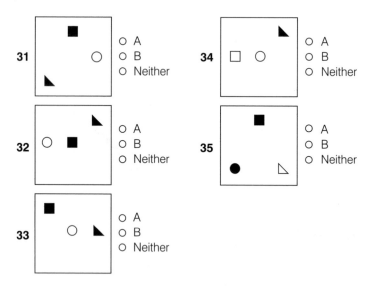

21 More difficult question

Set A   Set B

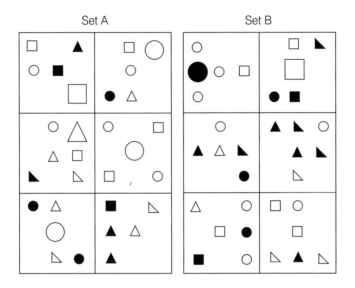

Text shapes 36 to 40:

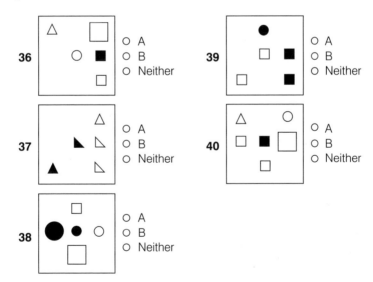

22 More difficult question

Set A   Set B

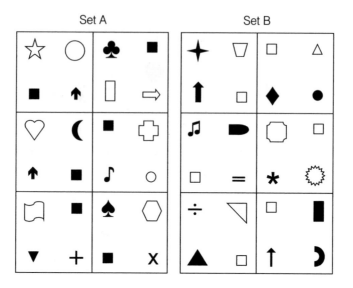

Text shapes 41 to 45:

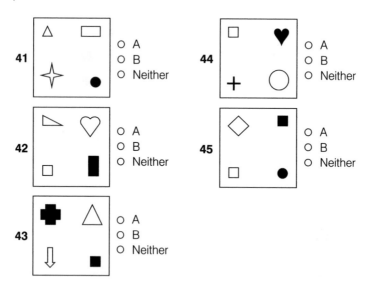

41   ○ A
        ○ B
        ○ Neither

42   ○ A
        ○ B
        ○ Neither

43   ○ A
        ○ B
        ○ Neither

44   ○ A
        ○ B
        ○ Neither

45   ○ A
        ○ B
        ○ Neither

23 More difficult question

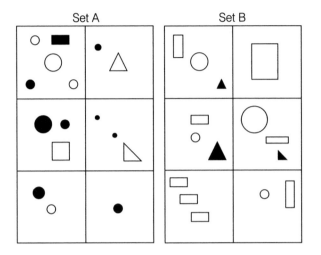

Text shapes 46 to 50:

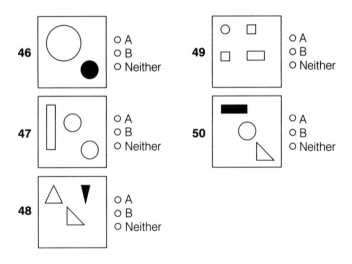

24 More difficult question

Set A   Set B

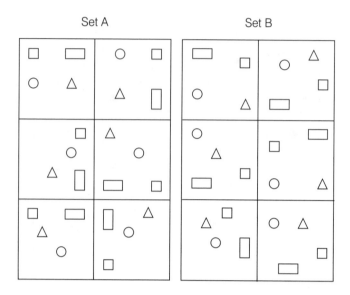

Text shapes 51 to 55:

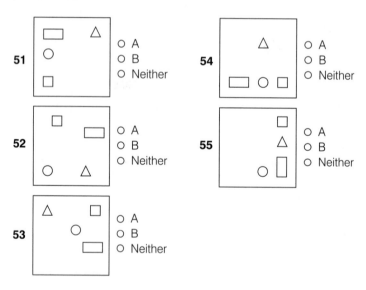

51
- ○ A
- ○ B
- ○ Neither

54
- ○ A
- ○ B
- ○ Neither

52
- ○ A
- ○ B
- ○ Neither

55
- ○ A
- ○ B
- ○ Neither

53
- ○ A
- ○ B
- ○ Neither

25 More difficult question

Set A   Set B

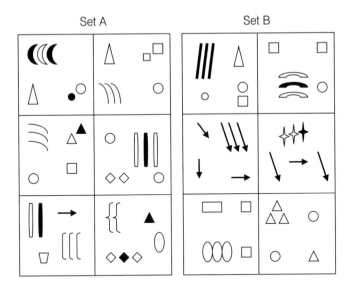

Text shapes 56 to 60:

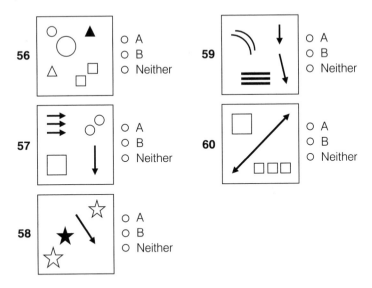

Part four

Answers with explanations

Chapter 1 Arithmetic

1 Warm-up exercise

1 two thousand five hundred and forty

2 four tens or 40

3 zero units

4 zero hundreds

5 10000

6 500000

7 95432

8 23459

9 fifty one million two hundred and forty thousand

10 50 000 000 and fifty million

2 Warm-up exercise

1 496

2 213

3 3147

4 617

5 429

6 252

7 214

8 311

3 Warm-up exercise

1 63

2 96

3 132

4 120

5 92

6 450

7 95

8 99

9 300

10 1000

4 Warm-up exercise

1	806	**5**	425
2	2528	**6**	10000
3	1200	**7**	5511
4	5080	**8**	5082

5 Warm-up exercise

1 280

2 6000

3 490

4 4900

5 49000

6 Warm-up exercise

1	4	**5**	410
2	62	**6**	59
3	113	**7**	244
4	53	**8**	125

7 Warm-up exercise

1	30	**6**	6
2	31	**7**	38
3	44	**8**	67
4	45	**9**	61
5	20	**10**	206

8 *Warm-up exercise*

1	14	**7**	9
2	13; (method: 10 + 3 = 13)	**8**	56
3	10	**9**	10
4	2; (method: 8 − 6 = 2)	**10**	6
5	14; (method: 10 + 4 = 14)	**11**	6
6	9	**12**	14; (method: 9 + 6 − 1 = 14)

9 *Warm-up exercise*

1	24	**7**	39
2	2	**8**	57
3	5	**9**	3
4	44	**10**	36
5	10; (method: 10 × 1 = 10)	**11**	5
6	21	**12**	9000

10 *Warm-up exercise*

1 1, 2, 3, 6

2 1, 2, 5, 10

3 1, 2, 4, 8, 16, 32

4 1, 2, 3, 5, 6, 9, 10, 15, 18, 30, 45, 90

5 1, 2, 4, 5, 10, 20, 25, 50, 100, 125, 250, 500

6 8; (method: factors of 24: 1, 2, 3, 4, 6, 8, 12, 24; factors of 32: for ease, look for the highest factors of 24 first and see if they fit 32: not 24, not 12; 8 × 4 = 32, so 8 is the highest common factor of 24 and 32).

7 15; (method: factors of 75: 1, 3, 5, 15, 25, 75; factors of 120; for ease look for the highest factors of 120 first and see if they are common to 75: not 120, not 60, not 30, not 20; 15 × 8 = 120, so 15 is the HCF of 75 and 120.)

8 4; (method: factors of 12: 1, 2, 3, 4, 6, 12; factors of 500; for ease look for the highest factors of 12 that will fit 500; not 12, not 6, 4 × 125 = 500, so 4 is the HCF of 12 and 500.)

11 Warm-up exercise

1   2×3

2   $2 \times 3 \times 5$

3   $3 \times 3 \times 7$

4   $2 \times 2 \times 3 \times 5 \times 7$

5   $3 \times 3 \times 3 \times 3$

6   $2 \times 2 \times 2 \times 3 \times 3 \times 3$

7   $5 \times 5 \times 5$

8   $7 \times 7 \times 7$

12 Warm-up exercise

1   2, 4, 6, 8

2   12, 24, 36, 48

3   20, 40, 60, 80

4   25, 50, 75, 100

5   100, 200, 300, 400

Method for questions 6 to 10: look at the larger number and find the lowest multiple that the smaller number will divide into.

6   6; (method: 3 goes twice and 2 goes three times)

7   60; (method: 20 goes three times and 12 goes five times)

8   72; (method: 36 goes twice and 24 goes three times)

9   150; (method: 75 goes twice and 30 goes five times)

10   200; (method: 40 goes five times and 25 goes eight times)

13 Warm-up exercise

1   70

2   130

3   0

4   140100

5   140000

6   hundred

7   ten

8   hundred

9   thousand

10   ten thousand

14 Warm-up exercise

1   2022

2   610

3   195

4   2592

5   108

6   64

7	5625	**22**	150
8	148473	**23**	1, 2, 4, 5, 10, 20
9	10500	**24**	2, 5
10	250000	**25**	1, 2, 3, 6, 7, 14, 21, 42
11	11	**26**	2, 3, 7
12	39	**27**	6, 12, 18, 24, 30, 36
13	224	**28**	9, 18, 27, 36, 45, 54
14	72	**29**	18
15	130	**30**	100
16	20	**31**	250
17	100	**32**	60
18	16	**33**	ten
19	54	**34**	hundred
20	80	**35**	thousand
21	26		

Chapter 2 Understanding fractions

1 Warm-up exercise

1 $\dfrac{1}{2}$ **6** $\dfrac{3}{5}$

2 $\dfrac{3}{4}$ **7** $\dfrac{1}{10}$

3 $\dfrac{1}{3}$ **8** $\dfrac{19}{20}$

4 $\dfrac{5}{9}$ **9** $\dfrac{2}{3}$

5 $\dfrac{2}{3}$ **10** $\dfrac{2}{5}$

2 Warm-up exercise

1 $\dfrac{7}{8}$

2 $\dfrac{5}{6}$

3 $\dfrac{11}{10}$

4 $\dfrac{5}{4}$

5 1

6 $\dfrac{1}{2}$

7 $\dfrac{2}{3}$

8 $\dfrac{1}{5}$

3 Warm-up exercise

1 15

2 12

3 16

4 $\dfrac{7}{15}$

5 $\dfrac{11}{12}$

6 $\dfrac{3}{16}$

4 Warm-up exercise

1 $\dfrac{3}{4}$

2 $\dfrac{2}{3}$

3 $\dfrac{2}{5}$

4 $\dfrac{7}{8}$

5 $\dfrac{16}{50}$

6 $\dfrac{75}{1000}$

5 Warm-up exercise

1   $\dfrac{2}{27}$

2   $\dfrac{8}{45}$

3   $\dfrac{16}{63}$

4   $\dfrac{2}{27}$

5   $\dfrac{3}{500}$

6   $\dfrac{1}{2}$

7   $\dfrac{1}{3}$

8   $\dfrac{1}{4}$

9   $\dfrac{2}{27}$

10 $\dfrac{3}{10}$

6 Warm-up exercise

1   $\dfrac{2}{3}$

2   $\dfrac{3}{5}$

3   $\dfrac{3}{4}$

4   $\dfrac{1}{2}$

5   $\dfrac{5}{6}$

6   $\dfrac{2}{5}$

7   $\dfrac{1}{25}$

8   $\dfrac{1}{200}$

9   $\dfrac{3}{20}$

10 $\dfrac{2}{3}$

7 Warm-up exercise

1   $\dfrac{25}{12}$

2   $\dfrac{1}{6}$

3   $\dfrac{15}{8}$

4   $\dfrac{1}{2}$

5   $\dfrac{49}{10}$

6   $\dfrac{8}{3}$

7   $\dfrac{20}{9}$

8   $\dfrac{50}{1}$

8 *Warm-up exercise*

1 $\dfrac{7}{4}$ **6** $\dfrac{119}{100}$

2 $\dfrac{11}{2}$ **7** $\dfrac{6}{5}$

3 $\dfrac{17}{6}$ **8** $\dfrac{12}{5}$

4 $\dfrac{27}{8}$ **9** $\dfrac{7}{5}$

5 $\dfrac{67}{10}$

9 *Warm-up exercise*

1 $4\dfrac{1}{2}$ **4** $16\dfrac{2}{3}$

2 $5\dfrac{3}{4}$ **5** $5\dfrac{1}{4}$

3 $5\dfrac{1}{3}$ **6** $12\dfrac{1}{2}$

10 *Warm-up exercise*

1 $2\dfrac{1}{2}$ **5** $7\dfrac{1}{2}$

2 $4\dfrac{1}{2}$ **6** $\dfrac{3}{20}$

3 $3\dfrac{1}{2}$ **7** $\dfrac{1}{36}$

4 $10\dfrac{4}{5}$ **8** $\dfrac{1}{24}$

11 *Warm-up exercise*

1 $1\frac{2}{5}$

2 $4\frac{1}{4}$

3 8

4 30

5 64

6 72

7 $\frac{5}{8}$

8 $\frac{1}{4}$

9 $\frac{9}{20}$

10 $\frac{1}{2}$

11 $\frac{1}{4}$

12 $\frac{1}{12}$

13 2

14 $3\frac{3}{5}$

15 $\frac{1}{400}$

12 *Warm-up exercise*

1 3

2 14

3 8

4 8

5 8

6 5

7 3

8 1

9 5

13 *Warm-up exercise*

1 50p:10p

2 £12:£18

3 95:30

4 300:200:100

5 125:100:25

14 Warm-up exercise

1 $\frac{2}{20}; \frac{5}{20}; \frac{11}{20}; \frac{19}{20}$ (method: no calculation necessary: smallest numerator = smallest fraction when the denominators are the same)

2 $\frac{5}{125}; \frac{5}{25}; \frac{5}{20}; \frac{5}{10}$ (method: no calculations necessary: largest denominator = smallest fraction when the numerators are the same)

3 $\frac{2}{3}$ and $\frac{6}{9}$ (method: these are the only equivalent fractions)

4 $\frac{1}{5}; \frac{12}{40}; \frac{5}{10}; \frac{11}{20}$; (method: convert all to 40ths: 8/40; 12/40; 20/40; 22/40)

5 3 (method: find the equivalent fraction: $\frac{6}{10}$ cancels to $\frac{3}{5}$ by dividing the top and bottom by 2)

6 12 (method: find the equivalent fraction: $\frac{2}{3} = \frac{8}{12}$; noting that 8 is 4 × 2 and 12 is 4 × 3)

7 $\frac{1}{5}$

8 $\frac{3}{5}$

9 $\frac{1}{6}$

10 $\frac{7}{20}$

11 $\frac{5}{6}$

12 $\frac{3}{5}$

13 $\frac{1}{4}$

14 $\frac{2}{9}$

15 $\frac{1}{32}$; (method: change $\frac{1}{8}$ to $\frac{4}{32}$; then $\frac{5}{32} - \frac{4}{32} = \frac{1}{32}$)

16 $\frac{1}{12}$; (method: convert to twelfths then subtract: $\frac{9}{12} - \frac{8}{12} = \frac{1}{12}$)

17 $\frac{3}{8}$

18 $\frac{1}{6}$

19 $\dfrac{1}{20}$; (method: dividing by 6 is the same as multiplying by one-sixth, so re-write $\dfrac{3}{10} \div 6$ as $\dfrac{3}{10} \times \dfrac{1}{6}$ which is $\dfrac{3}{60}$ or $\dfrac{1}{20}$)

20 6

21 $\dfrac{1}{3}$

22 $3\dfrac{6}{7}$

23 $\dfrac{9}{2}$

24 3

25 $2\dfrac{1}{2}$

26 40

27 50

28 $6\dfrac{1}{8}$

29 $\dfrac{5}{7}$; (method: (easiest) change 4 wholes to sevenths $4 \times \dfrac{7}{7} = \dfrac{28}{7}$ then subtract from $\dfrac{33}{7}$ to leave $\dfrac{5}{7}$; (alternative): convert $\dfrac{33}{7}$ to a mixed number to give $4\dfrac{5}{7}$, then subtract 4 to leave $\dfrac{5}{7}$)

30 $\dfrac{5}{7}$

31 15:21

32 14

33 i)   14
 ii)   18

15 *Easy questions*

1 37 (method: (easiest) one-fifth means divided by 5, change 185 into 200 − 15 because these numbers are easy to work with, then 185 ÷ 5 becomes (200 ÷ 5) − (15 ÷ 5) = 40 − 3 = 37 (by mental arithmetic without using paper); (alternative): double both numbers so that 185 ÷ 5 becomes 370 ÷ 10 = 37; you can double 185 as follows: 185 × 2 is (200 × 2) − (15 × 2) = 400 − 30 = 370).

2 180 (method: (most obvious) 1 out of 5 (one-fifth) do not own a phone, so we need $900 \div 5$; change this to $1800 \div 10$ (double both numbers) because these numbers are easier to work; $1800 \div 10 = 180$; (alternative): use the decimal equivalent of one-fifth; $1/5 = 0.2$; then $0.2 \times 900 = 2 \times 90 = 180$).

3 62 (method: (most obvious) find the fraction who are girls and multiply this fraction by the sample size (120); total pupils $= 290$ boys $+ 310$ girls $= 600$ pupils; fraction girls $= 310/600$ (no need to cancel at this time); now multiply this fraction by the sample of 120: $\frac{310}{600} \times 120 = 310 \times \frac{1}{5} = 62$; (alternative): same method except multiply by the decimal equivalent of one-fifth in the final step: $310 \times 0.2 = 31 \times 2 = 62$).

4 $\frac{1}{8}$; (method: for every pupil that takes single science, seven take double-science: $1 + 7 = 8$; so 1 in 8 takes single science and 7 out of 8 take double science, which expressed as fractions is $\frac{1}{8}$ single and $\frac{7}{8}$ double).

5 $5\frac{1}{7}$; (method: change the mixed number to an improper fraction, invert it and multiply it by the six: $6 \div 1\frac{1}{6}$ becomes $6 \div \frac{7}{6} = 6 \times \frac{6}{7} = \frac{36}{7} = 5\frac{1}{7}$).

6 $\frac{5}{9}$; (method: change both mixed numbers into improper fractions, invert the second fraction and multiply the two fractions: $2\frac{1}{3} \div 4\frac{1}{5} = \frac{7}{3} \div \frac{21}{5} = \frac{7}{3} \times \frac{5}{21} = \frac{1}{3} \times \frac{5}{3} = \frac{5}{9}$).

7 12; (method: the exact number of teachers is given by $172 \div 15$; however we need a whole number of teachers, so the answer must be the smallest *multiple* of 15 that lies above 172: $10 \times 15 = 150$; $11 \times 15 = 165$; $\underline{12 \times 15 = 180}$; $13 \times 15 = 195$).

8 $\frac{5}{8}$; (method: write 90 out of 144 as a fraction and cancel the top and bottom by dividing by small *primes*: $\frac{90}{144} = \frac{45}{72} = \frac{15}{24} = \frac{5}{8}$ (the small primes are 2 and 3)).

9 11; (method: calculate the total passengers (pupils + teachers) on all three coaches, then work out the *ratio* and the proportional parts: 40 (full) + 40 (full) + 30 (three-quarters full) = 110 passengers; teacher–pupil ratio = 1:9, so we have $1 + 9 = 10$ 'parts', and we want one part: $110 \div 10 = 11$; $11 \times 1 = 11$ teachers; (and $110 - 11 = 99$ pupils; ratio is correct at 1:9)).

10 i) false; (method: chemistry boys to girls $= 36:32 = 9:8$; false)
ii) true; (method: physics girls to boys $= 10:45 = 2:9$; true)
iii) false; (method: biology boys to girls $= 30:50 = 3:5$; false)

11 i) 4 kg; (method: find the total parts (the whole) and then the fraction that is fruit; multiply the fraction that is fruit by the weight of jam (12 kg): total parts = 2 (fruit) + 1 (water) + 3 (sugar) = 6 parts for the whole, and we needs 2 parts fruit = 2/6 or one-third fruit; 1/3 × 12 kg = 4 kg fruit).

    ii) 10 grams; (method: total parts = 75 + 3 + 2 = 80 parts and we want 2 parts yeast = 2/80 or one-fortieth; 1/40 × 400 gram loaf = 10 gram yeast).

12 30; (method: find the total parts and work out the fraction that are teachers then find the whole; pupil-teacher ratio = 9:1; total parts = 9 + 1 = 10; teachers = 1 part = 1/10 = 3 teachers; we have one part and we need to find ten parts, so we multiply by 10 to give 30 people (3 teachers and 27 pupils).

13 i) 1:4; ii) 5:4; (method: i) teachers to girls = 4:16 = 1:4; boys = 40 − 16 − 4 = 40 − 20 = 20 boys; ii) boys to girls = 20:16 = 5:4)

14 104; (method: (easiest) work out the total number of parts and how many pupils are <u>in one-part</u>, then multiply these two figures together to give the total number of pupils. 6:10 = 16 parts in total and we have 6 parts, where 6 parts equals 39 girls, so 1 part = 39 ÷ 6 = <u>6 ½ pupils per part</u>. Total parts = 16 so total pupils = 16 × 6 ½ = 96 + 8 = 104 pupils (39 girls and 104 − 39 = 65 boys).

16 More difficult question

a) i) 2/9;

    ii) 42;

b) 4:5

    (Method: find the total parts then find the fractions: maths (M) to English (E) to science: M:E:S = 4:6:8; total parts = 4 + 6 + 8 = 18 parts;

a) i) fraction from maths (M) = 4/18 = 2/9

    ii) mark in English = 6/18 × 126 = 1/3 × 126 = 126 ÷ 3 = 42;

b) mark in science (S) = 8/18 × 126 = 4/9 × 126 = 4/3 × 42 = 4 × 14 = 56; mark in maths (M) = 42 so mark in English (E) = 126 − 56 − 42 = 126 − 98 = 28; and M + E = 42 + 28 = 70; S: M+E = 56:70 = 4:5.

Alternative: for a) ii and b) calculate the *marks per part* as a first step; this allows you to multiply by the number of parts you have rather than work out the fractions. Marks per part = 126 ÷ 18 parts = 7 marks per part, so in a) ii) (English (E)) we have 6 parts, then 6 parts × 7 marks per part = 42 marks; similarly, mark in science (S) = 8 × 7 = 56.)

Chapter 3 Understanding decimals

1 Warm-up exercise

1   22.5

2   0.275

3   0.02

4   200.075

5   102.375

2 Warm-up exercise

	(a)	(b)	(c)	(d)
1	0.025	0.25	0.3	2.5
2	0.05	0.075	0.08	1.0
3	3.025	3.04	3.05	3.25
4	6.02	6.026	6.20	6.22
5	10.01	10.011	10.101	10.11

3 Warm-up exercise

1   1589.7

2   769.2105

3   3172.9

4   0.0175

5   17170.3

6   25

7   5.8

8   100

4 Warm-up exercise

1   8.96

2   20.02

3   0.3553

4   0.00544

5   1.5015

6   160

7   3

8   100.2

9   2032

10   14000

5 *Warm-up exercise*

1   1.7

2   12.45

3   8.03125

4   170; (method: 6.8 ÷ 0.04 becomes 680 ÷ 4 = 340 ÷ 2 = 170)

5   33.3; (method: 9.99 ÷ 0.3 becomes 99.9 ÷ 3 = 33.3)

6   11.1; (method: 5.55 ÷ 0.5 becomes 55.5 ÷ 5 = 11.1)

7   6; (method: 3.6 ÷ 0.6 becomes 36 ÷ 6 = 6)

8   60; (method: 9 ÷ 0.15 becomes 900 ÷ 15 = 300 ÷ 5 = 60)

9   1.2; (method: 1.44 ÷ 1.2 becomes 14.4 ÷ 12; we know that 12 × 12 is 144 from the times tables so 12 × 1.2 must be 14.4; answer 1.2)

10   62500; (method: 125 ÷ 0.002 becomes 125000 ÷ 2 = 62500)

11   20000; (method: 1000 ÷ 0.05 becomes 100000 ÷ 5 = 2000)

12   0.016

6 *Warm-up exercise*

1   2; (method: 6.08323 to 2 d.p.: 6.08323 = 6.08)

2   1; (method: 0.385426 to 5 d.p.: 0.385426 = 0.38543)

3   4; (method: 0.754 to 1 d.p. = 0.754 = 0.8)

4   3; (method: 7.956 to 2 d.p. = 7.956 = 7.96)

7 *Warm-up exercise*

1   4.17; (method: 25 ÷ 6 = 4.166 = 4.17 to 2 d.p.)

2   14.2857; (method: 100 ÷ 7 = 14.28571 = 14.2857 to 4 d.p.)

3   10.4; (method: 3.45 × 3 = 10.35 = 10.4 to 1 d.p.)

4   44; (method: 14.5 × 3 = 43.5 = 44 to 0 d.p.)

5   81; (method: 325 ÷ 4 = 81.25 = 81 to the nearest whole number)

6   160; (method: 1279 ÷ 8 = 159.8 = 160 to the nearest whole number)

7   66; (method: 655 ÷ 10 = 65.5 = 66 to the nearest whole number)

8 17; (method: 100 ÷ 6 = 16.6 = 17 to the nearest whole number)

9 3; (method: 73 ÷ 22 = 3.3 = 3 to the nearest whole number)

10 133; (method: 400 ÷ 3 = 133.3 = 133 to the nearest whole number)

8 Warm-up exercise

1 $\frac{3}{5}$; (method: 0.6 = 6/10 = 3/5)

2 $\frac{3}{4}$; (method: 0.75 = 75/100; cancel by 25 to give = 3/4)

3 $\frac{5}{8}$; (method: 0.625 = 625/1000 = 125/200 = 25/40 = 5/8; cancelling by 5s)

4 $\frac{9}{10}$; (method: 0.9 = 9/10)

5 $\frac{1}{1000}$; (method: 0.001 = 1/1000)

6 $\frac{2}{25}$; (method: 0.08 = 8/100 = 4/50 = 2/25)

7 $\frac{19}{20}$; (method: 0.95 = 95/100 = 19/20)

8 $\frac{7}{4}$; (method: 1.75 = 175/100; cancel by 25 to give = 7/4)

9 $\frac{19}{8}$; (method: 2.375 = 2375/1000; cancel by 25; 2500 is 25 × 100; we have 2375 which is 125 less, or 5 × 25 less, so 2375 ÷ 25 = (100 − 5) = 95; 1000 ÷ 25 = 40; so we have 95/40 = 19/8; alternative method: keep cancelling by 5s until you reach 19/8)

9 Warm-up exercise

1 0.3; (method: 3/10 = 0.3)

2 0.25; (method: 1/4 = 0.25)

3 0.4; (method: 2/5 = 4/10 = 0.4; alternative method to dividing 2.0 by 5)

4 1.25; (method: 5/4 = 5.00 ÷ 4 = 1.25)

5 0.12; (method: 3/25 = 12/100 (multiplying top and bottom by 4) = 0.12; alternative method to dividing 3.00 by 25)

6 0.875; (method: 7/8 = 7.000 ÷ 8 = 0.875)

7 0.85; (method: 17/20 = 85/100 (multiplying top and bottom by 5) = 0.85; alternative method to dividing 17.00 by 20)

8 0.105; (method: 21/200 = 10.5/100 (dividing top and bottom by 2) = 0.105)

9 1.8; (method: 27/15 = 9/5 (cancelling by 3) = 18/10 (multiplying top and bottom by 2) = 1.8; alternative method to dividing 27.0 by 15 (or 9 by 5))

10 *Warm-up exercise*

1 a); (method: 12 × 5 = 60; nearest is a) 58.69)

2 b); (method: 24 ÷ 10 = 2.4; nearest is b) 2.51)

3 d); (method: 100 × half = 50, divided by 25 = 2; nearest is d) 1.95)

11 *Warm-up exercise*

1	1589.7	**5**	0.000175
2	3172.9	**6**	0.0000058
3	17170.3	**7**	33
4	769.2105	**8**	91

9 2400; (method: 120 ÷ 0.05 = 12000 ÷ 5 (multiply both numbers by 100 to remove the decimal point); 12000 ÷ 5 = 24000 ÷ 10 = 2400)

12 *Easy questions*

1 2.025; (method: count along from 2.020 to 2.025 (midway) to 2.030; alternative: add the two numbers and divide by 2: (2.02 + 2.03) = 4.05; 4.05 ÷ 2 = 2.25)

2 $\frac{9}{20}$; (method: 0.45 = 45/100; cancel top and bottom by 5 to give 9/20)

3 0.025; (method: 25 thousandths = 25 ÷ 1000 = 0.025)

4 2.1; (method: 0.7 + 0.2 × 7 = 0.7 + 1.4 (seven 2s are 14 with one decimal place); 0.7 + 1.4 = 2.1)

5 0.92; (method (easiest): convert 23/25, meaning 23 twenty-fifths, to one-hundredths by multiplying the top and bottom by 4 to give: 92/100 = 0.92)

13 More difficult questions

1   7.58; (method: 45.5 ÷ 6 = 7.583 = 7.58 to 2 d.p.)

2 $\frac{4}{5}$; (method: 0.3 × 0.4 ÷ 0.15 = 3 × 4 ÷ 15 = 12/15 = 4/5)

3 $\frac{7}{8}$; (method: 0.875 = 875 ÷ 1000; divide both numbers by 25 to give 35/40 then divide by 5 again to give = 7/8; note that 875 is 125 less than 1000 or 5 × 25 less, so 875 ÷ 25 = (40 − 5) = 35; alternative method: keep cancelling by 5s until you reach 7/8)

4   0.5 or ½; (method: 2.7 ÷ (0.45 × 12) = 270 ÷ (45 × 12) = 90 ÷ (45 × 4) = 2 ÷ (4) = 0.5 or ½)

5   1.6; (method: 1/0.625 = 1000/625; cancel by 25, (noting that there are four 25s per hundred so 625 = 25 × 25) to give 40/25 = 8/5 = 1.6)

Chapter 4 Calculating percentages

1 Warm-up exercise

1 $\frac{1}{5}$; 0.2

2 $\frac{1}{4}$; 0.25

3 $\frac{1}{10}$; 0.1

4 $\frac{3}{4}$; 0.75

5 $\frac{9}{10}$; 0.9

6 $\frac{9}{20}$; 0.45

7 $\frac{7}{20}$; 0.35

8 $\frac{11}{50}$; 0.22

9 $\frac{1}{50}$; 0.02

10   90; (50% = 50/100 = ½; ½ × 180 = 180/2 = 90)

11   60; (30% = 30/100 = 3/10; 3/10 × 200 = 600/10 = 60)

12   25; (10% = 10/100 = 1/10; 1/10 × 250 = 250/10 = 25)

13   12.5; (5% = 5/100 = 1/20; 1/20 × 250 = 250/20 = 12.5)

14   125; (62.5% = 62.5 ÷ 100 = 0.625; 0.625 x 200 = 125)

15   25; (2½% = 2.5% = 2.5 ÷ 100 = 0.025; 0.025 × 1000 = 25)

16   50%

17   1.5%

18   75%

19	105%	**25**	85%
20	100%	**26**	50%
21	0.5%	**27**	40%
22	20%	**28**	60%
23	36%	**29**	25%
24	12.5%	**30**	25920

2 Easy questions

1	35%	**7**	62%
2	$\dfrac{3}{8}$	**8**	20%
3	12%	**9**	19
4	55%	**10**	42
5	20%	**11**	30%
6	60	**12**	25

Chapter 5 Aspects of algebra

1 Warm-up exercise

1	8	**11**	-9
2	4	**12**	-1
3	-4	**13**	-4
4	-8	**14**	-10
5	4	**15**	-4
6	-14	**16**	77
7	-18	**17**	-10
8	3	**18**	-10
9	-1	**19**	-100
10	-9	**20**	-20

2 *Warm-up exercise*

1	12	**7**	−3
2	−12	**8**	3
3	−18	**9**	−4
4	18	**10**	4
5	−36	**11**	−4
6	40	**12**	2

3 *Warm-up exercise*

1 $x = 3$

2 $x = 7$

3 $x = 15$

4 $x = 12$

5 $x = 9$

6 $x = 5 + y$

7 $x = 3$; (method: $2x + 3x = 5x$; $5x = 15$, so $x = 3$)

8 $x = 12$; (method: $9x - 4x = 67 - 7$; $5x = 60$, so $x = 12$)

9 $x = 22$

10 $x = 4$

11 $x = -9$; (method: $32 - 14 = -2x$; $18 = -2x$; then $2x = -18$ and $x = -9$; note: to arrive at $2x = -18$ from $18 = -2x$ you can either move each term to the opposite side of the equation and change its sign, or multiply both term by minus one).

12 $x = 48$

13 $x = \frac{3}{2}(25 - y)$; (method: multiply each term by 3 and divide each term by 2 to leave find x: $\frac{2}{3}x = 25 - y$ becomes $2x = 3(25 - y)$ then $x = \frac{3}{2}(25 - y)$.

4 *Warm-up exercise*

1 $x = \dfrac{8}{3}$; $(3(x + 2) = 14$; method: $3x + 6 = 14$; $3x = 8$ so $x = \dfrac{8}{3})$

2 $x = 3$; $(5(x - 1) = 10$; method: (easiest): divide both sides by 5 to give $x - 1 = 2$, so $x = 3)$

3 $x = 2$; $(3(x - 4) + 2(x + 3) = 4$; method: $3x - 12 + 2x + 6 = 4$; then $5x - 6 = 4$ so $5x = 10$ and $x = 2)$

4 $x = 1 - 2y$; $(2(x - y) + 3(x + 4y) - 5 = 0$; method: $2x - 2y + 3x + 12y - 5 = 0$; $5x + 10y - 5 = 0$, so $x + 2y - 1 = 0$ (dividing by 5), alternative: $x + 2y = 1)$

5 $7x^2 + 20xy + 6y^2 = 0$; $(7x(x + 2y) + 6y(x + y) = 0$; method: $7x^2 + 14xy + 6xy + 6y^2 = 0$; then $7x^2 + 14xy + 6xy + 6y^2 = 0$, so $7x^2 + 20xy + 6y^2 = 0)$

6 $12x^2 + 16$; (method: $\dfrac{4}{5}x(15x + 20)$; method: divide by the 5 as a first step to give: $4x(3x + 4)$, then expand to give $12x^2 + 16)$

5 *Warm-up exercise*

1 $2(x + y)$ **6** $5(2x^2 - 7)$

2 $5(2x - 3y)$ **7** $3x(3 - 4x)$

3 $2y(x + 1)$ **8** $7y(6x - 5)$

4 $6(2x + 3y)$ **9** $8(x + 3)$

5 $2x(x + 2)$

6 *Easy questions*

1   i)   31; (method: $3 \times 9 - (-4) = 27 + 4 = 31)$

       ii)   50; (method: $2(9 + (-4))^2 = 2(5)^2 = 2(25) = 50)$

2   i)   60; (method: $S = 0.5(5 + 15)6 = 0.5 \times 20 \times 6 = 60)$

       ii)   7.5; (method: $S = 0.5(0 + 30)0.5 = 0.5 \times 30 \times 0.5 = 15 \times 0.5 = 7.5)$

3   4; $(3x + 2y = 44$; method: $3 \times 12 + 2y = 44$; $36 + 2y = 44$; $2y = 8$; $y = 4)$

4 -3; $(2x - 3y = 29$; method: $2 \times 10 - 3y = 29$; $20 - 3y = 29$; $-3y = 9$; $y = -3)$

5   2; $(5x(y + 1) = 200$; method: $5x(19 + 1) = 200$; $5x(20) = 200$; $5x = 10$; $x = 2)$

6 $\frac{6}{5}$; $(11x - 6(x - 2) = 18$; method: $11x - 6x + 12 = 18$; $5x = 6$; $x = \frac{6}{5}$)

7   4; $(3x(2x - 5) - 5x(x - 3) = 16$; so: $6x^2 - 15x - 5x^2 + 15x = 16$; $x^2 = 16$; $x = 4$)

8 $x = 5, y = \frac{5}{2}$; (method: substitute the value of x in a) into b) so that we have only x term in b). We have a) $x = \underline{2y}$; b) $3x + \underline{2y} = 20$; so c) $3x + x = 20$; $4x = 20$; $x = 5$. To find y go back to equation a) and insert $x = 5$; $x = 2y$, so $5 = 2y$ and $y = 5/2$)

9 $x = 3, y = \frac{7}{2}$ (method: (easiest) subtract equation a) from equation b) to eliminate the y terms: b) $4x + 2y = 19$

a) $x + 2y = 10 - 3x + 0 = 9$

so $x = 3$; substitute $x = 3$ into b) $x + 2y = 10$ to give $3 + 2y = 10$; $2y = 7$; $y = \frac{7}{2}$)

10   14 (method: make the number x and write an equation for it from the information given: $20x + 45 = 325$; divide by 5: $4x + 9 = 65$; $4x = 56$; $x = 14$)

7 More difficult questions

1 $\frac{8}{3}$; (method $\frac{4}{5x} = \frac{3}{10}$; cross-multiply (this is a quick way of multiplying both sides by the common denominator of 50x and cancelling); cross-multiplying (diagonally) gives: $4(10) = 3(5x)$; or $4 \times 10 = 3 \times 5x$; then $40 = 15x$; then $8 = 3x$ and $x = 8/3$)

2   a)   (method: write the numbers of students who get off as fractions of S)
  i)   ½ S; (first stop: half get off: ½ S or S/2)
  ii)   ¼ S; (second stop: half of the remaining half, or one-quarter: ¼ S or S/4)
  iii)   ¼ S; (third stop: remainder get off, which is the final quarter: ¼ S or S/4)
  b)   48 students (method: final stop: 12 get off which is one-quarter; $12 \times 4 = 48$)

3   a)   i)   VC = 0.2x; (method: the variable cost (VC) is 20p per distance x, measured in quarter miles so VC = 20x pence; pounds VC = 0.2x
  ii)   C = 2.40 + 0.2x; (method: C = FC + VC = 2.40 + 0.2x)
  iii) $x = 5C - 12$; (method: start with C = 2.40 + 0.2x and multiply all the terms by five to get 1x: $5C = 12 + 1x$; rearrange to give $x = 5C - 12$; some methods of working will give $x = \frac{C - 2.40}{0.2}$ which is the same thing.

b)   8.5; (method: find x by substituting £10 for C in the equation $x = 5C - 12$; then $x = 5 \times 10 - 12 = 50 - 12 = 38$; note that x is in quarter miles so we can only travel $38 \div 4 = 19 \div 2 = 8.5$ miles for £10).

Chapter 6 Money and exchange rates

1 Warm-up exercise

£ \\ coin	£1	50p	20p	10p	5p	2p	1p
22p			1			1	
45p			2		1		
632p	6		1	1		1	
882p	8	1	1	1		1	
99p		1	2		1	2	
£1.74	1	1	1			2	
£2.65	2	1		1	1		
£3.79	3	1	1		1	2	
£4.50	4	1					
£5.96	5	1	2		1		1

2 Easy questions

1   £100; (method: $20 \times £7.50 - £50 = £150 - £50 = £100$)

2   £59.50; (method: $1 \times £9.95 - 40 = £99.50 - £40 = £59.50$)

3   75p; (method: $£10 - £1.85 \times 5 = £10 - £9.25 = £0.75$)

4   £13.90; (method: $£6950 \div 500$; double to $£13900 \div 1000 = £13.90$)

5   11; (method: $£100 \div £8.75$; use multiplications instead of division: $£8.75 \times 10 = £87.50$, add on £8.75 to get £96.25, so we can buy $10 + 1 = 11$ books (with £3.75 left over))

6   £13.60; (method: per book: 100 pages $\times$ 6 p $= £6$; $+ 30$ p $+ 25$p $\times 2 = £6.80$)

7   £80; (method: £50 + (200 ÷ 10) litres × £1.50 per litres
      = £50 + 20 × £1.50 = £50 + £30 = £80)

3 Easy questions

1   S3200; (method: £800 × ¼ = £200; £100 = S1600 so £200 = S3200)

2   SF225; (method: £600 × ¼ = £150; £2 = 3SF so £1 = 1.5SF, then £150 =
      150 × 1.5SF = 100 × 1.5 + 50 × 1.5 (half again) = 150 + 75 = 225)

3   €125; (method £720 × 0.15 = £720 (0.1 + 0.05) = £72 + £36 (half again)
      = £108; £108 × 1.16€/£ = 108(1 + 0.1 + 0.06)€ = 108 + 10.80 + 6.48 =
      €125.28)

4   2100Zl; (method: £375 × 0.2Zl/£ × 28 = 375 ÷ 5 × 28 = 75 × 28 = 300 × 7;
      multiply the 75 by 4 to give 300 (easy number) and divide the 28 by 4 to get
      7 to maintain the balance; 300 × 7 = 2100)

5   £77; (method: 1R = £0.07 so 1100R = 1100 × £0.07 = 11 × £7 = £77)

6   £2300; (method: €2645 ÷ €1.15/£; we can double to 5290 ÷ 2.3, then
      multiply by 10 to get 52900 ÷ 23, followed by long division)

7   £1 = $1.6; (method: we want £1 in dollars; we have £150 = $250 so divide
      both sides by 150 to get £1 = 250/150 = 5/3 (cancel by 50) = 1.6 dollars)

8     $592.5; (method: £400 − £5 = £395; £395 × $1.50/£ = 395 (1 + 0.5) =
      395 + 197.5 (half again) = 400 + 192.5 (add 5 and subtract 5) = $592.5)

9   a) 975K; (method: a £1 = 9.75K so £100 = 975K)
      b) £10000; (method: £100 = 975K (from a)) so £10000 = 975 × 100 =
          97500K)

10   £50; (method: £250 ÷ £10 = 25; then euros = 25 × 8.8 or 100 × 2.2 = €220;
      spends €176 leaving 24 + 20 (by adding back) = €44; we have €8.8 = £10
      (given this) so €88 = £100 and finally €44 = £50)

4 More difficult questions

1   £325; (method: fee of £10 = £3.50 + 2% × number of pounds; so the fee
      is £6.50 = 2% of pounds exchanged; multiply both sides by 50 to give:
      £16.50 × 50 = 100% of pounds (the number of pounds), so 100% pounds
      = £6.50 × 50; = £3.25 × 100 (half the £6.50 and double the 100 to
      maintain the balance); ie £325; check £325 × 2% = £6.50; the exchange
      rate is not used for this calculation).

2   a)   €445; (method: £1 = €1.15 so £300 = 300 × €1.15 = 3 × €115
                (shifting the decimal point to the other number) = €445)
        b)   £500; (method: £1 = $1.5, so £10 = $15, £50 = $75 so $750 = £500)
        c) $300; (method: change i) euros into pounds, then ii) pounds into
                dollars;
                i)   £1 = €1.15 so £100 = €115, so €230 = £200;
                ii)   £1 = $1.5 so £200 = $300)
        d)   1€ = $1.30; (method: from c) €230 = $300; €23 = $30;
                €1 = $30 ÷ 23 = $1.30)

Chapter 8 Indices and roots

1 Warm-up exercise

1   49 (method: 7 × 7)

2   14400 (method: 120 = 12 × 10, so 120 squared = 12 squared × 10
        squared = 144 × 100 = 14400)

3   0.16 (method: 0.4 = 4 ÷ 10, so 0.4 squared = 4 squared ÷ 10 squared =
        16 ÷ 100 = 0.16)

4   6.25 (method: 2.5 = 25 ÷ 10; so 2.5 squared = 25 squared ÷ 10 squared
        = 625 ÷ 10 = 6.25)

5   3 1/16 (method: 1 3/4 = 7/4; 7/4 squared = 7 × 7 ÷ (4 × 4) = 49/16 = 3
        1/16)

6   5 4/9 (method: 2 1/3 = 7/3; 7/3 squared = 7 × 7 ÷ (3 × 3) = 49/9 = 5 4/9)

2 Warm-up exercise

1   216 (method: 6 × 6 × 6 = 216)

2   8000 (method: 20 × 20 × 20 = 2 × 2 × 2 × 10 × 10 × 10;
        = 8 × 1000 = 8000)

3   0.027 (method: 0.3 × 0.3 × 0.3 = 3 × 3 × 3 ÷ (10 × 10 × 10) = 27 ÷
        1000 = 0.027)

4   1.331 (method 1.1 × 1.1 × 1.1 = 11 × 11 × 11 ÷ (10 × 10 × 10);
        = 121 × 11 ÷ 1000; = 1331 ÷ 1000 = 1.331)

5   3 3/8 (method: 1½ × 1½ × 1½ = 3/2 × 3/2 × 3/2 = 27/8 = 3 3/8)

3 *Warm-up exercise*

1   6 (method: square root 36 = root 6 × 6 = 6)

2   3/5 (method: square root 9 / square root 25 = root 3 × 3 / root 5 × 5 = 3/5)

3   7/2 or 3 ½ (method: square root 49/square root 4
       = root 7 × 7 / root 2 × 2 = 7/2)

4   80 (method: 6400 = 64 × 100; so square root 6400 = square root 64 ×
       square root 100 = 8 × 10 = 80)

5   12 (method: root 144 = root 12 × 12 = 12)

6   120 (method: root 14400 = root 144 × root 100 = 12 × 10 = 120)

4 *Warm-up exercise*

1   3 (method: cube root of 3 × 3 × 3 = 3)

2   1/3 (method: any root of 1 is 1/ cube root of 3 × 3 × 3 = 1/3)

3   6 (method: cube root of 6 × 6 × 6 = 6)

4   60 (method: cube root of 6 × 6 × 6 × cube root of 10 × 10 × 10
       = 6 × 10 = 60)

5 *Easy questions*

1   216

2   180

3 $n = 5$

4 $n = 5$

5   964

6 $n = 3$

7   16

8 $\dfrac{1}{16}$

9   2

10 $n = 3^3$

6 *More difficult questions*

1 $n = 2$; (method: we add the powers when multiplying, so add 40 and minus
       38 to give: $2^{40-38} = 2^2 = 4$)

2 $n = -0.5$ or $-½$; (method: any number to the power of a half is the square
       root, as in $10^{1/2} = \sqrt{10}$, and that any number to a negative power inverts the
       term; so $25^{1/2} = \sqrt{25} = 5$; and $25^{-1/2} = 1/\sqrt{25} = 1/5$)

3 $n = -5$; (method: $2^5 = 32$ so $2^{-5} = 1/2^5 = 1/32$)

4 $n = 4$; (method: $2^n = 16$ when $n = 4$; $2^4 = 16$; then $2^{-4} = 1/2^4 = 1/16$)

Chapter 9 Measurement

1 Easy questions

1   200; (method: area = length × breadth = 16 × 12.5 = 16 × 10 + 16 × 2.5 = 160 + 40 = 200)

2   35; (method: convert 1.5 m to cm then work out the number of full lengths and the number of full widths that can be cut from the sheet; 1.5 m = 150 cm; lengths = 150 cm ÷ 30 cm = 5 lengths; widths = 150 cm ÷ 20 cm = 7.5 (only 7 full widths); 5 × 7 = 35 full sheets.)

3   420 m; (method: perimeter = 2 lengths and 2 widths = 2 × 120 + 2 × 90 = 240 + 180 = 420 m)

4   60 inches; (method: convert metres to cm then cm to inches: 1.5 m = 150 cm; 150 cm ÷ 2.5 cm per inch = height in inches: remove the decimal point to give 1500 ÷ 25; multiply both sides by 4 to give 6000 ÷ 100, which is 60.)

5   8 cm; (method: convert m to cm then divide by 50; 4 metres = 400 cm; 400 ÷ 50; cancel to 40 ÷ 5 = 8 cm.)

6   12; (method: convert 3 miles to km, then convert to metres and divide by 400; 3 × 1.6 = 4.8 km; 4.8 km × 1000 m/km = 48 × 100 m = 4800 m; 4800 ÷ 400 cancels to 48 ÷ 4 = 12)

7   2/9; (method: write down 4.5 litres = 1 gallon; divide both sides by 4.5 to get one litre; then multiply the fraction of a gallon to remove the decimal point; 4.5 litres = 1 gal, so 1 litre = 1/4.5 gal; multiply top and bottom by 2 to get 2/9.)

8   88 lb; (method: convert kg to pounds by multiplying by 2.2, shifting the decimal point to the larger number; 40 × 2.2 = 4 × 22 = 88 lb.)

2 More difficult questions

1   a)   0.11 mm. (method: 5 reams × 500 sheets per ream = 2500 sheets; thickness = 27.5 cm = 275 mm; thickness of 1 sheet = 275 ÷ 2500; multiply both sides by 4 to make the divisor 10000; we have (275 × 4) ÷ 10000 = 1100 ÷ 10000 = 0.11 mm.)

b) i)   0.06 m². (method: 300 mm × 200 mm = 60000 mm²; 1 metre = 100 cm and 1 cm = 10 mm so 1 metre = 100 × 10 = 1000 mm; then 1 m² (1 m × 1 m) = 1000 mm × 1000 mm = 1000000 mm². So to convert mm² to m² we divide by 1 million (six noughts): 60000 mm² ÷ 1000000 cancels to = 6 ÷ 100 = 0.06 m²)

ii)   24 reams: (method: 1 ream = 500 sheets; = 500 × 0.06 m²; = 5 × 6 m² = 30 m². The pitch measures 100 m × 70 m = 700 m². Divide 700 m² by 30 m² to find the number of reams: 700 ÷ 30 = 70 ÷ 3 = 23.333 reams (24 reams).)

c) i)   4.8 gram; (method: weight of ream 2.4 kg = 2.4 × 1000 g = 2400 g; weight per sheet = 2400 ÷ 500 = 4800 ÷ 1000 = 4.8 g

ii)   80 g/m². We know that 1 sheet is 0.06 m² in area and 4.8 grams in weight, or 4.8 g per 0.06 m². We want the number of grams for 1.0 m²; multiply both terms by 100 to give 480 g/6 m²; divide both terms by 6 to give 80 g/m²)

Chapter 10 Averages

1 Warm-up exercise

1   3

2   5

3   30

4   17

5   115

2 Warm-up exercise

1   14

2   1

3   12

4   11.5 ((11+ 12) ÷ 2)

5   8 (15 − 7)

3 Easy questions

1   4; (method: sum of numbers = average × number of numbers = 6 × 5 = 30; then 30 = 3 + 10 + x + 5 + 8 = 26 + x; so x = 30 − 4)

2   21; (method: sum of numbers = average × number of numbers = 16 × 8
= 128; then 128 = 20 + y + 13 + 15 + 9 + 22 + 17 + 11; group in pairs
or three's to aid mental arithmetic: 128 = y + 33 + 24 + 50; 128 = y + 107;
y = 21.)

3   7; (method: sum of numbers = average × number of numbers = 8 × 9 =
72; then 72 = 7 + 10 + 8 + x + 9 + 8 + 6 + 10 + 7; group to aid mental
arithmetic: 72 = x + 25 + 17 + 16 + 7; 72 = x + 42 + 23 = 65;
72 = x + 65 = 7; so x = 7 and the mode is 7 (three 7's).)

4   5; (method: sum of numbers = average × number of numbers = 5 × 13 = 65;
then 65 = 7 + 3 + 5 + 8 + 7 + x + 4 + 4 + 6 + 8 + 2 + 2 + 8; 65 = x + 64;
x = 1
To find the median: 1, 2, 2, 3, 4, 4, 5, 6, 7, 7, 8, 8, 8)

5   2. (method: sum of scores = 1×5 + 2×1 + 3×3 + 4×1 + 5×0 = 5 + 2 + 9
+ 4 + 0 = 20; sum of frequencies (number of test takers) = 5 + 1 + 3 +1
+ 0 = 10; finally we have: mean = sum of (scores × frequency)/sum of
frequencies = 20/10 = 2)

6   a)   1.6. Average = total number of brothers/sister ÷ total number of pupils.
(0 × 7) + (1 × 8) + (2 × 6) + (3 × 3) + (4 × 1) = 7 + 8 + 12 + 9 + 4
= 40 brothers/sisters; total number of pupils = 25; 40 ÷ 25 = 8/5 = 1.6
per pupil

    b)   1 (occurs most frequently: 8 out of 25 pupils)

    c)   1 (occurs at the 13th pupil ((25+1) ÷ 2) when ordered low to high;
the 13th pupil is within the box of 8 pupils: pupils 8th, 9th, 10th, 11th,
12th, 13th, 14th, 15th; the full 25 are 0,0,0,0,0,0,0,1,1,1,1,1,1,1,1,2,2,2,2,
2,2,3,3,3,4)

4 More difficult questions

1   Method: first step: if the median is 5 then the fifth score must also be 5; if it
were less than 5, for example 4, then the median would be 4.5 (the average
of the two middle numbers). If there are two 5s there must be three 6s if
these are to be the mode.

1				5	5	6	6	6	10

Second step: the mean is 5 so the total of the scores must be 5 × 10 = 50.
We already have 1+ 5 + 5 + 6 + 6 + 6 + 10 = 39. This leaves 50 − 39 = 11
marks to be distributed amongst the remaining three boxes, ie 3 + 4 + 4 = 11

1	3	4	4	5	5	6	6	6	10

2 a) 15; the value of x must not exceed 15 otherwise the mode would not be 1 portion.

b) 26; we are told that the median is 1, so it lies in the middle group of 16 children; there are 27 children (16+8+2+1) who eat 1, 2, 3 or 4 portions, so there must be less than 27 who eat 0 portions, otherwise the median would fall into the 0 portions group.

c) 5; Mean average = total number of portions ÷ total number of children. mean average = 1.0 (given)

total number of portions = $(0 \times x + 1 \times 16 + 2 \times 8 + 3 \times 2 + 4 \times 1) = 42$

number of children = $x + 16 + 8 + 2 + 1 = 27 + x$

So $1.0 = 42 \div (27 + x)$; then $1(27 + x) = 42$; $27 + x = 42$, giving $x = 15$

(check: 42 children and 42 portions)

3 a) 15–19 (the modal class interval is the class with the highest frequency; it occurs on 10 day of the 31 days)

b) 10–14 (the median class interval is found in the middle of the 31 days at the 16th day (within the days = 8 box).

c) 13 days (estimate). Take the middle number of pupils in each of the class intervals and multiply by the number of pupils for that interval. For example 0–4 (0,1,2,3,4) the middle number of pupils is 2 and these lost 4 days; do this for all five of the class intervals: $(2 \times 4) + (7 \times 5) + (12 \times 8) + (10 \times 17) + (4 \times 23) = 8 + 35 + 96 + 170 + 92 = 401$ days lost (estimate) in 31 days; divide $401 \div 31$ to give 13 days lost.

Chapter 11 Speed, distance and time

1 Warm-up exercise

1 11 miles; (method: 10 mins = 1/6 hr; 1/6 hr × 66 mph = $66 \div 6$ = 11 miles)

2 1 mile; (method: 5 mins = 1/12 hr; 1/12 hr × 12 mph = 1 mile)

3 10 miles; (method: 15 mins = 1/4 hr; 1/4 hr × 40 mph = 10 miles)

4 2 miles; (method: 40 mins = 40/60 hr = 2/3; 2/3 hr × 3 mph = 6/3 = 2 miles)

5 22.5 miles; (method: 10 mph = 10 miles in 1 hour = 20 miles in 2 hours; similarly: 10 miles in 1 hour = 2.5 miles in ¼ hour or 15 mins; adding these gives us 2 hours + 15 minutes = 20 miles + 2.5 miles = 22.5 miles)

6 10 km; (method: 24 kmh = 24 km in 1 hour = 12 km in 30 mins; similarly 24 km in 1 hour = 2 km in 1/12 hour or 5 mins; subtracting these gives us 30 minutes − 5 minutes = 25 mins = 12 km − 2 km = 10 km)

7 13 miles; (method: 780 miles in 1 hour = $780 \div 60$ miles in 1 minute = $78 \div 6$ = 13 miles).

8   81 miles; (method: 36 mph = 36 miles in 1 hour = 72 miles in 2 hours, and 36/4 miles in ¼ hour = 9 miles in 15 minutes; 72 + 9 = 81 miles)

2 *Warm-up exercise*

1   18.6 miles; (method: 1 km = 0.62 miles; 30 km = 30 × 0.62 = 3 × 6.2 = 18.6 miles)

2   200 miles; (method: 320 km × 5/8 = 40 × 5 = 200 miles)

3   225 miles; (method: 360 km × 5/8 = 45 × 5 = 22.5 × 10 = 225 miles)

4   2.4 km; (method: 5 miles = 8 km so 0.5 miles = 0.8 km then 1.5 miles = 3 × 0.8 = 2.4 km)

3 *Warm-up exercise*

1   28 mph; (method: 84 miles in 3 hours = 84/3 miles in 1 hour = 28 mph)

2   50 mph; (method: 25 miles in 30 mins = 25 × 2 miles in 1 hour = 50 mph)

3   42 mph; (method: 7 miles in 10 mins = 7 × 6 miles in 60 mins = 42 mph)

4   28 km/h; (method: 21 km in 45 mins = 7 km in 15 mins (¼ hr) = 28 km/h)

5   60 km/h; (method: 140 km in 2 hr 20 min = 140 km in (120 + 20) = 140 min = 1 km in 1 min = 60 km in 60 min = 60 km/h; alternative more mathematical method: 2 hr 20 min = 2 and 1/3 hr = 6/3 hr + 1/3 hr = 7/3 hour; to change 7/3 hour to 1 hour you multiply 7/3 by 3/7 (or simply invert the fraction); so distance travelled in 1 hour = 140 × 3/7 = 20 × 3 = 60 km/h)

6   18 mph; (method: 12 miles in 40 mins = 3 miles in 10 min = 18 miles in 60 mins = 18 mph)

7   64 mph; (method: 16 miles in 15 mins = 16 miles in 60 mins = 64 mph)

8   36 km/h; (method: 27 km in 45 minutes = 9 km in 15 mins = 36 km in 60 mins = 36 km/h)

9   72 km/h; (method: 132 km in 1 hour and 50 minutes = 132 km in 110 mins = 12 km in 10 mins = 72 km in 1 hour = 72 km/h)

4 *Warm-up exercise*

1   525 seconds; (method: 8.75 × 60 = 8 × 60 + ¾ × 60 = 480 + 45 = 525)

2   205 minutes; (method: 3 hours 25 mins = 180 mins + 25 mins = 205 mins)

3   7; (method: 168 hours ÷ 24 hours = 7 hours)

4   0630 hrs (method: rewrite using the 24-hour clock 4-digit system)

5   2115 hrs; (method: 9.15 + 12 hours = 2115 hrs)

6   10:45 pm; (method: 2245 − 12 hours = 10.45 pm)

7   1810 hrs; (method: 1445 + 3 hrs and 25 mins = 1445 + 4 hours − 35 mins = 1845 − 35 mins = 1810 hrs)

8   1228 hrs; (method: 1410 − 1 hr 42 mins = 1410 − 2 hr + 18 mins = 1228 hrs)

5 Easy questions

1   0920 hrs; (method: 1200 hrs − (2 hrs 25 mins + 15 mins) = 1200 hrs − 2 hrs 40 mins = 1200 hrs − 3 hrs + 20 mins = 0920 hrs)

2   10.40 hrs

3   21 hrs; (method: 4 hours and 12 minutes × 5 days (not 7 days) = 4 × 5 hours + 12 minutes × 5 = 20 hours + 1 hour = 21 hours)

4   9 yrs 10 months; (method: 11 years and 4 months − 18 months = 11 years and 4 months − 1 yr and 6 mnth = 11 yr 4 mnth − 2 yr + 6 months = 9 yr 10 month)

5   10; (method: 0850 hours to 1530 hours = 6 hours 40 min (3 hours 10 min to midday then 3 hours 30 min after midday; subtract breaks of 1 hour 15 mins to leave 5 hours and 25 mins, which is enough for 10 half-hour lessons)

6   1545 hrs; (method: 10 × 30 mins + 90 mins = 5 hrs + 1 hr 30 min = 6 hr 30 min; 0915 hrs + 6 hr 30 min = 1545 hrs)

7   1315; (method: 50 + 50 + 10 = 1k mins = 1 hour 50 minutes; 1505 − 1 hour 50 minutes = 1315 hrs)

6 Easy questions

1   260 miles; (method: 60 mph = 60 miles in 1 hour = 240 miles in 4 hours and 20 miles in 20 minutes; total 240 + 20 = 260 miles)

2   312 miles; (method: 72 mph = 72 miles in 1 hour = 288 miles in 4 hours and 24 miles in 20 minutes = 312 miles)

3   90 miles; (method: 40 mph = 40 miles in 1 hour = 80 miles in 2 hours and 10 miles in 15 minutes; total 80 + 10 = 90 miles)

4   88 mph; (method: 44 km in 30 minutes = 88 km in 1 hour = 88 km/h)

5   48 km/h; (method: divide both terms by 7 to get the distance travelled in 5 minutes, then multiply by 12 to get the distance travelled in 1 hour (the speed); 17.5 miles in 35 mins = 2.5 miles in 5 minutes (dividing both terms by 7); then 2.5 × 12 = 30 mph in 60 minutes = multiple miles 1.6 to get km/h = 48 km/h).

6   55 mph; (method: 66 km in 45 minutes = 22 km in 15 mins = 88 km/hr; 88 km/hr = 88 ÷ 1.6 mph = 880 ÷ 16 = 110 ÷ 2 (dividing both terms by a factor of 8, or by 2 four times) = 55 mph)

7   1 hr 36 min; (method: use the SDT triangle: T = D/S so T = 6 miles (changed to kilometres) divided by 6 km/h = 6 × 1.6 ÷ 6 = 1.6 hours = 1 hour + 0.6 × 60 mins = 36 mins; total 1 hour 36 mins)

8   1 hr 15 minutes; (method: T = D/S = 140 km (changed to miles)/70 mph = 140 ÷ 1.6 ÷ 70 = 2 ÷ 1.6 = 20/16 = 10/8 = 5/4 hours = 1¼ hours)

9   1250 hrs; (method: 60 mph = 60 miles in 1 hour and 20 miles in 1/3 hr or 20 minutes (note that 60 mph is 'a mile a minute'); total time = 1 hour 20 minutes add this to 1130 hrs to give 1250 hrs)

7 More difficult question

1   a)   21 miles; (method: 5 miles = 8 km; 8 km = 5 miles; 1 km = 5/8 miles; 33.6 × 5/8 = 168/8 = 84/4 = 42/2 = 21 miles)

       b)   31.5 mph; (method; average speed = total distance ÷ total time; total distance = 21 × 2 = 42 miles; total time = time C to L + time L to C; T = D/S, for CL = 21/36 = 7/12 hour = 7 × 5 mins = 35 mins; for LC = 21/28 = 3/4 hour = 45 mins; total time = 80 minutes; average speed = 42 miles/80 minutes = 21 miles in 40 minutes = 10.5 miles in 20 minutes; adding these last two give us = 31.5 miles in 60 minutes or 31.5 mph)

Chapter 12 Charts, graphs and tables

1 Warm-up exercise

1   Food; (method: the largest sector for girls).

2   Appearance; (method: the smallest sector for boys).

3   Food; (method: similar size sector for boys and girls).

4   25%; (method: one-quarter of the circle (90° or a right angle) = 25%).

5   Boys spend 1/2 × girls on appearance: 1/2 × 1/4 = 1/8.

2 *Warm-up exercise*

1   20%; (method: read researchers = 20%).

2   1/5; (method: change 20% to a fraction; 20/100 = 1/5).

3   7/20; (method: 35% = 35/100 = 7/20).

4   4/25; (method: 16% = 16/100 = 8/50 = 4/25).

5   0.51; (method: 0.35 + 0.16 = 0.51).

6   32,000; (method: $0.2 \times 160,000 = 2 \times 16,000 = 32,000$).

7   1600; (method: $16\% + 20\% - 35\% = 1\%$; $1/100 \times 160,000 = 1600$).

8   14,400; (method: $0.09 \times 160,000 = 9 \times 1600 = 10 \times 1,600 - 1600 = 14,400$).

9   2400; (method: Ratio of male to female = 5:1 Total parts = 5 + 1 = 6 parts and we have 1 part: $1/6 \times 14,400 = 2,400$).

3 *Easy question*

1   False; (method: school A: $0.25 \times 400 = 100$; school B: $0.3 \times 330 = 99$).

2   True; (method: C or above: $25\% + 12\% + 29\% = 66\%$; $0.66 \times 400 = 264$).

3   True; (method: B: $30\% + 9\% + 33\% = 72\%$; A: $25\% + 13\% + 28\% = 66\%$).

4 *Warm-up exercise*

1   Maths; (method: longest bar = maths).

2   Design; (method: fifth longest = design).

3   English; (method: history = 4%; $4\% \times 3 = 12\%$ = English).

4   French; (method: science double = 9%; $2/3 \times 9\% = 6\%$ = French).

5   1/10 and 0.1; (method: 10% = 1/10 = 0.1).

6   1/4; (method: English 12% + maths 13% = 25% = 1/4).

7   5:6; (method: English Lit to English is 10:12 = 5:6).

8   150; (method: ratio of Lit to English is 10 parts to 12 parts; 12 parts English is 180 so 10 parts Lit = $10/12 \times 180 = 5/6 \times 180 = 5 \times 30 = 150$; alternative. 12 parts English is 180 so 1 part (unitary method) is $180 \div 12 = 15$, then 10 parts Lit is $10 \times 15 = 150$).

9 62%; (method: add bar heights; left to right = 12 + 10 + 6 + 8 + 4 + 9 + 13 = 62%).

10 0.38; (method: subtract 62% (seven subjects) from 100% and express the answer as a decimal fraction; 100% − 62% = 38% = 0.38).

5 *Easy question*

1 90; (method: 50% maths × 180 pupils = 90 pupils).

2 42; (method: we are told that history pupils = 1/3 maths pupils; so history = 1/3 × 180 maths = 60 history; 60 history × 70% grades A*–C = 60 × 0.7 = 6 × 7 = 42 history pupils gained grades A*–C).

3 18; (method: 180 took maths so 180 must have taken English if it is equally popular; grades A*–C: English: 180 × 60% (reading from the chart) and maths: is 180 × 50%; the difference is then 180 × 0.6 − 180 × 0.5 = 108 − 90 = 18; alternative method; subtract one bar length from the other and multiply the answer by 180: English: 60%; maths 50%; difference = 10%; 0.1 × 180 =18).

4 72; (method: 54 pupils = 75% (read from the chart) = 3/4; if three-quarters is 54 pupils then one-quarter is 54 ÷ 3 = 18; so four-quarters (4/4) is 72).

6 *Easy question*

1 True (method: compare the height of the bars to see that year 2004 is above year 2000 true for all five percentage intervals).

2 True (method: the highest proportion is 40% as read on the bottom (x) axis; the improvement from year 2000 to 2004 is visibly greater when comparing these two bars to any other pair of bars, so the statement is true).

3 False (method: there are no schools shown where 90% of the pupils were entitled to free school meals (maximum is 40%); the 10% and the 90% have been reversed in the statement).

7 *Easy question*

1 Level 4; (method: white bar A longer than black bar B).

2 3:2; (method: at Level 3: bar B = 50 − 20 = 30; bar A = 20 − 0 = 20; so the B:A ratio is 30:20 or 3:2).

8 Easy question

9/20 (method: English: 45% are boys (0 to 45) and 55% are girls (45 to 100); 45% boys = 45/100 = 9/20).

9 Easy question

1   40 mph: (method: 140 miles in 3.5 hours = 280 ÷ 7 = 40 mph).

2   30 minutes; (method: stationary = no distance travelled = line horizontal; so stationary between 1.5 hours and 2 hours, which is 0.5 hours or 30 minutes).

3   53 mph; (method: set out at 1000 so this is 0 hr on the Time axis; then midday is 2 hours later at 1200 hrs 1330 hrs is 3.5 hours later (the end of the journey), so we want the average speed between 2 hours and 3.5 hours: distance travelled = 140 miles (after 3.5 hours) − 60 miles (after 2 hours) = 80 miles in 1.5 hours; average speed = 80 ÷ 1.5 = 160 ÷ 3 = 53.3 = 53 mph).

4   (3,120); (method: locate 1300 hrs on the Time axis; it is 3 hours after the start at 10.00 (the origin 0,0), so the x-coordinate is 3; read vertically up from the x-coordinate 3, until you reach the line, then read across to the y-axis to find the y-coordinate of 120 miles).

10 Warm-up exercise

1   Chemistry; (method: the results show the least fluctuation (least range)).

2   150; (method: range = maximum minus minimum = 450 − 300 = 150).

3   100; (method: range = maximum minus minimum = 500 − 400 = 100).

4   200; (method; extend the line (extrapolate) from 700 in 1990 down through 600 in 1992 to reach 200 by the year 2000 using a ruler; mathematically the rate of descent is 700 − 600 = 100 from 1990 to 1992 or 100 in 2 years, which is 50 per year (the common difference); if this continues then after 10 years the decline will be 50 per year × 10 years = 500, to leave 700 − 500 = 200 maths passes after 10 years).

11 Easy question

1   70%; (method: read 70% off the vertical axis (y-axis) for Levels 5–8)

2   25%; (method: 2004: 'less than Level 5' = Levels 3–8 (top line) minus Levels 5–8 (lower line) = 95% − 70% = 25% in 2004)

3   3/4; (read 75% off the y-axis for 2005; 75% = 3/4)

4 1/5; (method: 2005: 'less than Level 5' = Levels 3–8 (top line) minus Levels 5–8 (lower line) = 95% − 75% = 20% in 2005).

12 *Easy question*

2004; (method: as a first step look for the greatest distance of separation between the lines for the years given; the separation must exceed 10%. The greatest separation is in 2003 and the second greatest separation is in 2004; however, 2003 is the wrong answer because the LA's performance exceeded that of the school in 2003 and we want the school above the LA as in 2004).

13 *More difficult questions*

1 72%; (method: 23 half days = 11.5 days; read up from the x-axis (dotted line) and across to the y-axis (dotted line) to see that 72% are expected to achieve Level 4).

2 Worse; (method: co-ordinate point (10 days,70%) is below the diagonal line.)

3 Better; (method: co-ordinate point (8 days,90%) is above the diagonal line.)

14 *More difficult question*

1 Pupil E lies on a diagonal line that shows equal performance (same × and y co-ordinates) in both tests.

2 10 pupils below the diagonal line = better in writing.

3 9 pupils above the diagonal line = better in arithmetic.

4 12 pupils on or above the horizontal line.

5 14 pupils to the right of the horizontal line.

6 11 pupils in the top right-hand corner.

7 5 pupils in the bottom left-hand corner.

8 Pupils F and O the furthest away from the diagonal.

9 Total the x-coordinates of the 20 pupils A to G to give 240 marks. Average = 240 ÷ 20 = 12 marks in the writing test.

10 Total the y-coordinates of the 20 pupils A to G to give 232 marks. Average = 234 ÷ 20 = 11.7 marks in the arithmetic test.

11 The line of best fit goes from the origin (0,0) through the point (11.7, 12).

12 The line of best fit is just below the dashed diagonal line.

15 Warm-up exercise

1	St Moritz	9	Lake Lugano
2	July	10	September
3	Interlaken and Lake Geneva	11	23°C
4	September	12	6.1°C
5	Five	13	10.6°C
6	Four	14	Lake Lugano
7	All nine	15	Adelboden
8	10°C	16	11°C

16 Easy question

0815 hrs (method: arriving back in Dublin means that we need consider only the right-hand side of the table, that is to say, the Dublin to Holyhead journey. There are two possible ferries/arrival times: 1130 (Cruise ferry) and 1045 (Swift ferry); both of these are suitable ferries. However, the Swift ferry has the later departure time (0845) which is the one we want because the question asks for the latest check-in time. The latest check-in time is 30 minutes before departure (see bottom of table), so we subtract 30 minutes from 0845 to give an answer of 0815 hrs).

17 Easy question

1   34; (method: $7 \times 1 + 6 \times 2 + 5 \times 3 = 7 + 12 + 15 = 34$ points)

2   5.67 (method: $34 \div 6$ subjects = 5.67 to 2 d.p.)

18 More difficult question

1   45; (method: points = $6 \times 7 + 3 = 42 + 3 = 45$).

2   Grade B; (method: nearest to 45 points).

3   Grade D; (method: $6 \times 5 + 3 = 30 + 3 = 33$).

4   Level 7; (method: grade B = 46 points; $46 = 6 \times$ KS3 level + 3; rearrange this to give KS3 on its own: $46 - 3 = 6$KS3; so $43 = 6$KS3; KS3 $= 43 \div 6 = 7.2$).

5   43; (method: points = $45 + 45 + 39 = 129$; average points = $129 \div 3 = 43$).

6   360; (method: 45×8 subjects = $320 + 40 = 360$ points).

7 40; (method: 46 × 2 + 40 × 4 + 34 × 2 = 92 + 160 + 68 = 320; 320 ÷ 8 = 40).

8 Grade F; (method: 5 × 40 + 46 × 2 = 292; then points of remaining grade = 314 − 292 = 22 = grade F, according to the table).

19 *More difficult question*

1 True; (method: add the five percentages for English and divide by 5: 75 + 75 + 75 + 77 + 79 = 381; 381 ÷ 5 = 76.2%).

2 False; (method: find the missing percentage in the maths column by i) multiplying the mean by 5 (for the five years) to give the total of the percentages, and then ii) add the four known percentages and subtract the answer from the total in i). We have i) mean × 5 = 73.2 × 5 = 366 (mental arithmetic: 70 × 5 + 3 × 5 + 0.2 × 5); ii): 71 + 73 + 74 + 75 = 293 (mental arithmetic: 70 × 4, + 1 + 3 + 4 + 5). Finally: 366 − 293 = 73 (mental arithmetic: 366 − 300 + 7), so the answer is 73 not 72 (false)).

3 False; (method: the mode is the number that occurs the most often; it is 86% in Science (occurs three times) so this part of the question is true. The median is the middle number; we have 5 numbers so the median is the third number in the ranking: 86, 86, 86, 87, 87 (median found at (5 + 1) ÷ 2 = third position); so the median is 86 not 86.5 making this part of the question false).

20 *More difficult question*

Reading; (method: i) convert the highest scores in each subject to percentages, then ii) subtract the lowest mark from the highest mark in each subject to find the ranges. i) Reading = 36 out of 40 = 90% (36/40 = 9/10 = 90%); writing = 43 out of 50 (43/50 = 86/100 = 86%); arithmetic: 54 out of 60 = 90% (54/60 = 9/10 = 90%). We have two subjects with the highest tests scores: reading and arithmetic (both 90%) so writing can be discarded as an answer option. ii) reading: range = 36 − 15 = 21; arithmetic: range = 54 − 25 = 29; so reading has the highest percentage mark and the smallest range).

21 *More difficult question*

1 80%; (method: in English, top to bottom, person by person for Level 5 or above: Aziz, Bethan, Carl, Harry, Josh, Phoebe, Ruby and Zak achieved Level 5 or above = 8/10 pupils = 80%; alternative: Level 4 and below: Eleri and Yasmin = 2/10 leaving 8/10 at 5 or above).

2 60%; (method: i) identify those who achieved Level 5 or above in science as a first step, then ii) find what proportion of these (as a fraction) achieved

Level 5 or above in maths; i) only one person (Eleri) did not achieve Level 5 or above in science meaning that 9 people did achieve the level; ii) person by person, top to bottom: Aziz, (not Bethan), Carl, Harry, (not Josh), Phoebe, Ruby, (not Yasmin), and Zak; meaning that 6 out of 9 or 2/3 meet the requirement).

3   60%; (method: top to bottom, person by person, all three subjects, Aziz, Carl, Harry, Phoebe, Ruby and Zak = 6/10 = 60%).

22 *Warm-up exercise*

1   4; (method: read down from grade C and across from grade C to find 4).

2   9; (method: read across from grade C: 1 + 2 + 4 + 2 = 9; alternative: see total for the column).

3   7; (method: read down from grade A: 2 + 2 + 2 + 1 = 7; alternative: see total for the column).

4   35; (method: the total for French and the total for Spanish (bottom corner)).

5   C; (method: modal grade for French = most popular grade = grade C, it occurs 9 times: 1 + 2 + 4 + 2 = 9, or see the total for the column; note that the answer is C not 9).

6   27 pupils; (method: grade C or above in Spanish = C + B + A + A* grades = 9 + 9 + 5 + 4 = 27 pupils.)

7   77.1%; (method: 27 pupils (from question 6) ÷ 35 pupils in total × 100% = 2700 ÷ 35 = 77.1%, by long division).

8   10; (method:10 pupils lie to the left of the diagonal line drawn from A*A* to GG, meaning that these pupils achieved a lower grade in Spanish than in French. Reading from the table, the ten pupils/grades are (higher French grade followed by Spanish grade): A*A; A*B; AB × 2; AC; BC × 2; CD × 2; and DE).

23 *More difficult question*

1   150 students; (method: tally all 7 bars (pairing method shown): (1 + 2) + (14 + 26) + (39 + 52) + 16 = (3 + 40) + (91 + 16) = 43 + 107 = 150.)

2   88.7% (method: grade C or above = 26 + 39 + 52 + 16 = 133; 133 ÷ 150 × 100% = 13300 ÷ 150 = 1330 ÷ 15 = 88.7% by long division).

3   A grade; (method: modal = occurs most frequently = A grade).

4   B grade; Median = (n + 1) ÷ 2 = 151 ÷ 2 = 75.5 (75th to 76th pupil);
so the median lies in the B grade bar which extends from the 44th student
(1 + 2 + 12 + 26 = 43) to the 83rd pupil (1 + 2 + 14 + 26 + 39 = 83).

5   144; (96% = 0.96; 0.96 × 150 = 96 × 1.5 = 96 + 48 = 144 pupils).

24 *More difficult question*

1   64%; (method: i) find the number who scored more than 6 points and ii)
express this as a percentage of the total students; i) reading from the table,
total the ranges above 6: 6.1 to 6.5 = 43; 6.6 to 7.0 = 25; 7.1 to 7.5 = 9 and
7.6 to 8.0 = 4; then 43 + 25 + 8 + 4 = 80; alternative: add the four bars
above 6.0 in the histogram); ii) total number of students = 125 (given in
question); to calculate the percentage: 80 out of 125 scored more than 6
points; convert 80/125 to a percentage as follows: 80/125 = 16/25 = 64/100
= 64%; alternative calculation for the percentage: 80/125 × 100% = 80 × 4/5
= 16 × 4 = 64%).

2   16:9; (method: 80 scored more than 6 points so (125 − 80) = 45 scored
6 points or less; so ratio = 80:45 = 16:9).

3   76%; (method: 5.5 < × ≤ 7.0 means that the range 'X' is above 5.5 but less
than or equal to 7, in other words the three centre bars = 27 + 43 + 25 =
95 (or read from the table); as a percentage: 95 ÷ 125 × 100% = 19/25 ×
100 = 19 × 4 = 76%).

25 *More difficult question*

1   35; (method: for C and below read off the CF axis (y-axis) for grade C).

2   46; (method: for B and below read off the CF axis (y-axis) for grade B).

3   50; (method: for A and below read off the CF axis (y-axis) for grade A).

4   16; (method: total 51 minus C and below in question 1 above: 51 − 35 = 16).

5   5; (method: total 51 minus B and below in question 2 above: 51 − 46 = 5).

6   1; (method: total 51 minus A and below in question 3 above: 51 − 50 = 1).

7   34; (method: total 51 minus D and below: 51 − 17 = 34 or read the values
from the table: 18 + 11 + 4 + 1).

8   46; (method: 51 minus E and below: 51 − 5 = 46 (or read values from table).

9   2/3; (method: divide 34 (the answer in question 7) by 51: 34/51 = 2/3).

10 90.2% (method: divide 46 (the answer in question 8) by 51 and express the answer as a percentage: 46/51 × 100% = 46 ÷ 51 × 100 = 4600 ÷ 51 = 90.2% by long division).

11 31.4% (method: grade B and above = 51 minus grade C and below = 51 − 35 = 16; 16 ÷ 51 × 100 = 1600 ÷ 51 = 31.4% by long division).

26 More difficult question

1 58; (method: highest points as read from the graph or the table).

2 22; (method: lowest points as read from the graph or the table).

3 36; (method: range = highest − lowest = 58 − 22 = 36).

4 46; (method: median is the 80th student (given); cuts the line at 46 points).

5 140; (method: read from the CF axis (y-axis) at 52 points (x-axis).

6 20; (method: total minus 52 points and below = 160 − 140 = 20).

7 148; (method: 34 points or lower = 12; more than 34 = 160 − 12 = 148. Note that the y-axis divisions are 4 units apart (4, 8, 12, 16, 20 etc; not 2, 4, 6, 8, 10 etc).

27 More difficult question

1 18; (method: read across from 50% CF until you meet the curve, then vertically down to a mark of 18 on the x-axis).

2 20; (method: read across from 70% CF until you meet the curve, then vertically down to a mark of 20 on the x-axis).

3 13; (method: read across from 12% CF until you meet the curve, then vertically down to a mark of 13 on the x-axis).

4 30; (method: read up from 16 marks on the x-axis until you meet the curve, then horizontally across to 30% on the y-axis; 30% means 30 out of 100 so we can convert 30% to 30 students because 100 students sat the test).

5 70; (method: to pass, a student needs 17 marks or higher, so those with 16 marks or lower will fail; read up from 16 marks on the x-axis until you hit the curve at 30% CF; this means that 30% will fail, so 100 − 30 = 70 will pass (100 students minus those with 16 marks and below)).

28 Easy question

1   True; (method: the highest mark was 72, so at least one pupil achieved it).

2   True; (method: the inter-quartile range is from 38 to 54; 54 − 38 = 16).

3   False; (method: three-quarters scored more than 38 marks).

29 More difficult question

1   Maths; (method: the lowest mark at the end of the bottom whisker).

2   English; (method: the box containing the highest 'white line').

3   Science; (method: the subject with the shortest box).

4   Maths; (method: greatest minimum–maximum span; the whisker ends have the greatest separation).

5   English; (method: the median lies at 57 in English, so half the marks lie above this level and half the marks lie below it).

6   Science (method: similar length whiskers at the top and bottom in science).

7   60%; (method: the upper quartile starts here for science; whisker begins).

8   Maths (the range of marks for the top 25% of pupils is shown by the length of the upper quartile whiskers, and the whisker is longest in maths).

9   40; (method: half the marks lie in the inter-quartile range (inside the box); half of 80 = 40).

10   English; (method: all three subjects have their upper quartiles (whiskers) extending above 60% but only English has a proportion of the inter-quartile range above 60%).

Chapter 13 Probability

1 Warm-up exercise

a)   3/5; (method: walk = 2/5; so not walk = 1 − 2/5 = 3/5 (mutually exclusive))

b)   7/10; (method: bus = 3/10; so not bus = 1 − 3/10 = 7/10 (mutually exclusive))

c)   11/15; (method: car = 4/15; so not car = 1− 4/15 = 11/15 (mutually exclusive))

d)   29/30; (method: add walk, bus and car by converting each to thirtieths (the common denominator): 2/5 + 3/10 + 4/15 = 12/30 + 9/30 + 8/30 = 29/30)

e)   1/30: (method: cycles is the same as not walk, not bus and not car; we know that walk + bus + car = 29/30; so not walk, not bus and not car = 1 − 29/30 = 1/30 cycles (meaning that 1 in every 30 pupils are expected to cycle to school, so if, for example, 300 pupils attend the school then 'in theory' 10 of these would cycle).

f)   9/30 (method: cycles is 1/30 and car is 4/15 = 8/30; (1+8)/30= 9/30)

2 Easy questions

1   a)   3x (method: add the probabilities for 3 and 4: x + 2x = 3x)
        b)   0.1 (method: the probabilities must add up to 1.0 because it is 100% certain to land on one of the six numbers: 0.1 + 0.15 + 3x + 0.2 + 0.25 = 1.0; then we have: 0.7 + 3x = 1.0, giving 3x = 1.0 − 0.7 = 0.3, so x = 0.1

2   a)   i)   0.45 (method: 1.0 − 0.3 − 0.25 = 0.45)
            ii)   0.25; (method: P red or blue = P not green = 1.0 − 0.75 = 0.25)
            iii) 0.55; (method: P not blue = P red or P green = 0.3 + 0.25 = 0.55)
        b)   40; (method: total balls × P red = 12 red; total balls × 0.3 red = 12; then total balls = 12 ÷ 0.3 = 120 ÷ 3 = 40)

3 Easy question

1   a)   i)   1/36; (method: 1 possibility)
            ii)   1/12; (method: 3 possibilities)
            iii) 5/36; (method: 5 possibilities)
            iv)   1/9; (method: 4 possibilities)

        b)   i)   13/18; (26 possibilities)
            ii)   7/12; (21 possibilities)
            iii) 1/6; (6 possibilities)
            iv)   5/6; (method: 1− 4 or less = 1 − 1/6 = 5/6)

        c)   i)   8/9 (method: P(NOT 5) = 1 − P(5) = 1 − 4/36 = 1 − 1/9 = 8/9)
            ii)   5/6 (method: P(NOT 7) = 1 − P(7) = 1 − 6/36 = 1 − 1/6 = 5/6)

        d)   i)   1/6; (method: 6 possible 'doubles' = 6/36 = 1/6)
            ii)   5/6; (method: 1− 1/6 = 5/6)
            iii) 5/12; (method: primes totals: one 2, two 3s, four 5s; six 7s and two 11s = 15/36 = 5/12)
            iv)   5/9; (method: a six on one die only means total all the scores of 7 or more with the exception of 12 (double six); there are 20 such possibilities = 20/36).

4 More difficult question

1st bag						
	1	2	3	4	5	6
1	2	3	4	5	6	7
2	3	4	5	6	7	8
3	4	5	6	7	8	9
4	5	6	7	8	9	10

(2nd bag labels 1, 2, 3, 4 on left)

1
a) 1/6; (method: 4 possibilities (out of 24 total possibilities))

b) 5/12; (method: 10 possibilities)

c) 1/6; (method: 4 possibilities, which are 1,1; 2,2; 3,3; and 4,4)

d) 1/2; (method: even totals are 2, 4, 6, 8, 10; there are 12 of these; 12/24 = 1/2)

e) 1/24; (method: 1 possibility which is 3, 3 = 1/24)

f) 1/12 (method: 2 possibilities which are 2, 3 and 3, 2 = 2/24 =1/12)

5 Easy question

1
a) i) 2/3; (method: P white = 8/12 = 2/3)
ii) 4/9; (method: 2/3 × 2/3 = 4/9)
iii) 1/3; (method: P black = 4/12 = 1/3)
iv) 1/9; (method: 1/3 × 1/3 = 1/9)
v) 2/9; (method: 2/3 × 1/3 = 2/9)
vi) 2/9; (method: 1/3 × 2/3 = 2/9)

b) i) 8/27; (method: 2/3 × 2/3 × 2/3 = 8/27)
ii) 4/27; (method: 2/3 × 2/3 × 1/3 = 4/27)
iii) 4/27; (method: 1/3 × 2/3 × 2/3 = 4/27)
iv) 1/27; (method: 1/3 × 1/3 × 1/3 = 1/27)
v) 2/27; (method: 2/3 × 1/3 × 1/3 = 2/27)

6 Warm-up exercise

1
a) 3/4; (method: P 1st red (8 balls in bag) = 6/8 = 3/4)

b) 5/7; (method: P 2nd red (7 balls remain, 5 reds) = (6 − 1)/(8 − 1) = 5/7)

c) 2/3; (method: P 3rd red (6 balls remain, 4 reds) = (5 − 1)/(7 − 1) = 4/6 = 2/3)

  d) 5/14; (method: multiply a) × b) × c): 3/4 × 5/7 × 2/3 = 30/84 = 15/42 = 5/14)

  e) 3/14; (method: P 1st red: 6/8 = 3/4; P 2nd black = 2/7; 3/4 × 2/7 = 6/28 = 3/14)

7 More difficult question

1 a) 2/7; (method: 6 girls; 21 children; 6/21 = 2/7)

  b) 5/7; (method: 15 boys, 21 children; 15/21 = 5/7)

  c) 1/14: (6/21 × 5/20 = 2/7 × 1/4 = 2/28 = 1/14)

  d) 3/7; (boy-girl = 15/21 × 6/20 = 5/7 × 3/10 = 3/14; girl-boy = 6/21 × 15/20 = 2/7 × 3/4 = 6/28 = 3/14; total = 3/14 + 3/14 = 6/14 = 3/7)

8 More difficult question

1 a) $x = 2/3$; $y = 1/3$; (method: white branch (W): P(W) 1st ball = 6/16 = 3/8; then P(WW) 2nd ball = 5/15 = 1/3 = y; then $x = 1 - y$ (complementary events; $x + y = 1$) so $x = 1 - 1/3 = 2/3$)

  b) i) 1/2; (method: BW + WB; BW = 10/16 × 6/15 = 5/8 × 2/5 = 10/40 = 1/4; WB is 6/16 times x, or 3/8 × 2/3 = 6/24 = 1/4; so BW + WB = 1/4 + 1/4 = 1/2)

  ii) 7/8; BB added to the answer i); BB = 10/16 × 9/15 = 5/8 × 3/5 = 15/40 = 3/8; 1/2 + 3/8 = 7/8. Alternative: at least one ball is black means none are white; WW is 3/8 times y or 3/8 × 1/3 = 3/24 = 1/8 and 1 − WW = 1 − 1/8 = 7/8

9 More difficult questions

1 a) 0.04; (method: pass first time = 0.8 so fail first time = 1.0 − 0.8 = 0.2; fail the second attempt = 0.2 × 0.2 again = 0.04)

  b) 96%; (method: pass first time = 0.8; pass second time (having failed the first time) = 0.2 × 0.8 = 0.16; so pass at either of the first two attempts = 0.8 + 0.16 = 0.96 = 96%.)

  c) 0.032; (method: fail once = 0.2; fail twice = 0.2 × 0.2 = 0.04; then finally pass = 0.04 × 0.8 = 0.032)

  d) 0.008; (method: not pass at all = 0.2 × 0.2 × 0.2 = 0.008 (this means that if 1000 students take the test then by the third attempt only 0.008 × 1000 = 8 are expected to fail, meaning that 1 − 0.008 = 0.992 or 99.2% have passed)

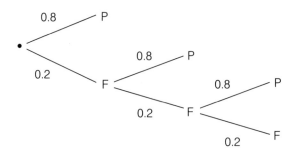

2   3/16; (method: we have 25% of the marks at 39 or below, so 75% (3/4) of
the marks are 40 or above; we have 75% of the marks at 69 or below so
25% (1/4) of the marks are at 70 or above; then 3/4 × 3/4 = 3/16. See data
presentation chapter for more information on box plots. The key values are:
22 = lowest mark; 92 highest mark; 51 = median mark; lower quartile = 39
and the upper quartile = 69; the box shows the inter-quartile range (half the
marks fall inside the box).

10 Easy questions

1   a)   1/2; (method: 26 out of 52; 26/52 = 1/2 or 0.5)
     b)   1/4; (method: 13 out of 52; 13/52 = 1/4 or 0.25)
     c)   13/204; (method: 13/52 × 13/51 = 1/4 × 13/51 = 13/204)
     d)   1/17; (method: 13/52 × 12/51 = 1/4 × 12/51 = 12/204 = 6/102
          = 3/51 = 1/17)

2   5/6; (method: work out the probability that the fifth card will be a face card and
subtract the answer from one (complementary events); there are 52 cards and
4 × 3 = 12 face cards; four of the face cards have been drawn to leave 8 face
cards in 48 cards; 8/48 = 1/6; so NOT another face card = 1 − 1/6 = 5/6)

3   a)   11/24; (method: the first four cards are black so this leaves 22 black
          cards in the remaining 48 cards; 22/48 = 11/24)
     b)   13/24; (method: the first four cards are black so this leaves 26 red
          cards in the remaining 48 cards; 26/48 = 13/24)
     c)   1/4; (method: the first four cards are not a picture (face) card so this
          leaves 12 face cards in the remaining 48 cards; 12/48 = 1/4)

4   1/78; (method: there are four sixes in a pack of 52 playing cards; 4/52 = 1/13;
and there is one six on a dice with six numbers; 1/6. Multiplying these
probabilities gives 1/13 × 1/6 = 1/78)

11 More difficult question

1   20/221; (method: picture card = 12/52; second card picture card = 11/51
so NOT a picture card = 1 − 11/51 = 51/51 − 11/51 = 40/51; dice shows
an even number = 1/2; multiply the probabilities: 12/52 × 40/51 × 1/2;
cancelling gives: 3/13 × 40/51 × 1/2 = 3/13 × 20/51 = 60/663 = 20/221)

12 Easy question

1   a)   0.08; (method: the relative frequency is the experimental probability; we have 20 tails in 250 flips; 20/250 = 2/25 = 8/100 = 0.08)

b)   0.92; (method: obtaining a head or a tail are mutually exclusive events, in which case: P head + P tail = 1.0; so P head = 1.0 − P tail = 1.0 − 0.08 = 0.92)

c)   1150; (method: multiply the number of trials by the probability: 1250 × 0.92 = 92 × 12.5 = 1150)

d)   11.5 (method: compare the probabilities: heads = 0.92 and tails = 0.08; this means the ratio of heads to tails is 0.92 to 0.08, which is the same as 92:8 (multiplying both numbers by 100), 92:8 = 46:4 = 23:2 = 11.5:1; so the chances of obtaining a head are 11.5 times greater than the chances of obtaining a tail with this biased coin.

Chapter 14 Venn diagrams and sets

1 Easy question

a)   13 (method: E(30) = 21 − x + x + 16 − x + 6; so 30 = 43 − x, giving x = 13)

b)   8 (method: 21 − x = French only; 21 − 13 = 8)

c)   3 (method: 16 − x = Spanish only; 16 − 13 = 3)

2 More difficult question

a)   i)   18 − p (method: p + x = 18, so x = 18 − p)

ii)   15 − q (method: q + x = 15, so x = 15 − q)

iii)   12 (method: add p + x = 18 and q + x = 15 to get p + q + 2x = 33; then substitute p + q = 9 (given this); so 9 + 2x = 33; 2x = 33 − 9 = 24; x = 12)

iv)   6 (method: p = B − x; p = 18 − 12 = 6)

v)   24 (method: E = p + x + q + y; E = (p + q) + x + y; E = 9 +12 + 3 = 24)

b)   i)   6:5 (method: B = 18 and C = 15 (given); ratio is 18:15; cancel to 6:5)

ii)   75% (method: B = 18 and E = 24; fraction is 18/24 = 3/4 = 75%)

iii)   1:3 (method: B only (p) = 6 (from iv); B = 18; ratio p: B = 6:18 = 1:3)

iv)   1/8 (method: C only (q): p+ q = 9 (given); p = 6 so q = 3; E = 24; 3/24 = 1/8)

c)   i)   0.625 (method: C = 15; E = 24; probability C = 15/24 = 5/8 = 0.625 (by any mental arithmetic method, for example 1/8 = 0.125 so 5/8 = 0.625)

ii) 0.375 (method: not C = 1.0 − probability C; so not C = 1.0 − 0.625 = 0.375)

iii) 0.5 (method: both B and C = the overlap (x); x = 12 (from iii); 12/24 = 0.5)

iv) 0.5 (method: B = p = 6; C = q = 3; neither = y = 3; 6 + 3 + 3 = 12; 12/24)

3 Warm-up exercise

a) Set P

b) P∩Q

c) (P∪Q)′

d) P∩Q′

e) P′

f) P′∪Q

g) P∩R

h) P∪Q∪R

i) E

j) P∩Q∩R′

4 Warm-up exercise

a) {1,2,3,4,5,6,7,8,9,10}

b) {1,2,4,8}

c) {2,3,5,7,10}

d) {3,5,6,7,9,10}

e) {1,4,6,8,9}

f) {2}

g) {1,2,3,4,5,7,8,10}

h) {6,9}

i) {1,2,4,6,8,9}

j) {1,4,8}

k) {2,3,5,7,10}

l) {3,5,7,10}

5 Warm-up exercise

a) {2,3,5,15}

b) {2,3}

c) {2,3,4,5,8,9,15}

d) {2,3,8,9}

e) {4,18,19,20}

f) {4}

g) {9}

h) {5,15}

i) {1,4,6,8,11,18,19,20}

j) {4,18,19,20}

k) {1,6,11,18,19,20}

l) {18,19,20}

m) {9}

6 *Easy question*

a)   i)   30 (method: E = 100, so 2 + y + 35 + 25 + 8 = 100; y + 70 = 100;
            y = 30)

     ii) 65 (method: B = y + 35; B = 30 + 35; B = 65)

    iii) 40 (method: not C = A + B only (y) + 8 (outside circles) = 2 + 30 + 8
            = 40)

    iv) 90 (method: B∪C = y + 35 + 25; = 30 + 35 + 25; = 90)

     v) 8 (method: (A∪B∪C)′ = everything outside all three circles = 8;
            alternatively: (A∪B∪C)′ = E − (A∪B∪C) = 100 − (2 + 90) =
            100 − 92 = 8)

b)   Students who study chemistry only

c)   7/13 (method: B = 65, B∩C = 35; 35/65 = 7/13)

d)   0 (disjoint set)

e)   35% (method: B∪C = 35; 35/100 = 35%)

f)   0.4 (method: C = 35+25 = 60; p(C) = 60/100 = 0.6;
     not C = 1.0 − 0.6 = 0.4)

g)   6:13 (method: biology only (y) = 30; biology (B) = 30: 65 or 6:13)

7 *Difficult question*

a)   shade (P∩R)∩Q′ as shown (method: the region where P and R overlap that
     is outside of Q)

     Next step: complete the three set, P, Q and R

     P = {2,3,5,7,11} noting that 1 is not a prime number

     Q = {1,2,3,4,5,6,7,8,9}

     R = {2,4,6,8,10,12}

     Complete the Venn diagram (easier than trying to compare sets directly)

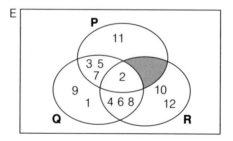

b) i)   11; (method: RQ = {1,2,3,4,5,6,7,8,9,10,12); so n(RQ) = 11 elements)

     ii) 6; (method: R′ = {1,3,5,7,9,11}; so n(R′) = 6 elements)

     iii) 2,3,4,5,6,7,8,11; (method: everything in P together with the overlap of Q and R; see completed Venn diagram)

     iv) 2,3,5,7; (method: those elements in P that overlap with those elements in both Q and R (includes empty shaded region); see completed Venn diagram)

c) i)   3/4; (method: Q = {1,2,3,4,5,6,7,8,9}; n(set Q) = 9; probability = 9/12 = 3/4)

     ii) 1/2; (method: R′ = {1,3,5,7,9,11}; n(set R′) = 6; probability = 6/12 = 1/2)

Chapter 15 Flowcharts

1 Warm-up exercise

1   i)   4

     ii) 24

     iii) 44

     iv) 64

2   Add 12

2 Easy question

1   Input °F then the mathematical steps are reversed: subtract 32; divide by 9; multiply by 5.

3 More difficult question

1   Probability = 2/9; win if throw 7 or 11

2   Probability = 4/27; no win, no lose at the first throw, so roll the dice again; probability = 2/3 first throw (roll again) then 2/9 (win) on the second throw; 2/3 × 2/9 = 4/27.

Chapter 16 Spelling

Answers to spelling tests 1 and 2

	Test 1	Test 2		Test 1	Test 2
1	B	B	11	A	B
2	B	B	12	A	A
3	B	B	13	A	B
4	A	B	14	A	A
5	B	B	15	B	A
6	B	B	16	B	B
7	B	A	17	B	A
8	B	A	18	A	A
9	A	B	19	A	A
10	A	A	20	A	A

Answers to spelling test 3

1	A. absence	17	C. benefited
2	D. accidentally	18	B. Britain
3	B. accessible	19	A. business
4	B. accommodate	20	D. careful
5	B. achieve	21	A. cemetery
6	A. addresses	22	B. chargeable
7	D. aggressive	23	D. colleagues
8	C. all right	24	C. committee
9	C. announcement	25	B. conscientious
10	B. anonymous	26	B. controversial
11	A. argument	27	C. copies
12	D. auxiliary	28	D. decisive
13	B. appealing	29	A. definitely
14	D. beginning	30	D. deterrent
15	C. believed	31	B. difference
16	A. believable	32	D. discernible

33	A. disappoint	**62**	A. occasionally
34	B. disappear	**63**	B. occurrence
35	D. discreetly	**64**	A. opulence
36	B. endeavour	**65**	A. parallel
37	C. embarrass	**66**	D. pavilion
38	B. existence	**67**	A. pedlar
39	D. ecstasy	**68**	B. permissible
40	D. enrolment	**69**	C. presence
41	C. fulfil	**70**	A. precede
42	B. forgettable	**71**	C. profession
43	C. grateful	**72**	A. privileged
44	B. grievance	**73**	C. questionnaire
45	A. harass	**74**	D. receipt
46	D. humorous	**75**	A. recognise and B. recognize are both correct
47	D. illegible		
48	C. immediately	**76**	A. recommend
49	B. inoculate	**77**	B. recuperate
50	C. irresistible	**78**	D. ridiculous
51	D. jeopardy	**79**	C. referring
52	B. jewellery	**80**	A. reference
53	A. laboratory	**81**	C. relevance
54	D. livelihood	**82**	D. rhythm
55	A. maintenance	**83**	C. schedule
56	D. millennium	**84**	B. separately
57	B. karaoke	**85**	C. successful
58	C. liaise	**86**	C. supersede
59	A. manoeuvre	**87**	A. susceptible
60	C. mischievous	**88**	B. temporary
61	B. necessary	**89**	C. tolerant

90	A. tomorrow		**96**	A. wholly
91	B. umbrella		**97**	B. xylophone
92	D. unnecessary		**98**	D. yacht
93	C. vacuum		**99**	C. yoghurt
94	B. vandalism		**100**	C. zealot
95	D. veterinary			

Answers to spelling test 4

1   Disruptive behaviour may be .... by poor classroom management.
aggravated, agravated, agrivated, aggrivated

2   We have a green, yellow and red card system for dealing with insolent, rude or .... behaviour.
beligerent, **belligerent**, belligerant, beligerant

3   Both student teachers and pupils have .... from lessons in citizenship.
benefitted, benifited, benifitted, **benefited**

4   Our football team lost the match because we had become too .... and underestimated the opposition.
complaicent, complaisant, **complacent**, complaisent

5   Many schools are making a .... effort to offset their carbon-footprint.
consious, **conscious**, consciouse, concious

6   There has been much .... over school selection policies.
controversey, contraversy, controvercy, **controversy**

7   Higher education workers took part in a 'day of .... '.
descent, discent, **dissent**, disent

8   Classroom .... is essential for efficient teaching and learning.
disipline, dicipline, disciplin, **discipline**

9   My two B's and a C were mildly ....
dissappointing, dissapointing, **disappointing**, disapointing

10 It would be .... to make a simple spelling mistake.
embarrassing, embarassing, embarrasing, embarasing

11   The debt crisis could . . . . teacher shortages.
ecsacerbate, exsacerbate, exaserbate, **exacerbate**

12   I sprained my ankle playing five-a-side football and it was . . . . painful.
extremely, extremelly, extreamly, extremley

13   The x-axis is used to plot the . . . . variable.
independent, independant, indipendent, indapendent

14   Unhealthy snack foods have become . . . . for some pupils.
irrisistible, **irresistible**, irrisistable, irresistable

15   There will be a meeting of the parents' . . . . committee on Friday week.
liason, **liaison**, liasion, liaision

16   Some university students may be eligible for a non-refundable
. . . . grant.
maintainance, maintenence, **maintenance**, maintainence

17   A temporary post led to a . . . . position.
permenant, permanant, **permanent**, permenent

18   Her story stressed the virtues of hard work and . . . .
perseverence, **perseverance**, persaverance, persaverence

19   Our tutor spoke . . . . about his own problems with maths.
poiniantly, poingnantly, **poignantly**, poynantly

20   Their sixth form college has a careers . . . . library where resources may
be viewed but not borrowed.
reference, refrence, referance, refference

21   Should teachers dress more . . . . or at least appropriately?
professionaly, proffesionally, profesionally, **professionally**

22   It is . . . . that pupils with packed lunches are seated separately from
those having hot dinners.
regrettable, regretable, reggretable, reggrettable

23   Prejudice and discrimination are part of . . . . education.
religous, **religious**, relligious, religouis

24   A letter starting Dear Mr or Mrs should end Yours . . . .
sincerly, sinserely, **sincerely**, sincerley

25 Old technology has been .... by interactive whiteboards,
   superseded, superceded, superceeded, superseeded

26 The group booking was an .... good deal.
   unbelievabley, **unbelievably**, unbelieveably, unbellievably

27 Children who behave .... at school may find themselves being sent home.
   unacceptably, unacceptabley, unnacceptabley, unaceptably

28 Excessive testing can cause .... stress for pupils and teachers alike.
   uneccesary, unnecceccary, unnecesary, **unnecessary**

29 OFSTED stated .... that teaching was better in small schools with proportionately more good teachers.
   unequivicolly, uniquivacally, **unequivocally**, uniquivacolly

30 The teacher proved that sound does not travel in a .... by pumping the air out of a bell-jar with the bell ringing.
   vaccuum, **vacuum**, vaccum, vacume

Chapter 17 Punctuation

Answers to punctuation test 1

1 Boys do better in maths, girls in English and languages. ✗

   (ie A run-on sentence. Boys do better in maths. Girls do better in English and languages. Boys do better in maths, but girls do better in English and languages.)

2 The Labour Government of 1964, and subsequent governments, supported the phasing out of grammar schools. ✓

3 However there are still more than 150 grammar schools in England, and they remain popular with parents and young people. ✗
   (The comma is missing after 'However'.)

4 To be certain of being seen, all pupils should wear clothing with yellow, orange, or light green fluorescent strips. ✗ (There is a comma missing; clearly all three colours are meant to be fluorescent: To be certain of being seen, all pupils should wear clothing with yellow, orange, or light green, fluorescent strips.)

5 Semi-colons have several uses in punctuation, one of them is to hold two linked sentences together. ✗ (Semi-colons have several uses in punctuation; one of them is to hold two linked sentences together.)

6   Pupil behaviour will improve by adopting the following ✗ (missing a colon after the word 'following').

7   A student's expectations of the course can be unrealistic. ✓ (Singular noun with possession.)

8   Students' expectations of the course can be unrealistic. ✓
(Plural noun ending in s with possession.)

9   Our school's rating was comparable with the average schools' rating for the Local Authority. ✓ (Ordinary noun used in the singular case (one owner add 's) and in the plural case (more than one owner add').)

10   Parents expressed concerns about their children's safety, which meant that the school's annual trip had to be cancelled. ✓
(Plural noun not ending in s and singular noun not ending in s.)

11   Most library's allow books to be renewed on-line. ✗
(ie Use the plural noun without an apostrophe (libraries).)

12   Twelve books' can be taken out on your card at any one time. ✗
(No apostrophe needed with an ordinary plural noun (books).)

13   If I had foreseen my low mark I might of studied harder. ✗
(If I had foreseen my low mark I might have studied harder.)

14   It's not easy working with mixed ability classes. ✓ (It is.)

15   The school has achieved its LEA targets. ✓

16   "I'm not surprised that foreign language teaching is in decline," said the head teacher. "Languages are no longer compulsory for 14 to 16 year olds, and there aren't enough jobs to go around." ✓

Answers to punctuation test 2

Should calculators be banned from the classroom?(1)

Calculators were invented to increase the speed of basic arithmetic calculations.(2) They(3) were not intended to replace mental agility with numbers. However,(4) if too much time is spent on basic calculations then maths becomes tedious and pupils have less time to develop more advanced mathematical skills.

Problems involving fractions can rarely be solved with a calculator, even though addition, subtraction,(5) multiplication and division remain as key elements. On the other hand,(6) problems involving trigonometry,(7) calculus and graphs are greatly assisted by calculators.

Pupils'(8) dependency on calculators can impair number skills that require rough checks, such as rounding, approximation and estimation. In these situations, calculators need only be used when precision and accuracy are essential. Calculators should be allowed into the classroom, but not at the expense of paper and pencil skills.(9) After(10) all,(11) speed is not everything, and what happens in the real world when a calculator is not available?(12)

Answers to punctuation test 3

Working children

If you're(1) under 13,(2) then apart from a few exceptions,(3) you cannot do paid work. At age 14,(4) you can be employed in a wide range of jobs,(5) but these must not harm your health and development,(6) or affect your attendance at school.

By law,(7) young people aged 14 to 16 can only do light work. It is illegal to work on a building site or with heavy machinery.(8) You(9) must not drive vehicles (including tractors on farms) and you cannot work in kitchens and chip shops,(10) or serve alcohol, cigarettes and medicines.

It is illegal for 14 to 16 year olds to work for more than:(11)

two hours on any school day;(12)

one hour before school starts;(13)

twelve hours in any school week.

Chapter 18 Grammar

Answers to grammar test 1

1   Is the team ready? ✓

2   We are happy if she is. ✓

3   We (were) ill after he was. ✗

4   It (was) faster than he was. ✗

5   Either you are right or I am. ✓

6   I (was) late and left alone. ✗

7   It was you who was last. ✓

8   The choir (is) singing. ✗

9   The teacher was late and so (missed) his train. ✗

10   It was extremely cold and the pipes had (frozen). ✗

11   They shook hands and made up. ✓

12   Carl speaks too (loudly) in class. ✗

13   Josh writes slowly and carefully. ✓

14   Lucy and (I) are friends. ✗

15   Emma can go with you and me. ✓

16   It was they all along. ✓

17   Jack, Ben and Steve are tall, but Steve is the tallest. ✓

18   Neither Moira nor Jane bring lunch. ✓

19   Twenty per cent of the class (is) missing. ✗

20   No pupils are ready. ✓

21   Our team is ready so (it) will bat first. ✗

22   Our pupils are ready so they will leave first. ✓

23   The head teacher, along with the other teachers, (is) in class. ✗

24   Homework compliance for the worst performing classes (is) the most improved. ✗

25   The improvement in results for the schools with the highest proportion of pupils on free school meals was the greatest. ✓

26   Every child, including those with special needs, (has) a fundamental right to education. ✗

Answers to grammar test 2

1   How many pupils are at grade C or above? ✓

2   Are school dinners still unhealthy? ✓

3   A well-balanced, healthy diet, low in saturated fat. ✗ (missing verb)

4   It's now or never. ✓

5   Assessed by the popularity of A-level subjects last year, maths and science are making a comeback. ✓

6   Seen as a candidate for A* grades at A-level, the teacher thought (the candidate) had every chance of a place at medical school. ✗

7   Teaching will benefit from reflective practitioners having acquired the skills of self-assessment and self-evaluation. ✗

8   Recognizing the possibility of plagiarism, students must use the Harvard system of referencing for information taken off the internet. ✓

9 Widely acknowledged as a seminal work on classroom management, Kounin (1970) explored the many facets of poor pupil behaviour. ✗

10 Shaken by the breach in confidentiality, the head implemented changes to prevent any more disclosures from taking place. ✗

11 Between you and me. ✗ (missing verb)

12 That's all right then. ✓

13 Between you and me, that's all right then. ✓

14 It was disappointing for us to have lost the match, even though I had not expected to be on the winning team. ✗

15 To avoid disrupting other users, Sarah went outside the library building to use the phone. ✗

16 Jackson states that the traditional method of teaching mathematics has failed pupils of low ability, believing that a whole-class interactive approach is the best way to reduce ability gaps. ✓

Answers to grammar test 3

1 d) Our school trip to France will cost £15 more per pupil this year because of the falling value of the pound against the euro.

The main clause of the sentence is <Our school trip to France will cost £15 more per pupil this year>; this sentence is complete in itself making it the main clause. It should not be interrupted if the message is to remain clear. Answer a) is incorrect because the subordinate clause <because of the falling value of the pound against the euro> should come at the end. Answer b) is likewise incorrect, and a more logical order of words would be <£15 more per pupil this year>. Answer c) is incorrect because the meaning is ambiguous; it could mean either that the trip to France will cost £15 per pupil (eg more than the £10 charged last year) or it could mean that the trip will cost an extra £15 per pupil when compared with last year.

2 b) Judged by their evaluation forms, students did not find that larger class sizes were detrimental to their learning experiences.

The noun is at the beginning of the clause, as near as possible to the participle <Judged> and so avoids any ambiguity.

3 c) GCSE results were very good again this year. The percentage that gained grades A* and A rose to 35%.

The first sentence of the stem uses the past tense <were> as does the second sentence of the stem <gained>. For consistency, the answer should use the past tense <rose> of the irregular verb <rise>, not the present participle <rising>, or the past participle <risen>, or the future tense <will rise>.

Chapter 20 Reasoning skills

1 Warm-up exercise: numerical reasoning

1	200	**11**	38
2	50	**12**	16
3	6	**13**	4.6
4	1.7	**14**	M
5	13	**15**	Q
6	16	**16**	R
7	36	**17**	10
8	31	**18**	108
9	6	**19**	1
10	8	**20**	2.55

2 Easy questions: numerical reasoning

1   81

2   4

3   6.4

4 $\frac{1}{72}$ (dividing by 6 each time; finally $\frac{1}{12} \div 6 = \frac{1}{72}$)

5   125 (cubes; 5×5×5 = 125)

6   4

7   15 (double and add 1)

8   2

9   36 (times 3 times 2 times 3 times 2)

10   10

11 15

12 4.05 (multiply by 3 three from right to left)

13 13, 15

14 128, 512

15 90, 81

16 91, 136

17 −30, −60

18 45, 55 (mirror image, increasing again)

19 $\frac{5}{32}, \frac{1}{8}$ (convert all to 32nd's then it becomes obvious)

20 $6\frac{1}{4}, 5$

21 $\frac{1}{8}, \frac{1}{2} (\frac{1}{16} \times 4 = \frac{1}{4}; \frac{1}{12} \times 4 = \frac{1}{3}; \frac{1}{8} \times 4 = \frac{1}{2}$; denominators 16, 12, 8; 4, 3, 2)

22 0.75, 0.5 (subtract 1.25, 1.0, 0.75, 0.5 (= 0.75), 0.25 (= 0.5))

23 JI LK

24 TSR QPO

3 Easy questions: numerical reasoning

1 5.0

2 1 (subtract $1\frac{3}{8}$ each time; alternative method: convert to eighths (largest denominator) as a first step and then subtract $\frac{11}{8}: \frac{41}{8}, \frac{30}{8}, \frac{19}{8}, \frac{8}{8} = 1$)

3 20, 20

4 166, 342 (+11, +22, +44, +88, +176)

5 S, Z

6 JI, HG

7 D, F

8 TSR, QPO, NML

9 G, I, H

10 P, S, V,

11 $3\ (\frac{1}{4};$ 1/32 is to 4/32 as 1/16 is to 4/16 = ¼)

12 $\frac{2}{5}$

13   1.1 litres

14   8.56 (0.0214 × 400 = 2.14 × 4 = 8.56)

15   635 (25.4 ÷ 0.04 = 2540 ÷ 4 = 635)

16   989.9 (1000g − 10g − 0.1 g = 990 − 0.1 = 989.9g)

17   1.667 (15/9 = 5/3 = $1\frac{2}{3}$ = 1.66666 recurring = 1.667 to 3 d.p.)

18 $\frac{3}{4}$ (12:16 = 3: 4 = ¾)

4 *More difficult questions: numerical reasoning*

1   4, 30 kg. (Intuitive method: cancel the first ratio from to 60:100 to 6 kg:10 kg to make it easier to work with, noting that we have 18 kg which is three times bigger than 6 kg so the answer must be three times greater than 10 kg, ie 30 kg. Fractions method: write the ratios as fractions using x as an unknown eg 60:100 = 60/100 = 6/10; 18:x = 18/x; then we have $\frac{18}{x} = \frac{6}{10}$; $\frac{3}{x} = \frac{1}{10}$; cross-multiply to give 3 × 10 = x × 1; so x = 30)

2   a)   10 drops (because 10 × 0.1 ml = 1 ml)
      b)   20 drops/minute (because 1 minute = 60 seconds and 1 drop every 3 secs)
      c)   3 litres (20 drops per minute = 20 × 0.1 ml/min = 2 ml/min = 120 ml/hr; we have 25 hours, so water wasted = 25 hr × 120 ml/hr = 250 × 12 = 2500 + 500 = 3000 ml = 3 litres)

3   6 ($3\frac{3}{16} \times 1\frac{7}{17} \times 1\frac{1}{3} = \frac{51}{16} \times \frac{24}{17} \times \frac{4}{3}$; cancel the 51 at the top with the 17 and the 3 at the bottom to leave $\frac{24}{16} \times \frac{4}{1}$; cancel the 4 and the 16 to leave $\frac{24}{4}$ = 6)

4 $1\frac{1}{7}$ ($\frac{5x}{8} = \frac{x+1}{3}$; 'cross-multiply' which is the same as multiplying both sides by the common denominator of 24 (8×3), to give 3(5x) = 8(x + 1); expand the expressions to get 15x = 8x + 8; from which 7x = 8, so x = $\frac{8}{7}$ or $1\frac{1}{7}$)

5 $\frac{1}{9}$ ($\frac{2}{3} = \sqrt{4x}$; square both sides to remove the root sign: $\frac{4}{9}$ = 4x, so $\frac{1}{9}$ = x)

5 Warm-up exercise: verbal reasoning

1	4. forbid	15	5 mammals
2	3. meet	16	4. opaque
3	2. determine	17	1. success
4	1. conceal	18	4. pressure
5	2. expound	19	4. cauliflower
6	3. digest	20	3. tree
7	1. reactive	21	1. student
8	2. jump, 3. leap	22	1. waist
9	1. fair, 3. honest	23	4. digest
10	3. disguise, 2. conceal	24	3. ruler
11	1 sarcasm, 1 irony	25	2. devout
12	2. repudiate, 2 reject	26	4. inch
13	2 prohibit, 3 forbid	27	2. calories
14	5 bullet		

6 Easy questions: verbal reasoning

1	FLIT	6	8462
2	TONS	7	LUCID
3	TOUR	8	TEACHER
4	R	9	DISK
5	L	10	4, 26, 2

7 Warm-up exercise: Oxbridge (expanded answers follow on)

1	D	**8**	FALSE
2	A	**9**	TRUE
3	B	**10**	NOT GIVEN
4	C	**11**	I
5	TRUE	**12**	D
6	FALSE	**13**	H
7	NOT GIVEN	**14**	G

7 Warm-up exercise: Oxbridge expanded answers

1 D. (first paragraph) '*In the past Oxbridge has been seen as.* **a place that represents the highest educational standards**'. This answer is reflected in. 'Traditionally, a degree from Oxbridge symbolized the pinnacle of academic achievement.'

2 A. (second paragraph) 'Everybody agrees that. **too many Oxbridge students have had a private education.**' This answer is reflected in. 'It cannot be disputed that a disproportionate number of Oxbridge entrants went to a fee-paying private school rather than to a free, state school.' (Q68 distracter: Some people believe that Oxbridge is part of a social class system that favours the privileged few)

3 B. (third paragraph) 'In the passage, there is an example of how Oxbridge. **has made the application process fairer**'. This answer is reflected in. 'Indeed, in some subjects the application process includes admissions and aptitude tests that help to ensure a level playing field.'

4 C. (second paragraph) 'In the passage, a link is made between a degree at Oxbridge and. **a successful career**.' This answer is reflected in. 'Oxbridge graduates are rewarded with the best paying jobs.'

5 TRUE. (third paragraph) **The 'Oxbridge advantage' refers to better prospects in life.**
The statement is true because 'Oxbridge helps to maintain the "social divide" where the rich get richer and the poor remain poor. Some people would argue that this "Oxbridge advantage" ……'.

6   FALSE. (third paragraph) **Some Oxbridge candidates are offered a place whether they deserve it or not**. The statement is false because There is no evidence to suggest that Oxbridge selects students on anything other than merit.

7   NOT GIVEN. (third paragraph) **A student from an ordinary background is unlikely to do well at Oxbridge**. There is no information on this in the passage. Whilst a student from an ordinary background is less likely to secure a place at Oxbridge, no information is given about how well they do once whilst at Oxbridge.
     (Distracter: some pupils from an ordinary background are not comfortable with the idea of attending Oxbridge; this says nothing about the student's performance at Oxbridge)

8   FALSE. (third paragraph) **A lack of applications from state schools is the only reason for the low number of state school students at Oxbridge**. The answer is false because 'Alternatively, the low aspiration of some pupils' parents may fail to drive gifted pupils onwards and upwards.' In other words, there is another reason (a second one). Q73 'distracter' offers a third possibility (a third alternative).

9   TRUE. (fourth paragraph) **The author does not believe that Oxbridge is responsible for social inequalities**. The answer is true because 'Inequalities in our society do not begin and end with Oxbridge.'

10   NOT GIVEN. (fourth paragraph) **There are few good schools in the state sector**. There is no information given about the number of good state schools or the proportion of state schools that are good.

11   Answer **I. prosperous.** (fourth paragraph) The answer is 'prosperous' **because it means the same as** affluent in 'The best state schools tend to be found in the most **affluent** areas'.

12   Answer **D. fairness**. (fourth paragraph) The answer is 'fairness' **because** 'a lack of fairness in the state school system' summarizes 'Injustices can arise when parents move house to secure a child's place at a more desirable school.'

13   Answer **H. privately**. (fourth paragraph) The answer is 'privately' because 'pay for them to be educated privately' is the same as 'will pay for their children to be educated at a private school.'

14   Answer **G. important**. (fourth paragraph) The answer is 'important' **because** 'more important' is the same as 'outweighs'.

8 *Warm-up exercise: Home-schooling (expanded answers follow on)*

1   Section B iii) Problems at school

2   Section C ix) Parents as teachers

3   Section D v) Overcoming a weakness

4   Section E ii) Range of benefits

5   Section F vii) Shared responsibility

6   FALSE

7   TRUE

8   NOT GIVEN

9   TRUE

10   FALSE

11   FALSE

12   TRUE

8 *Warm-up exercise: Home-schooling expanded answers*

1   Paragraph **B. iii)** The paragraph deals with 'Problems at school'. The key phrase is 'removed from a school following negative experiences.'

2   Paragraph **C. ix)** The paragraph deals with 'Parents as teachers'. The word 'parents' is mentioned five times and the key phrase is 'Parents are not professional teachers'.

   Answer i) 'Disadvantages' is a distracter linked to 'education in the home can have its limitations'.

3   Paragraph **D. v)** The paragraph deals with 'Overcoming a weakness' (lack of socialization) as indicated by 'Socialization outside of the home can negate some of these shortcomings'. Answer i) 'Disadvantages' is a distracter linked to 'the main criticism of home-schooling', noting that 'Main disadvantage' (one only) would fit with this paragraph.

4   Paragraph **E. ii)** The paragraph explains the 'Range of benefits' when referring to 'Whilst home-schooling has its shortcomings it also offers (Q218) several advantages. Answer iv) 'Main advantage' is a distracter, noting that the paragraph explains many advantages, not just one.

5   Paragraph **F. vii)** The paragraph explains the 'Shared responsibility' when referring to 'it is the duty of the state and the parents.'

FALSE. (Paragraph A) **In the US has there are four times as many home-educated children as in the UK**. This statement is false because 'In the UK... 100,000 pupils. In the US... approximately two million children.' Noting that the figures of 1 per cent and 4 per cent are distracters.

7 **TRUE.** (Paragraph A) **There is much disagreement about the merits of home-schooling**. This statement is true because. 'Home-schooling is a controversial issue.'

8 **NOT GIVEN. School children with disabilities are the most discriminated against**. Discrimination is referred to in paragraph B but not in relation to disabilities.

9 **TRUE.** (Paragraph C) **There is nothing unusual about children learning from their parents at home**. This statement is true because 'Whilst home-schooling of a child is unusual, learning from parents is not.'

10 **FALSE.** (Paragraph D) **Only children who attend school can be favourably socialized**. This statement is false because 'socialization experienced in the natural setting of a community is preferable to that within the confines of a school.'

11 **FALSE.** (Paragraph E) **Pupils in school achieve higher grades than home-school children**. This statement is false because home-educated children usually outperform their schooled counterparts academically.'

12 **TRUE.** (Paragraph E) **Children from better-off homes are more likely to complete their homework**. This statement is true because 'Parents who home-school their children tend to be ..... in a higher... income bracket. ... more likely .... encouraging compliance with homework.'

9 Easy question: religious education

1 FALSE: the second paragraph states that the programme of learning will include Christianity and five other principal religions, ie six main religions.

2 TRUE: the first sentence of the first paragraph states that the programme of learning will be non-statutory.

3 NOT GIVEN: there is no information on whether students will have a religious faith or not.

4 TRUE: the last sentence of the fourth paragraph indicates that schools will have a duty to promote community cohesion.

5 FALSE: the third paragraph states that lessons will include thinking about responses to ethical questions; and moral issues are part of ethics.

10 Easy question: school uniforms

1 TRUE: the first paragraph indicates that from 2003 to 2007 (4 years) the cost of schooling has risen by 4%.

2 NOT GIVEN: the first paragraph indicates that almost four in ten found it very difficult or quite difficult to meet the overall costs; this means that at least six in ten did not find it very difficult or quite difficult, but this does not mean that they found it easy.

3 TRUE: the statement is reflected in the first sentence of the third paragraph which states that setting exclusive uniform deals with retailers disadvantages low income families.

4 FALSE: the first and last sentences of the final paragraph indicate parents should not have to contribute towards trips that are part of the curriculum.

5 TRUE: the last but one sentence in the final paragraph states that over nine out of ten paid the full cost of the residential trips. ie over 90%.

11 More difficult question: our guarantee

1 FALSE: the second sentence of the first paragraph indicates that the guarantee applies to the first year of secondary school, so not all pupils.

2 TRUE: the third sentence of the first paragraph indicates that the head-teachers can take action against parents who ignore their responsibilities.

3 TRUE: the first sentence of the third paragraph implies that pupils starting Key Stage 2 are expected to make two levels of progress by age 11.

4 FALSE: the first sentence of the second paragraph explains that the need for 'no contact policies' is a myth where bad behaviour is concerned.

5 NOT GIVEN: the fourth paragraph explains that parents can expect clear information on several issues, but there is no mention of university courses.

6 NOT GIVEN: the final paragraph concludes that behaviour in school since 2008 is still good and improving, but makes no mention of behaviour prior to 2008.

12 More difficult question: world's language

1 FALSE: first paragraph, second sentence: one billion speakers of Mandarin compared with 330 million English speakers, so just over three times as many.

2 TRUE: first paragraph, sixth sentence: belies the notion that the number of speakers of a language determines its status.

3   FALSE: first paragraph, fourth sentence: China has more English Language teaching jobs than in any other country.

4   NOT GIVEN: 300,000 of the one-million IELTS tests were in China but we do not know whether it is more popular in China than in any other country.

5   NOT GIVEN: start of second paragraph: we know that Latin has declined but its displacement by English is not confirmed.

6   TRUE: second paragraph: last but one sentence: Globally there are almost three times as many non-native speakers of English as native speakers.

7   NOT GIVEN: second paragraph, last sentence: United States is before India and Nigeria is before the UK but the position of Nigeria in relation to India is unknown.

13 Warm-up exercise: abstract reasoning

1   3

2   2

3   4

4   4

5   4 (3 sides to 6 sides; 4 sides to 8 sides)

6   2 (one-quarter of the area is shaded; others one-half)

7   2 (shape built from 5 blocks instead of 4)

8   2 (the other shapes come in pairs)

14 Easy questions: abstract reasoning

1   2 (has 3 bars, the rest have 4 bars)

2   2 (split into 4 parts but no interior triangles)

3   4 (position of the right arrow head is different)

4   1 (not a rotation; shapes 2,3,4, and 5 are all the same, just rotated)

5   5 (mirror image)

6   1 (90° rotation)

7   2 (90° rotation)

8   1 (small shape becomes large shape; large shape becomes smaller shape)

9   4 (180° rotation)

10   1 (square circle triangle, repeat pattern, and one of the three is shaded)

11   5 (count down 4,3,2,1 and the 1 is shaded)

12   2 (90° rotation three times; draw the first shape on a sheet of paper and rotate is if unsure)

13   5 (120° rotation = turn through one-third of a circle)

14   4 (mirror image with the mirror in the vertical plane)

15   2 (mirror image with the mirror in the vertical plane)

16   3 (copy the process: reverse the diagonal, turn the shapes upside down and reverse the shading)

15 *More difficult questions: abstract reasoning*

(Questions 1 to 60)

Example 1: Set A = straight lines; Set B = curved lines

1   A   **4**   B

2   A   **5**   Neither

3   Neither

Example 2: Set A = divided into triangles; Set B = divided into squares/rectangles

6   A   **9**   A

7   B   **10**   B

8   Neither

16 *More difficult questions:*

Set A = at least one line of symmetry; Set B = no lines of symmetry

11   A   **14**   B

12   A   **15**   A

13   B

17 *More difficult questions:*

Set A = straight lines and curved lines; Set B = straight lines only or curved lines only

16	B	**19**	A
17	B	**20**	A
18	A		

18 *More difficult questions:*

Set A = at least one-right angle; Set B = no right-angles

21	B	**24**	B
22	B	**25**	A
23	A		

19 *More difficult questions:*

Set A = shapes are the same with a line of reflection (mirror image); same; Set B = shapes are the same without a line of reflection

26	B	**29**	Neither
27	B	**30**	A
28	A		

20 *More difficult questions:*

Set A = circle square triangle left to right; Set B = square circle triangle left to right

31	Neither	**34**	B
32	A	**35**	A
33	B		

21 *More difficult questions:*

Set A = three similar shapes in a diagonal row; Set B = three similar shapes in a vertical or horizontal row

36	B	**39**	Neither
37	A	**40**	B
38	B		

22 *More difficult questions:*

Set A = one shaded square; Set B = one unshaded square (all the remaining shapes are incidental/distracters)

41	Neither	**44**	B
42	B	**45**	Neither
43	A		

23 *More difficult questions:*

Set A = at least one shaded circle; Set B = at least one unshaded rectangle (all the remaining shapes are incidental/distracters)

46	A	**49**	B
47	B	**50**	Neither
48	Neither		

24 *More difficult questions:*

Set A = the square and the rectangle are adjacent to one side of the square; they are orientated in line with each other and they rotate clockwise around the set as a pair; Set B = the square and the rectangle are adjacent to different sides; they are not orientated towards each other and they do not rotate around the set. The triangle and the circle are incidental/ distracters.

51	Neither	**54**	A
52	B	**55**	A
53	Neither		

25 *More difficult questions:*

Set A = a group of three similar shapes and a group of two similar shapes; Set B = a group of three similar shapes only. All other shapes are incidental/distracters

56	Neither	**59**	A
57	A	**60**	B
58	Neither		